REBOUND FAITH

CHAYAH!

_647·627·4006_

The Grit to Survive, Revive, and Thrive from Devastation
and Depression to Deliverance

NICOLA MCFADDEN

A Spiritual Empowerment
and Life Transformation Series

Dedication

Lord Jesus, thank you for all the seasons of my life, the courage, strength, and faith to know you as the Provider of abundant life.

I dedicate this book to my mother, Audrey Young-Lynch, as well as my two sons, Nicholas Stanley and Matthew Chambers. Thank you for believing, challenging, and supporting me.

To my readers:

I pray that the Lord may use this book as a source of spiritual empowerment and life transformation; for you to live victoriously, righteously, prosperously, and zealously.

May you experience a divine encounter with God, being confident of.

His love to keep you,

His power to defend you,

His Word to empower you,

His strength to protect you,

His hands to provide for you,

His eyes to look ahead of you,

His light to illuminate your path,

His desire to give you a renewed life.

May God use my story to influence, inspire and ignite your faith for you to rebound and 'really' live. Chayah!

Foreword

I remember when I first met Nicola. It was in High School of 1990. However, it was in 1989 that I first heard about her. I remember the Math teacher telling the class that someone scored very high on the same Math test he administered at another High School. I had to wait until the following year to finally meet her, and surprisingly, she was in most of my classes: Math, Chemistry, and General Paper. Even though I was a new student at St. Jago High School, St Catherine, Jamaica, Nicola and her friends created a welcoming atmosphere.

Throughout my time at St. Jago High, she remained friendly. Somehow, we felt we had a lot in common – background, circumstances, and ambitions - and it was quite noticeable by a few. On the other hand, I was too selfish (wrapped up in myself) and judgmental to find all that out on my own.

After high school, I saw Nicola again at the University of the West Indies, where I found out we were in the same program. Still being new to the university, Nicola remained friendly, and I naturally felt comfortable in her study groups. I guessed Nicola wanted to let everyone know that she knew me for a very long time. I remember Nicola was working while in undergrad and would usually try to sit close to me whenever slightly late. In retrospect, I guess she did not want me to feel left out or too lonely. At one point, a student questioned if Nicola reserved the seat next to me.

One prominent thing I remember is that Nicola was very driven and always tried to get and give as much help as possible; unlike me, who wanted to sort out everything all by myself. However, I would still fail in doing that and Nicola would let it sink in. It was like we exchanged grades, or she had some power to figure it out. Throughout undergrad and especially in my third year, we were in a study group with mostly Nicola's friends. Night and day, the group would meet before finals. I remember Nicola would always start a conversation with me no matter what mood I was in; and even though I was a loner and only kept few friends, I never felt she was someone who would brush me aside or make me feel somewhat inferior to anyone. She let them know I am smart and relevant to the group, but after the study group, she would accuse me of being selfish with my knowledge. I thought Nicola had a positive influence on me; harsh criticisms came from others that she played a role in the courses I registered for, especially some of my electives. Still many admired, recognized and respected Nicola. She is inspirational, influential and impactful in other's progress to make positive choices.

It's funny that after undergrad, I found out she was enrolled in the same Management Information Systems (MIS) graduate program as I was. This time, we were in different cohorts. That did not stop a few students from telling me stories about her or asking how long I knew her. We did not see each other much due to the class schedules, but it was like I always kept informed about the things that were happening in her life; where she worked, the car she drove, and so on. Even after Nicola moved to Canada, we would still talk on the phone about old times and still have her stuck it to me about my wrong ways and judgmental views. I guess I finally learned from that.

For some reason, Nicola's success inspired me and made me feel like I was not trying hard enough to accomplish my real potential, not sure if it was luck on her side... Alternatively, is this what she devised and coined as Rebound Faith?

~ Dr. Tyrone Cadenhead (Ph.D.)

Table of Contents

Dedication iii

Foreword... v

Table of Contents vii

VOLUME ONE 1

My Rebound Faith Story to Chayah!............................2

One Legend's Venture to Legacy............................... 2

Let's get started.. 5

Her Story Continues.. 10

The Pain of Being Pregnant with Purpose! 11

Rebound to Live an Abundant Life! 17

Transforming Business, Leaders, and Life 21

To Sum It All Up.. 24

Becoming a Legend and Building a Legacy 28

Pre-Game Warm-Up Drills 30

What does it mean to Rebound? 30

Faith says, "Take Your Sandals Off; It's Rebound Time!".......... 36

What is Faith?... 43

What is Rebound Faith? The Grit! 52

The Rebound Faith Prophetic Prayer Strategy (5Rs) 64

Rebound and 'Really' Live!....................................... 69

Be Transformed from Ordinary to Legendary.......................... 80

Despite It All; Chayah! 87

VOLUME TWO 93

1st Quarter 94

Live Victoriously... Chayah! 94

Rebound Faith Transformative Change Process (5Vs) 94

His Grace Is Sufficient and Always Available to You! 119

2nd Quarter 128

Live Righteously... Chayah! 128

Jesus' Demonstration of Rebound Faith 150

Request to Revelation 154

Revelation to Response 163

Response to Receive 181

Receive to Rejoice 184

VOLUME THREE 197

3rd Quarter 198

Live Prosperously... Chayah! 198

Rebound Faith Antidote for Depression 198

Mental Wellness is the Mind-Blowing Wealth! 208

Renewed Mind for Mental Wellness (Shalom) 217

4th Quarter 248

Live Zealously... Chayah! 248

Her Story: The Zest for Life! 253

Post-Game Review 273

The Manifestation of Rebound Faith to Chayah! 273

Claiming God's Promises for Your Rebound to Chayah! 297

REBOUND FAITH

CHAYAH!

VOLUME ONE

My Rebound Faith Story to Chayah!

One Legend's Venture to Legacy

A man who puts on his armour to go to battle should not boast like the man who takes it off after the battle has been won.

~ 1 Kings 20 Amplified Bible (AMP)

My name is Nicola McFadden, fondly called Niki. I am a Christian, a mother, and a senior Transformational Change Consultant. I am an advocate for mental wellness, empowerment speaker, and a multi-certified Project and Change Management Leader. I have my own company, which I founded in late 2011. My vision was simple; it was to offer business consulting services. Since then, it became something much more significant. Nikimac Solutions Inc. (the name of my consulting company) has since successfully transformed various companies, leaders, and individuals for the better. It has helped the up-and-coming in its unique way; inspiring, influencing, impacting, and implementing Changes globally.

My success didn't just come to me. I would say it occurred to me later than I would have liked it to happen. Life and its hardships were in the way, somehow, moulding and making me.

However, everyone stumbles upon life difficulties. I realized no one ever talks about their hardships. Some people are too afraid of being judged; others are private about who they are and where they come from, and others never mix business with personal life.

I cannot entirely agree with all these perceptions. I believe that one's, mine as I can't speak for anyone else, personal life shapes who one is; not just personally, but rather professionally. I don't think I would be where I am today if it weren't for my past. Harsh life lessons have re-shaped, re-established, and re-positioned me; building my grit, courage in pain and adversities; developed my strength of mind and character, resilience, bravery, endurance, and faith. So, in enabling Change as a Transformational Leader, I learn to lead with more empathy, compassion, and emotional intelligence because I understand the effect of change transitions not only at the organizational level, but to the affected individuals as well. I know that Change, regardless of work, school, home, or life events is hard and painful. The fear of the unknown brings denial, resistance, and can lead to despair. As such, I drive from the heart and not just my head; loving people and nurturing relationships as a servant and a thoughtful leader.

With all that in mind, it can be a therapeutic process sometimes to see what I have been through, examine what I have achieved since then, and think of what I will accomplish in the future. Not only that, but I believe that if I tell my story, it might help another individual who is struggling personally, professionally or even both. Moreover, especially as a woman, I think that my faith, family trials, and triumphs, professional accomplishments, career path and choices in ministry and the marketplace have been strongly dependant on my personal life.

I was doing a self-reflection recently. I looked at my two miraculous sons. Then I looked at my family, my household, and our lives. I reviewed my resume, online presence, and profile, my company websites, social media network and community. Then I analyzed my faith journey, my career, my professional life, and my personal growth. I tried to look at them as a first-time observer; Nikimac, 'U Power Up, and the Rebound Faith book series are all an impressive work! I made a big realization – you know what I do professionally now and what I'd done in the past few years. However, there's so much more to tell for you understand my story and describe my zeal for God and my zest for life. My Rebound Faith testimony has matured into a Spiritual Empowerment and Life Transformation Series that provide a strategy and solution to empower and transform you in how to overcome your setbacks, despairs, and hindrances; using God's power and His light to strengthen you and demolish the evil of darkness.

Never affirm your fears; They are afraid of your strengths!

When I thought of the shape or form to tell you my story, I knew I wanted it to be authentic. I tried to explain my story uniquely, in a way that is challenging to me, and yet motivational to you. Why is that, you ask? One thing you should already know about me is that I always seek ways to challenge myself. I had never authored a book. I never considered myself a good writer or a public speaker. I still struggled with my pronunciation and grammar; though I had attempted to write several blogs, had delivered many speeches and messages, and shared many inspirational posts but a book, oh no, I thought initially! However, I decided it was the perfect way to summon myself and share my life story: My past (what shaped me and how), and finally, my present (what I do now), and my tomorrow (what I hope to achieve).

Let's get started

The Beginning

Nicola McFadden was born in Jamaica to a teenage single mom. Nicola's mother was 18, unwed, and a secondary school dropout when her daughter was born. However, Nicola wasn't an only child; she had three other siblings. Her mother worked in a clothing factory until she was laid off, and later worked as a dressmaker (seamstress) and made custom clothes for clients from home.

Because of her upbringing, Nicola felt unloved as a child and had low self-esteem. Nonetheless, she had no time for any nonsense. Instead, Nicola was purpose-driven, hungry for success, and focused on her learning. At a very early age, she figured education would be the key to break the generational poverty in her bloodline. However, her journey during schooling wasn't an easy one. Nicola was forced to miss out on school regularly due to the lack of some necessities, such as school shoes and money for the bus fare.

Because of the financial situation, Nicola's mother was only qualified to have the funds for a small house consisting of only two rooms, a tiny bathroom, and a kitchenette. The development of the house that Nicola's mother purchased took longer than expected due to delay in the construction by several years. She almost lost the home due to increased fees, so Nicola's mother was forced to co-own the place with Nicola's step-dad. While the house was in development, Nicola's family lived on rent. However, due to an inability to pay, the family got kicked out by the landlord. They got another place they could eventually afford, but the living arrangements were dreadful. The living situation only worsened, so Nicola's mother had no choice but to move the family with her boyfriend, Nicola's stepfather. He was an unkind man, and was abusive towards Nicola, both emotionally and mentally.

The commute between Nicola's stepfather's house to school was hours long. Nicola's bus route began at 3:30 AM and ended at 8:30 AM. Classes would finish at 2:30 PM, and Nicola would only arrive home by 9:30 PM. Often, the bus would break down due to mechanical glitches, and Nicola and the other students would be left on the road accommodated by a kind pleasant until alternative transportation would be available. Her mother reported Nicola missing several times due to these types of situations because there was no way of communicating; there was no such thing as a mobile phone or even a home phone at the time, and there was no alternative transportation. Nicola tried to live with her father, but it was a dreadful experience for her, and the situation was proven to be impossible. Nicola stayed with several other families but eventually moved back in with her mother.

The tiny two-room house was finally ready for Nicola's mother to move. So, she did just that with her four children and a granddaughter (Nicola's niece). From then on, Nicola became more and more determined to make something of herself. She didn't want her future to be limited by her lack of resources nor by her past. Nicola was an exceptional student and frequently set new academic standards and received academic awards for excellence. After a lot of hard work and determination, Nicola's university acceptance letter came.

Nicola initially wanted to be a medical doctor. However, that dream quickly faded away as the harsh financial reality kicked in. During her first year of post-secondary school, Nicola continued the administrative job that she managed to secure during the summertime. She had to do it if she wanted to be in

University because her mother had no way of providing her financial support for her education. Nicola was the first person in the family to ever go to college. Nicola seemed to manage to be a full-time student, as well as a full-time employee just fine; until she got called by the financial controller, who gave her an ultimatum – either full-time study or full-time employment. After much deliberation, Nicola chose her schooling. She still worked during the summer but was forced to change her programme to a double major in Management Studies and Computer Science. Nicola did everything she could to save money to fund her studies until she graduated with first-class honours in 1995.

The Bold Move

Nicola made some tough decisions as she was offered and got a full scholarship to continue her education in the Masters' Programme as a full-time student. She eventually decided to decline that offer. She felt she needed to support her family. As an alternative, Nicola acquired decent high-paying jobs, later purchased her first home, and gave birth to her son, Nicholas. She eventually completed her Masters in 2000, holding a MSc. in Management Information System.

At that point, Nicola didn't make decisions for her well-being anymore, but rather for the welfare of her son. In August 2000, when her firstborn was only eight months old, Nicola left an abusive romantic relationship, took the bold move and immigrated to Canada so that she and, most importantly, her son could have a better life with more resources and opportunities at their reach. Nicola was a determined single mom, with no family or known support system in Canada. However, eventually Nicola followed her heart to what she thought was her happy ending; she got married and had another son,

Matthew. Nicola continued the climb, nurturing for her family, and pursuing her dreams in Corporate Canada; in a short time, she was at the pinnacle of her full-time career, a successful Director in a high-profile global organization.

Nikimac Solutions Inc.

Now we finally get to Nicola's "third baby." It is what she's most proud of in her career. Not to say that she isn't proud of everything else that she's done. However, everything that she's done in her career led to this, Nikimac Solutions Inc. Nicola founded the company on November 20th, 2011. Her vision was simple when she worked on bringing her business to life – it was to offer consulting services to organizations.

However, since then, Nicola's life journey has reshaped, matured, and extended Nikimac to its current Purpose to establish Nikimac as an agent of transformation in business, leadership, and life.

Once Nikimac began operating, it became something different; it became more meaningful, purposeful and impacting.

Today, Nicola leads Nikimac as a top-performing innovative team working collaboratively to engage, educate, and elevate clients through Transformative Change.

Nikimac focuses on the corporate, government, and entrepreneurial clients and provides pioneer breakthrough solutions for businesses, leadership, and individuals; navigating the complexities and ambiguity of the emerging digital transformation era and other organizational, initiative, and individual changes. Nikimac tailors the approach to each client, helping them to operate their companies uniquely, efficiently, and effectively; delivering the strategy, structures, systems, and services to:

- **Investigate** the current state and future state vision
- **Identify** gaps and optimization opportunities
- **Influence** change and transformation
- **Inspire** leaders and stakeholders
- **Ignite** individuals and teams
- **Improve** capacity and capabilities
- **Implement** innovative solutions
- **Impact** bottom-line growth, market position, and performance
- **Increase** social responsibility and social good

In 2017, Nicola pursued her purpose and her passionate love for people. That was when 'U Power Up was launched as the life transformation, spiritual empowerment, and social responsibility arm of Nikimac. The site provides a partnership network, events, programme, and social projects to support people to overcome adverse life events and transformative experiences, with the favourite and inspiring tagline, Life Happens, Stay Strong!

Life is not always comfortable, but no one is a prisoner to his or her past or present situation; the future is exciting, victory is imminent and success abiding. Moreover, God continues to reveal that:

- He is faithful to perform His Word!
- Delay is not denial! Even if the wait seems extended and the process is painful; the shift is coming! Suddenly, God will catapult you in a way that is fast and furious!
- The outcome will be better than expected, prayed or imagined!

Her Story Continues

"Strength and honour are her clothing, and she shall rejoice in time to come."

~ *Proverbs 31:25 New King James (KJV)*

There was the mention of Nicola's family life previously. To rewind a little, Nicola was married and had two sons, Nick and Matt. She finally got her happy ending that she deserved after living through such harsh experiences so early in life. She got her happy ending; well at least for a little while. Nicola sadly got a divorce. Just like anything else that she'd ever been through in her life, Nicola didn't let this bring her down for long. This time, however, she didn't just put a positive spin for herself, but her clients, potential clients, and others who might only find out about her life, leadership, business, ministry, and its existence. Who knows, maybe they'll use her services in the future, or they know someone who may find her services useful.

During the time of her divorce, Nicola began her long and hard battle with situational depression. To cope with her life's new hardship, Nicola turned to God; and coined her testimony as Rebound Faith. She used her faith in God to empower her to successfully get through her pain in the process and pursue her purpose. Nicola decided to help others as God helped her. She started applying her belief in God into her consultation, coaching and offering mentorship and motivation as part of her leadership.

The Pain of Being Pregnant with Purpose!

*The perils of your past have prepared and produced
you, like a pretty, precious and priceless Pearl!*

During the period 2010 to 2015, all hell broke loose! Nicola experienced the passing of her biological father, a brutal divorce, and family court battle resulting in her situational depression, significant financial crisis, the loss of her family home, the injury of her corporate leadership career, the critical illness and surgery of her mother, as well as neglect of many friends and family. But God!

When the enemy shall come in like a flood, the Spirit of the Lord will lift a standard against him and put him to flight (Isaiah 59:19).

No pressure; No Diamond!

No cocoon; No Butterfly!

Nicola lost everything; her career, home, finances, family, and friends. Determined to overcome, she fought desperately for her mental wellness and her children. She needed to stay strong; having the power to survive, strengthen, and succeed. Nicola was profoundly distressed and fearful of losing her children because of this painful adverse life event. However, she was encouraged and found her strength in the Lord, her God. Nicola had a divine encounter with God, and got the power, hope, and direction to move forward; the strategy and solution for Rebound Faith.

11

Today, Nicola boldly shares her story to effect change, disrupt the stigma, and help others suffering silently in solitude behind closed doors due to the shame associated with depression in our culture, the Corporate workplace, the church, and the local community. As she becomes naked, she allows many others to feel liberated to speak out and share their stories, seek the support required for survival, and the strength to overcome.

Nicola is determined to be an advocate for mental wellness and a voice for individuals traumatized by fear, shame, and discrimination, which prevent them from seeking support. This stigma has resulted in people feeling abused, rejected, and isolated without hope for mental health care.

By preparing her presentation and this book, Nicola aims to show to her audience and listeners that God is there for them all the time. God promised never to leave nor forsake us. He is there with us even through the hard times. Hard times are there to teach us a lesson. Hard times are there to make us stronger. Hard times develop us into Agents of Transformation and the masterpieces, which God designed us to be at creation; after all the whole creation awaits us! God has a way with timing, and we need the faith to believe in Him for our rebound. We shouldn't live in the perception and realm of our fears and feelings; instead, we should live in the promises and reality of Faith to a God, who can and will do the impossible and have a favourable outcome for us.

The same goes with all the challenges you may encounter in having a business, working as an employee, leading a church, keeping the household, parenting as a single mother, enduring a stressful life experience, or thriving to live the abundant life. God is there in the big dreams, the adverse life events, the surprising life experiences, everyday activities and the menial things of our lives. He promises never to leave us nor forsake us.

God promises to strengthen us and to be with us always, and through all things. He promised to bless, prosper, provide, heal, comfort, rescue, protect, support, sustain, keep, and save us. He is our Redeemer, Friend that sticks closer than a Brother, Our Lord and Saviour. We should keep our eyes focused and affixed on Him, the Resurrection and the Life, and the Light of the World; bringing us to the fullness of life regardless of the circumstance, lightening every-darkness and increasing our faith for the rebound.

> *"Looking away from all that will distract us and focusing our eyes on Jesus, who is the Author and Perfectionist of faith, the first incentive for our belief and the One who brings our faith to maturity], who for the joy of accomplishing the goal set before Him endured the cross, disregarding the shame, and sat down at the right hand of the throne of God revealing His deity, His authority, and the completion of His work."*
>
> *~ Hebrews 12:2 Amplified Bible (AMP)*

The Birth of the Rebound Faith Series

Out of devastation; comes excellent innovation!

As mentioned earlier, in 2011, Nicola founded Nikimac Solutions Inc. Initially, her vision was simple: to provide up and coming business consultation services. However, as she journeyed through her years of divorce, depression, and devastation; God's grace extended the vision and repositioned her for purpose and deliverance. Nicola became naked and transparent about how pain can turn to gain if we depend on God's power and dwell in His presence. She began posting spiritual, motivational and inspirational posts through the Nikimac, Facebook Community to engage, encourage, and empower herself; instead, she was also refreshing, reviving and restoring many others with positivity.

It was during one of her inspirational devotions, while amid the fiery furnace, that Nicola began searching through the scriptures in desperation for God's presence to power her up, for revival, restoration, and recovery. She came across Deuteronomy 5:32-33, 30:6, 30:19-20.

"Therefore, you shall pay attention and be careful to do just as the Lord your God has commanded you; you shall not turn aside to the right or to the left [deviating from My commandments]. You shall walk [that is, live each and every day] in all the ways which the Lord your God has commanded you, so that you may live and so that it may be well with you, and that you may live long in the land which you will possess."

~ Deuteronomy 5:32-33 Amplified Bible (AMP)

"God, your God, will cut away the thick calluses on your heart and your children's hearts, freeing you to love God, your God, with your whole heart and soul and live, really live."

~ Deuteronomy 30:6-7 The Message (MSG)

I call heaven and earth as witnesses against you today, that I have set before you, life and death, the blessing and the curse; therefore, you shall choose life in order that you may live, you and your descendants, by loving the Lord your God, by obeying His voice, and by holding closely to Him; for He is your life [your good life, your abundant life, your fulfillment] and the length of your days, that you may live in the land which the Lord promised (swore) to give to your fathers, to Abraham, Isaac, and Jacob."

~ Deuteronomy 30:19-20 Amplified Bible (AMP)

Chayah!

That day, Nicola learnt a new Hebrew word, Chayah!

The Hebrew word, Chayah pronounced 'khaw-yaw' is rich in its definition and means to live, to survive, to revive, to thrive, to recover, to be restored to life, to rebound, and to 'really' live!

The website https://www.biblestudytools.com explains the following:

Chayah means to live, have life, to remain alive, to live whether literally or figuratively; causatively, to revive: —keep, leave, make alive, certainly give you the promised life, let it suffer and then resurrect to live, nourish up, and preserve alive.

Chayah is defined as to come alive, recover, repair, and restore to life. God saved your life, keeping you alive. God gave you a new life, so you live, be whole, and rebound from illness, weariness, faintness, abuse, and addiction; to live victoriously, righteously, prosperously, and zealously; to rebound from every defeat, devastation, depression, disease, disappointment, discouragement, debt, drama, divorce, disaster, and even death.

Chayah is to live forever, be active, to preserve alive, to live abundantly, to continue in life, to cause to grow, to sustain life, to live on or upon God, and to be quicken to life!

This revelation spoke to Nicola profoundly and gave her spiritual empowerment for her life, as well as the lives of her children. God promised to revive, restore, and rebound her, according to His Word, His Love, His Ways, His Will and in His Timing. She was fighting a fierce custody battle for her boys; they were hurting and trying to adjust to the many changes; lost their home, friends, school, and all familiar things which would have probably helped ease the transitions were gone; comfort zones wholly ruffled.

She needed hope to assure her that though she was still in the fire, in the miry pit, and in the dungeon; there was hope for a new life and not just for her, but for her children, and their future generation. Nicola's boys had listened to her praying! They had seen her crying many times at the altar! She suffered severe panic attacks. They had seen her depressed and unable to get out of bed. They knew she was broke and broken! However, they also knew that she believed in God, and she trusted Him; somehow, they knew she had faith in Him for her rebound.

God's Word promised her that He would heal our broken hearts and free us to love Him fully, and in seeking, finding and loving Him, through this painful process of life transformation, we would live; rebound and 'really' live… Chayah!

However, Nicola treasured up all these things, pondering them in her heart! It gave her hope that one day, she would chayah! One day Nicola's children would chayah! One day, our stories of Rebound Faith will also cause you too to chayah!

Though Nicola was at rock bottom and in a mess, she believed! After all, Jesus, crucified, resurrected and He lives, so that we too can live. Nicola and her children shall chayah against all the odds, despite the many obstacles, oppositions, and opponents. So, will you too!

Rebound to Live an Abundant Life!

As the storm raged, Nicola sought God, and He kept her! God progressively revealed the *game-changing secret* of abundance and restoration for the grit, wisdom, knowledge, and information for the Rebound Faith Spiritual Empowerment and Life Transformation series. God disclosed four principles of Rebound Faith as described in the three volumes of this book:

VOLUME ONE - *Her Background and Your Warm-Up!*

VOLUME TWO - *The Game Plan to...*

Live victoriously:

You evolve to a new level of progress along the Transformative Change Process.

The five stages (5Vs):

- *Violation*
- *Venting*
- *Valley*
- *Vision*
- *Vow*

Live righteously:

Praying for the unlocking of your envisioned future state by applying an effective Prophetic Prayer Strategy.

The five milestones (5 Rs):

- *Request*
- *Revelation*
- *Response*
- *Receive*
- *Rejoice.*

VOLUME THREE - *The Game Plan to...*

Live prosperously:

Enabling a renewed mind for mental wellness and equipping you with:

- *Positivity*
- *Perseverance*
- *Praise*
- *Prophecy*
- *Prayers.*

Live zealously:

Enthusiastically sharing your Rebound Faith stories as testimonies to empower others and bring glory to the Lord.

The Prophetic Prayer Strategy (5 Rs)

God divulged five milestones (Rs) of the Rebound Faith Prophetic Prayer Strategy to achieve a prosperous destiny and unlock the promised abundant life.

Request: Amid what seems like the ending, Nicola asks God for a new beginning.

Revelation: God reveals His word in alignment to her circumstances, makes His commitment as a covenant to Nicola, her children, and their future generation; for a good life, abundant life and the fulfillment of all the days of their lives.

Response: Nicola believes, receives, declares, and decides to activate God's truth and faithfully stand on His Word in prayers to evolve her through the transformation stages.

Receive: Her reaction to God's revelation changes her mind set to inspire positivity; think, speak, expect, and produce a positive outcome. God consistently delivers and manifests His promises. By God's grace, Nicola continues to live abundantly; to survive, revive, and thrive!

Rejoice: Nicola doesn't wait until the battle is over to praise God! She exalts the greatness, goodness, grace, and glory of God. She brings adorations to the Lord by sharing her story, prayers, declarations, and inspirational devotions during her storm, encouraging many others; leading even when she is bleeding!

Nicola knows pain, failure, loss, and suffering; but she encounters success, happiness, affluence, and influence as the reward of God's faithfulness.

God continues to manifest His honour, favour, and power through Nicola. The Holy Spirit has counselled and instructed her to:

- Develop *Rebound Faith*, as a personal Vision for her future state.

- Create *"Chayah"* as her Vow to come alive, survive, revive and thrive continuously, despite it all.

- Expand the Nikimac vision to transforming business, leaders and life.

- Invent the *'U Power Up* concept to empower and help others.

- Share her God story as her life-transformational testimony; offering her talents to encourage, empower and equip others.

- Seek, trust, obey and love the Lord.

God did it for Nicola, and He will undoubtedly do it even more spectacularly for you!

Rest assured that we can make mistakes, move on, let go, begin late, start over, look different, endure the seemingly impossible circumstances, be unsettled and still be significantly successful and beautiful!

We are confident, calm, and composed in God's plan for our future. We are courageous during the battle, with a state of dependence upon God to rebound us to live victoriously, righteously, prosperously and zealously!

Transforming Business, Leaders, and Life

Through Nikimac, Nicola teaches her clients to apply Rebound Faith for their chayah. Trusting in God and having the courage to face and overcome situations in their lives, homes, schools, ministries, workplaces, and their businesses. She helps leaders and entrepreneurs to believe in God for their visions and successes. She helps individuals to encounter God, to have hope and find happiness in life.

Let's face it, life is tough! We are either entering, enduring, or exiting a battle! How do we sustain and overcome adverse life events and experiences that knock the wind out of us? We must present our pain to the divine power of God and watch Him bring exaltation in every area of our afflictions. We must focus on the purpose rather than the pain of the process.

However, don't get the wrong impression – Nicola is frequently leading even when she is bleeding! With great calling come extraordinary challenges, responsibilities, demonic attacks, and spiritual warfare. She had to learn to put on the Whole Armour of God. She recognizes who the real enemy is and applies the weapons of war that work to consume and conquer the enemy. Cripples Satan and his plots before he attempts to destroy her life, children, character, household, career, business, finances, ministry, her support network, and her clients; each day and in their future.

"The weapons of our warfare are not physical [weapons of flesh and blood]. Our weapons are divinely powerful for the destruction of fortresses. We are destroying sophisticated arguments and every exalted and proud thing that sets itself up against the [true] knowledge of God, and we are taking every thought and purpose captive to the obedience of Christ, being ready to punish every act of disobedience, when your own obedience [as a church] is complete."

~ 2 Corinthians 10:4-6 Amplified Bible (AMP)

All prayed up, Nicola helps her clients to develop the most realistic goals and objectives for themselves, their families, and their businesses. Women, as well as men, are encouraged that despite the hardship of life, they can reset, recover, and rebound to greatness and chayah! On an individual basis, leaders and entrepreneurs are transformed and empowered to know their identity, find their purpose, and take charge of their own lives:

- Developing confidence
- Overcoming weakness and applying strengths
- Setting and attaining personal and professional goals
- Thinking and making positive choices
- Maximizing potential to be successful and self-sufficient
- Being elevated to move forward

Nicola views everyone as a leader, within themselves, innate and blessed by God and not based on a status or title, but on that which God has given everyone; authority, dominion, and the power to lead their own lives, to overcome the power of the enemy and to have a light that disperses all darkness.

"...to open their [spiritual] eyes so that they may turn from darkness to light and from the power of Satan to God, that they may receive forgiveness and release from their sins and an inheritance among those who have been sanctified (set apart, made holy) by faith in Me."

~ Acts 26:18 Amplified Bible (AMP)

Some leaders are called, hired or, chosen to lead others; however, we are role models in life; whether business or ministries or households; for we are all created by God to lead, to be fruitful, to multiply, to fill and conquer the earth, to rule and dominate it. So build your faith in God as a leader and develop an unshakeable belief in God to claim your dominion to conquer, rebound from failures and setback, with resilience to come back, the rest will happen on its own. There will be evidence of

- Successes in your household, children, and family to enjoy peace and prosperity

- Business or ministries you lead will see the rewards and positive performance

- Employees will be happy to work there; new long-term visions, short-term goals, and objectives will be creative, well thought-out and achieved

- A positive and engaging environment will be in place

- The manifestation of God's grace, victory and freedom for His glory in your life and the lives of others impacted

To Sum It All Up

We can talk about professional skills and qualifications all day long. However, what are most important are our life experiences and how our faith shapes what we take through them. The rest comes naturally. We learn all the most common skills like communication, time management, and customer service by being at the workplace or in the household, and like you, Nicola has developed many skills in her life. Not just in her career, but her personal life as well. During her difficult times growing up with her mother and brothers, Nicola learnt the value of determination and being independent. It was vital for her to develop these skills to prepare her for motherhood and her move to Canada. Being diligent, disciplined, and determined matured her to become exclusively independent; yet poverty and pain provided the dependence on God as her source of provision, protection, peace, and prosperity. These attributes became even more important to her when she got divorced and had to learn to start her life and career all anew, to live on her own again and stand on her own two feet; not just for herself, but for her two sons as well.

After a painful divorce, there was a sense of freedom and fear; facing so many unknowns in the future, yet the excitement and enthusiasm of a new beginning. Nicola had to rediscover herself, whom she was created and wired to be, the passion that drives her, and the unshakeable faith required for the rebound. She positively addressed all areas of her career, self-worth, self-esteem, starting over, singleness, social life, children, as well as single-parenting, dating, new relationships; achieving emotional, physical, spiritual, financial, and mental wellness. God was not punishing her; He was preparing her for His plan and promises. He was positioning her for Purpose! Nicola learnt to trust the process and focus on the mission despite the pain. God's divine power in her empowered her to overcome her struggle and the shame. She developed the capacity to grow and be innovative; be more resilient and recover quickly from difficulties; the Rebound Faith to get up again and again; the determination to grow deeper in her faith and climb higher in her success. The key to Rebound Faith is to thrive on moving forward despite the attacks, the accusations, the aggravations and the agony of defeat. Resisting, resetting, and recovering; to rebound again and again!

> *"But resist him, be firm in your faith [against his attack—rooted, established, immovable], knowing that the same experiences of suffering are being experienced by your brothers and sisters throughout the world. [You do not suffer alone.] After you have suffered for a little while, the God of all grace [Who imparts His blessing and favour], who called you to His own eternal glory in Christ, will Himself complete, confirm, strengthen, and establish you [making you what you ought to be]."*
>
> *~ 1 Peter 5:9-10 Amplified Bible (AMP)*

Starting over is not easy, but through life's hardships, you grow in strength, knowledge, and confidence in God to take hold of a new life despite the setbacks. You start being determined to rebound and 'really' live again.

Nicola learnt the importance of mental wellness, and how it could quickly destroy a reputation, a character, a career, one's family, finances, friendship, faith, and fun. Nicola's depression could have either made her or wholly broken her. However, for her own sake and the sake of her family, she got on her own two feet and made lemonade out of the lemons that life handed her. She took the chance and chose to change, to make something better of her rather than continue to mope around being bitter and feeling sorry for herself.

A critical character test in life is not during one's seasons of comfort, contentment, and convenience; but how one copes with challenging circumstances, contradictions, and controversies.

Nicola survived with her depression through her belief in God, exercising the faith to rebound. Moreover, it motivated her to get better and empowered her and others. With that, Nicola learnt how to bounce back and really live; live victoriously, righteously, prosperously, and zealously – to restore her family, to reconstruct her future, to redeem by God from her sins; to respond to God's calling to help others in the way that He helped her. She desires to see the magnificence of God and His excellence in the households, families, missions, ministries and the marketplace, as well as in the lives of individuals and leaders. She aims to help those that do not feel strong, confident, and self-assured in their trials and to power them up with hope in God, which she has known, throughout her life, to be dependable.

Right where you are is to be encouraged today!

The Lord is your hiding place. He will protect and defend you from every trouble, fill and heal your broken heart, and surround you with songs of deliverance.

The Lord is your shelter in the storm. He is your light and your Salvation so why should you be afraid? The Lord is your fortress protecting you from danger, so why should you tremble?

Every day is a new beginning to be inspired by the joyfulness of the Lord as your strength. Also, that should limit your sadness.

God will never forget you as your name is engraved on the palm of His hands (Is 49:16). He knows your name! God knows who you are. He knows your fears and failures. God knows your weakness and concerns. God remembers the plans and promises in store for you, and His nail scars remind Him of you. His wounds are evidence of the price He paid for you, your healing, your freedom; and the victory that He has already won on your behalf in every battle. So, no matter who has forgotten and failed you in the past, not God, He will never fail, fall, forget nor forsake you. The Lord's great love protects us, and the enemy will not consume us; for God's compassions never fail! God has chosen you! He loves you!

So, remain courageous, compassionate, and confident with composure, for what is coming is so much more significant than what's happening. Let God finish the work which He started in you! Be patient and convinced that God who began a good job in you will perfect and complete it. God will bring you mind-blowing miracles and dream-like blessings that will bring tears of gladness to your eyes, awe-inspired reverence to God, controversy among onlookers, dancing in your feet, and shouts songs of thanksgiving, praises and rejoice from your lips.

> *When the Lord brought back the captives to Zion (Jerusalem), we were like those who dream [it seemed so unreal]. Then our mouth was filled with laughter and our tongue with joyful shouting; then they said among the nations, "The Lord has done great things for them." The Lord has done great things for us; We are glad!*
>
> *Psalm 126:1-3 Amplified Bible (AMP)*

Becoming a Legend and Building a Legacy

Isn't it interesting that located on the top floors are many executive offices and penthouses, where you will find influential leaders and icons. The usual indicative of the testament to the Legends occupy them and their achievements, their fame and fortunes, game-changing success and accomplishments.

Legends achieve their dream and destiny despite the hardship; taking ownership of the highs and lows of life. Their achievements take sacrifice (blood), hard work (toil), determination (sweat), and discipline (tears). The process takes focused work to pursue, survive the pain and attain one's Purpose against all the odds, and to walk confidently through opened doors by faith and with the favour of God.

As you thrive for your goals and reap the gain of others opening doors for you, don't forget to invest in a Legacy; returning the great sentiment to help by holding the doors for others coming behind you. As you climb to the top and occupy those top floors in executive offices and penthouses, remember to send the elevator down!

Along life's journey, what you do and accomplish builds you as a Legend; while who you are, how you have lived, and how you have allowed what happened to you to positively impact others is establishing a Legacy that outlives and outlasts you.

You show yourself strong when you help others, being a light that illuminates their paths, even if you are hurting and leading while you bleed! After each fall, get up and rebound again, each time higher and higher, until you shatter glass ceilings!

Nicola is not done learning and shattering glass ceilings herself, and she never will be. She continues to thrive for new dimensions, to learn more patience, practise what she preaches while helping others to accomplish their goals. Nicola aims to increase others in inspiration, influence, impact, and income. As she strives to become a Legend, she is determined to leave a Legacy of Rebound Faith; to encourage you to gain the energy that will power you up.

As God continues to bless her; her desire becomes a channel of God's blessings to others and a spiritual and financial pillar to nations. She aspires to be a servant leader who leads with empathy, compassion, and integrity; knowing that a good leader is only possible by being a good follower, who serves and genuinely love others.

Nicola doesn't just want to teach her employees, clients, community, family, and friends how to be better leaders and how to live a purpose-filled life; she also wants to learn, support, and grow from, though, and with them. Together, they can chayah; to revive and live victoriously, righteously, prosperously, and zealously.

By His grace and all for His glory!

Pre-Game Warm-Up Drills

Preparing your Faith to believe your Rebound

What does it mean to Rebound?

- To bounce back from a forceful impact

- To revive from sickness or discouragement

- In Basketball; to acquire hold of rebounds by boxing-out the opponents. Boxing-out, in basketball, is achieved by positioning yourself, as the player, between an opponent and the basket, and efficiently guarding against the opponent with your body contact.

Boxing-Out is an essential and strategic technique to keep opponents from capturing the rebounds. It is a valid tactic that is utilized by a player to be able to get the most extraordinary comeback after missing a shot (basket); even a weaker and shorter player can block-out and gain the rebound over a stronger and taller player.

Player rebound effectiveness is measured by dividing the number of rebounds by the games played.

An analogy of Life to Basketball:
Box-Out the Opponent to Gain the Rebound

The definition of rebound in the game of basketball stands out to me. It makes me wonder what your rebound effectiveness in life battles is; especially when knowing that with Christ, your victory abounds and is imminent. Why do you give up? Why do you become discouraged and hopeless? Whose lens are you viewing the scoreboards?

Mind you, I am neither a sports expert nor an enthusiast, but let's compare the journey of life with the game of basketball.

In layman's terms, there are the:

- Team (players: families, friends, and other relationships)
- Coaches (teachers, parents, pastors, mentors)
- Referees (facilitators)
- Cheerleaders (support network)
- Role models (The Lord, legends, and leaders)
- Playbook (The Bible). The Bible provides the Truth, the revelation, knowledge, and information to navigate the plays, and apply the winning strategies – obedience, faith, and trust in the LORD. The covenant promises to govern the outcome as your victory already were pledged, predestined, and prophesied.
- Scoreboard (our successes - awards, titles, merits as well as the record of our failures)
- Distractions from the spectators (the haters, hinderers, and the hypocrites)
- Opponents: The opposing teams and their supporters (the enemy of our soul and his evil workers)

- Calls, Technical and Fouls (surprise and the suddenness of life)

- Injuries (adverse life events and challenges)

- Change of possession and turnovers (spiritual, physical, emotional, mental, financial, and other highs and lows)

- Stops/Starts/Timeouts (delays, denials, disappointments)

- Setups/setbacks (sometimes felt undeserved)

- Buzzer signifying the end of a quarter (a season in life), and the final buzzer signifying the end of the game (end of life on earth). Games are likened here to each battle faced in life; the preparation for the grand finale - The Championship Game.

- Moreover, there you are **a player**, not a spectator but an active participant in the game. You are experiencing the violation, the venting, the valley of despair, then the upturn, *'U Power Up*, establishing a new vision, and making a vow to come back with the victorious rebound.

You have something great in you to give; the determination to win and privilege to contribute to each game, the desire to gain victory and ignite the power in others. You bring skills, talents, gifts, and experiences to the game and the team. You play as an individual contributing to your household, organizations, community, and society. You aim to leave a legacy behind for future generation by inspiring, influencing and impacting lives. You celebrate the many victories. You murmur, mourn, and move-forward from each loss and seeming defeat. You make the vow to overcome the many setbacks; never to give up. Each quarter within the game, each game within the tournament, and each tournament season is a second chance for a new beginning. There is always hope! You fall, and with a little strength, you push yourself up again! You fail, but you don't beat yourself up for the mistakes. Instead, you try again, and again! It's OK not to be OK because it's going to be OK! You forgive quickly those who hurt you; you love profoundly and fight earnestly to refocus on your comeback; establish a new standard, game plan and strategy for victory. Never stop believing in yourself and your team! Ignore the noise, the distractions, and the naysayers – God-focused on the time-bounded game.

Your questions should challenge you; they should inflame your motive for encouragement and empowerment through setbacks and disappointments.

- How are you?
- Why are you afraid?
- What are your fears?
- What is possible, if you believe?
- What is this heaviness that you are carrying that is weighing you down?

You silent all other voices; press through the noise of the crowd, the lies, and of the enemy. You listen deeply to your inner soul; boldly speaking, positively, and profoundly to the hope in you for a victorious rebound.

SELF-TALK:

"I am not a convict to my past mistakes or my current circumstances. There are lessons to be learnt, not a life sentence to take my future captive. There is always hope! I am still alive! I will survive, revive and thrive... Chayah! I own this moment, this play, and this game! I believe in myself; my victory, my destiny, and my dream! Failure is not an option – I was born and built for this! It doesn't matter who doesn't like me, but merely tolerates or refuses to celebrate me. Your opinion of me is

useless. I am priceless! I am not a failure. I am not my setbacks, or past, or mistakes. I am a winner! I am more than enough. I am complete. Each day, I have the choice to give up or to let go – Today, I choose to let go of my mistakes, bitterness, and forgiveness, but never to give up! I decided to forgive myself and forgive others. The beginning or current scenes of my story may show that I began late, encountered setbacks, started over, was uncertain, looked and acted unlike others; But I am blessed to finish well, be fruitful and even more beautiful!

I am proud of me, after all, I have been through, I'm still here, still fighting, even in the game and failure is not an option. I thought of throwing in the towel, but no, I won't give up... I will use this towel to dry my tears, my sweat and even my blood! I am an overcomer, more than a conqueror, a mighty warrior, a winner, a world-changer! Each day, I make a new commitment to do well, better than I did yesterday – letting myself be my most significant competition!"

So, you get up, get dressed, and get moving! You show up early, rest well, sleep well, and eat well. Drink plenty of water, proper nutrition, exercise correctly, and do the drills. Determined, driven, and dedicated; you hustle! Meditate on the Book of Life (The Bible); seeking the strategy regarding the game and each play.

You are desperately and continuously working to improve your weakness to maximizing your potentials and capacity. You dream big dreams; never settling for mediocrity. You listen attentively to the Coach (Greatest Teacher, The Holy Spirit) in humility, obedience, and repentance. You forgive quickly and love genuinely. You show kindness, gratitude, and thoughtfulness to others. You know that there are consequences for bad choices and corrective discipline for your actions; and more grace, forgiveness, and mercy from Your Heavenly Father.

You are learning, growing, and developing the strength and stamina through the many defeats, denials, and disappointments. You know your game! You are setting new standards! You are creating a new order! You keep your eyes on the prize! Missed opportunities are tools used to mature your faith as an assurance to bounce back, blocking-out the opposition and gaining; The victorious Rebound!

You are leaving a legacy of Rebound Faith that will outlive and outlast you! You stop viewing the situation through the lens of your doubts and allow God to resurrect your hope to see the performance of His promises for your rebound to greatness and the continuous supply of God's goodness.

Rebound Faith Prayer and Declaration

Lord, I trust You to take me higher to have a more profound encounter and personal experience with You. The pruning, purging and purifying process is painful as You position me for purpose and prepare my promotion. Though I don't understand, I know that I am not here by accident, you know all things, and I am in Your hands. Though I am weak, I know that *is it not by might nor by power but by the Holy Spirit!* I trust Your plan wholly and wholeheartedly. I stand on Your Words, and I remember in the dark everything You told me in the light. I will not be afraid! I believe Lord that You are the Resurrection and the Life! I know that You are the great Physician. I am confident that You are my Shepherd and I shall not be in want... God says, *"Get moving and take charge, I have already set up your Rebound!"*

> Then the LORD said to Moses, "Why are you crying out to me? Tell the people to get moving!"
> ~ *Exodus 14:15 New Living Translation (NLT)*

Faith says, "Take Your Sandals Off; It's Rebound Time!"

No one puts new wine into old wineskins; otherwise, the [fermenting] wine will [expand and] burst the skins, and the wine is lost as well as the wineskins. But new wine must be put into new wineskins."

~ Mark 2:22 Amplified Bible (AMP)

New wine calls for new wineskins! To rebound from your current state and claim the manifestation of the empowered future state, you must rid yourself of *old* mindset, mentality, and thinking that are holding you back as a captive to your past. Wherever you find yourself in the path of life today, may God increase your greatness (honour) and turn to comfort you (Psalm 71:21).

God is saying to you, *"My Child, take your 'old' sandals off! I have positioned you for a victorious Rebound!"*

...saying, 'I am the God of your fathers—the God of Abraham, the God of Isaac, and the God of Jacob.' And Moses trembled and dared not look. Then the Lord said to him, "Take your sandals off your feet, for the place where you stand is holy ground. I have surely seen the oppression of My people who are in Egypt; I have heard their groaning and have come down to deliver them. And now come, I will send you to Egypt."

~ Acts 7:32-34 New King James Version (NKJV)

So, He said, "No, but as Commander of the army of the Lord I have now come." And Joshua fell on his face to the earth and worshiped, and said to Him, "What does my Lord say to His servant?" Then the Commander of the Lord's army said to Joshua, "Take your sandal off your foot, for the place where you stand is holy." And Joshua did so.

~ Joshua 5:14-15 New King James Version (NKJV)

Rebound from your 'old' self, relationships, attitudes and actions that are holding you back.

- *Rebound from your mediocrity living*
- *Rebound yourself from a toxic relationship*
- *Rebound yourself from abuse and manipulation*
- *Rebound yourself from stagnation*
- *Rebound yourself from sins*
- *Rebound yourself from unforgiveness*
- *Rebound yourself from people who don't tolerate nor celebrate you*
- *Rebound yourself from low standards*
- *Rebound yourself from negative thoughts and judgements*
- *Rebound to your promoted and esteemed position*
- *Rebound to possess your possession*
- *Rebound to your authority, dominion, and power*
- *Rebound to your fruitfulness and abundant harvest*
- *Rebound to the prophecies spoken over your life*
- *Rebound to your purpose and God-ordained destiny*
- *Rebound to 1st priority relationship with God*
- *Rebound to your identity as a Child of God*
- *Rebound to your Godly heritage and inheritance*
- *Rebound to God's plans and promises for you*
- *Rebound to a renewed mindset*

Rebound yourself **from** situations causing:

Hurt	Lack of character
Pain	Low self-esteem
Bitterness	Anger
Fear	Negative environment
Anxiety	
Stress	Unhealthy abusive relationships
Procrastination	Refusing to be coached or instructed
Lateness	
Doubt	
Low self-worth	Small mind thinking and low ambition
Laziness	
Low self-control	Sadness
Insecurity	Self-centeredness
No motivation	Disbelief
No creativity	No self-care nor mind-care
Frustration	Giving up
Comfort zone	Selfishness

Know that the place you are standing is Holy Ground! Right there in your devastation and depression, God says it's a Holy Ground; you are hand-picked, positioned, and anointed for deliverance.

Renew your mind with the right thoughts as limitless light – positivity, patience, prophecy, praise, prayers, and a personal relationship with Jesus.

> *And now, dear brothers and sisters; one final thing: Fix your thoughts on what is true, and honourable, and right, and pure, and lovely, and admirable. Think about things that are excellent and worthy of praise.*
> *~ Philippians 4:8 New Living Translation (NLT)*

There is a Well in Your Wilderness!

One morning, I was feeling so broken during the battle, I was crying out to God because desperate for my breakthrough. God led me to Gen 26:19. He revealed to me that right there in my valley experience was where I had an everlasting flowing well. It was a ground-breaking and world-shattering revelation! It shifted the atmosphere to reliable, positive energy. I began dancing, rejoicing and declaring, "I am claiming this Word for my Rebound Faith!"

> *But when Isaac's servants dug in the valley and found there a well of flowing [spring] water.*
> *~ Genesis 26:19 Amplified Bible (AMP)*

Beloved, you are never broken beyond repair but broken with a purpose and a promise! You may have suffered through various devastations, and history may have written damage in your past, but God takes all the broken pieces and makes you more beautiful! Wear the scars of your battles proudly; show the enemy that you are strong, brave, and more courageous. You overcame that which he intended to kill you!

Your pain attracts God's power in you!

Your anointing repels attacks and accusations. It is God's goodness in you; therefore, it shall be well!

Your wounds become why you worship!

Every disgrace testifies to His grace!

There is no testimony without a test, and the mess gives birth to the Message - *Christ is in you. Therefore, you can look forward to sharing in God's glory.*

From brokenness is the manifestation of Jesus' glorious blessings!

Not only those but all the broken and dislocated pieces of the universe - people and things, animals, and molecules - get properly fixed and fit together in vibrant harmonies, all because of his death, His blood that poured down from the Cross.

You yourselves are a case study of what He does. At one time you all had your backs turned to God, thinking rebellious thoughts of him, giving him trouble every chance you got. But now, by giving himself completely at the Cross, actually dying for you, Christ brought you over to God's side and put your lives together, whole and holy in his presence. You don't walk away from a gift like that! You stay grounded and steady in that bond of trust, constantly tuned in to the Message, careful not to be distracted or diverted. There is no other Message - just this one. Every creature under heaven gets this same Message.

I, Paul, am a messenger of this Message. I want you to know how glad I am that it's me sitting here in this jail and not you. There's a lot of suffering to be entered into in this world - the kind of suffering Christ takes on. I welcome the chance to take my share in the church's part of that suffering.

When I became a servant in this church, I experienced this suffering as a sheer gift, God's way of helping me serve you, laying out the whole truth. This mystery has been kept in the dark for a long time, but now it's out in the open. God wanted everyone, not just Jews, to know this rich and glorious secret inside and out, regardless of their background, regardless of their religious standing.

The mystery, in a nutshell, is just this: Christ is in you; therefore, you can look forward to sharing in God's glory. It's that simple. That is the substance of our Message.

We preach Christ, warning people not to add to the Message. We teach in a spirit of profound common sense so that we can bring each person to maturity. To be mature is to be basic. Christ! No more, no less. That's what I'm working so hard at day after day, year after year; doing my best with the energy God so generously gives me.
~ Colossians 1:20-29 The Message (MSG)

So rather than vent constant negativity; say, *"God, this violation hurts like crazy, I am amid the valley of darkness, I have no idea how You are going to make this all beautiful, but You promise to work things together for my good and Your glory. With this truth and Your power, I am shifting my thoughts and self-talks to positivity. I believe in a new vision of Rebound Faith for my future as such I make a vow to move forward and chayah! I am growing, glowing and glorifying God!"*

You could *go* through the storms or *grow* through the storms. As you rebound from your current situation to your envisioned future state, you have a choice to face down the giants that were holding you back. You arise with new hope, possibilities, and opportunities. Out of devastation, your greatness, excellence, innovation and high creativity all come together. You are created by the Creator to be creative! You give birth to new businesses, new ministries, new ideas and product/service concepts. You create, as a Legend and contribute to a Legacy that outlives and outlasts you.

> *Overwhelmed? Kneel and let God fight your battle!*
> *Every next level of your life will require a new you!*

As you lay down your focus on traditional accomplishments; you go through the eye of the needle. You take hold of Christ as your priority, and you evolve in a new you with a renewed life to achieve significant success on earth and eternal life in heaven.

You begin to:

- Experience your Salvation and have a personal relationship with Jesus

- Encounter God's power and presence for your transformation

- Establish a new vision and vow of a future aligned with your Purpose, which is part of God's divine plan

What is Faith?

Faith is confidence and trust in God, in who He is (His Character and Attributes), and what He can do (His Conduct and Actions) that absolutely nothing is too difficult or impossible for Him. Therefore, when we put our belief in God and in what we hope for will happen, it gives us a blessed assurance and an expectation of a favourable outcome of the things we cannot yet see.

*"**Faith** is not a mere feeling, and it is not the absence of fear but a deliberate action. It is the determination to trust God even when you don't understand and especially when the path ahead is unknown and seems uncertain."*

We have Faith in what we don't or can not yet see. So, don't let what our eyes see dictate what we ought to believe.

It is by faith that we act!

It is by faith that we live!

It is by faith that we fight!

It is by faith that we stand!

It is by faith that we speak!

It is by faith that we believe!

It is by faith that we understand!

It is by faith that we please God!

It is by faith that we move forward!

It is by faith that we walk and not by sight!

It is by faith that we prophesy our rebound!

Therefore, you shall focus your faith to rebound through every cycle of life.

Hebrews 11 explains and provides examples to demonstrate faith. Faith means being sure of the things we hope for and knowing that something is real even if we do not see it. Faith is the reason we remember great people who lived in the past. It is by faith we understand that God's command made the whole world. So, we believe that what we see was made by something that is unseen. Without faith, no one can please God. Anyone who comes to God must believe that He is real and that He rewards those who truly want to find Him.

- Now faith is confidence in what we hope for and assurance about what we do not see. ~ Hebrews 11:1 (NIV)

- Now faith is the substance of things hoped for, the evidence of things not seen. ~ Hebrews 11:1 (NKJV)

- Faith shows the reality of what we hope for; it is the evidence of things we cannot see. ~ Hebrews 11:1 (NLT)

- Now faith is assurance of things hoped for, a conviction of things not seen. ~ Hebrews 11:1 (ASV)

- The fundamental fact of existence is that this trust in God, this faith, is the firm foundation under everything that makes life worth living. It's our handle on what we can't see. The act of faith is what distinguished our ancestors, set them above the crowd. ~ Hebrews 11:1-2 (MSG)

Faith brings you Hope; Hope gives Happiness, and Happiness Drives Healing.

For in this hope we were saved [by faith]. But hope [the object of] which is seen is not hope. For who hopes for what he already sees? But if we hope for what we do not see, we wait eagerly for it with patience and composure.

~ Romans 8:24-26 Amplified Bible (AMP)

Faith gives you a new perspective and mindfulness that each moment is only temporary and will eventually pass, and God has a more significant outcome in store for you.

Therefore, we do not become discouraged [spiritless, disappointed, or afraid]. Though our outer self is [progressively] wasting away, yet our inner self is being [progressively] renewed day by day. For our momentary, light distress [this passing trouble] is producing for us an eternal weight of glory [a fullness] beyond all measure [surpassing all comparisons, a transcendent splendour, and an endless blessedness]! So, we look not at the things which are seen, but at the things which are unseen; for the things which are visible are temporal [just brief and fleeting], but the things which are invisible are everlasting and imperishable.

~ 2 Corinthians 4:16-18 Amplified Bible (AMP)

Faith must be deeply rooted in Christ's faithfulness, not your fear, failures nor fragility; even if you are faithless, He remains faithful— for He cannot deny himself. (2 Timothy 2:13)

But, Christ is faithful as a Son over His [Father's] house. And we are His house if we hold fast our confidence and sense of triumph in our hope [in Christ].

~ Hebrews 3:6 Amplified Bible (AMP)

Faith keeps you moving forward to live a purposeful life, in hope, confidence, and courage; despite what your eyes see.

Now He who has made us and prepared us for this very purpose is God, who gave us the [Holy] Spirit as a pledge [a guarantee, a down payment on the fulfillment of His promise]. So then, is always filled with good courage and confident hope, and knowing that while we are at home in the body, we are absent from the Lord— for we walk by faith, not by sight [living our lives in a manner consistent with our confident belief in God's promises].

~ 2 Corinthians 5:5-7 Amplified Bible (AMP)

Faith warrants you to share in the secured promises and victory of Christ, when you hold firmly, persevere and trust Christ to the end.

For we [believers] have become partakers of Christ [sharing in all that the Messiah has for us], if only we hold firm our newborn confidence [which originally led us to Him] until the end...

~ Hebrews 3:14 Amplified Bible (AMP)

Faith in Christ's resurrection sustains, strengthens, and supports you; therefore, you don't give up as your circumstances will not defeat you.

But our way is not that of those who shrink back to destruction, but [we are] of those who believe [relying on God through faith in Jesus Christ, the Messiah], and by this confident faith preserve the soul.

~ Hebrews 10:39 Amplified Bible (AMP)

Faith pleases God, and God rewards your faithfulness and righteousness for trusting and believing in Him.

But without faith, it is impossible to [walk with God and] please Him, for whoever comes [near] to God must [necessarily] believe that God exists and that He rewards those who [earnestly and diligently] seek Him.

~ Hebrews 11:6 Amplified Bible (AMP)

Faith gives you steadfast and unwavering trust in God; therefore, you do not fear men or facts!

By faith Moses left Egypt, being unafraid of the wrath of the king; for he endured [steadfastly], as seeing Him who is unseen. By faith, he kept the Passover and the sprinkling of the blood [on the doorposts], so that the destroyer of the firstborn would not touch them (the firstborn of Israel). By faith, the people [of Israel] crossed the Red Sea as though they were passing through dry land, but when the Egyptians attempted it, they were drowned.

~ Hebrews 11:27-29 Amplified Bible (AMP)

Faith makes you a Legend! When you believe God and take Him at His Word; you become a hero, an Icon of Righteousness and leave a Legacy of Glory for the future generation.

By faith [with confidence in God and His word] Noah, being warned by God about events not yet seen, in reverence prepared an ark for the salvation of his family. By this [act of obedience] he condemned the world and became an heir of the righteousness which comes by faith.

~ Hebrews 11:7 Amplified Bible (AMP)

Faith causes you to believe that nothing is impossible with God. He will bring victory even out of problematic tasks that He asks you to do or even the painful journey that God allows in your life; to bring you to the beautiful destination, He has already prepared for you.

By faith Abraham, when he was called [by God], obeyed by going to a place which he was to receive as an inheritance; and he went, not knowing where he was going. By faith, he lived as a foreigner in the Promised Land, as in a strange land, living in tents [as nomads] with Isaac and Jacob, who were fellow heirs of the same promise. For he was [waiting expectantly and confidently] looking forward to the city which has foundations, [an eternal, heavenly city] whose architect and builder is God. By faith even Sarah herself received the ability to conceive [a child], even [when she was long] past the normal age for it, because she considered Him who had given her the promise to be reliable and true [to His word]. So, from one man, though he was [physically] as good as dead, were born as many descendants as the stars of heaven in number and innumerable as the sand on the seashore.

~ Hebrews 11:9-12 Amplified Bible (AMP)

Faith makes you strong, even in your weakness, and mighty in the battle for your victory.

[11]Because of faith also Sarah herself received physical power to conceive a child, even when she was long past the age for it because she considered [God] Who had given her the promise to be reliable and trustworthy and true to His word.

[17]By faith Abraham, when he was put to the test [while the testing of his faith was still in progress], had already brought Isaac for an offering; he who had gladly received and welcomed [God's] promises was ready to sacrifice his only son.

[29] [Urged on] by faith the people crossed the Red Sea as [though] on dry land, but when the Egyptians tried to do the same thing they were swallowed up [by the sea].

[30] Because of faith, the walls of Jericho fell down after they had been encompassed for seven days [by the Israelites].

[31] Prompted by faith, Rahab the prostitute was not destroyed along with those who refused to believe and obey, because she had received the spies in peace [without enmity].

[32-34] And what shall I say further? For time would fail me to tell of Gideon, Barak, Samson, Jephthah, of David and Samuel and the prophets, who by [the help of] faith subdued kingdoms, administered justice, obtained promised blessings, closed the mouths of lions, extinguished the power of raging fire, escaped the devouring of the sword, out of frailty and weakness won strength and became stalwart, even mighty and resistless in battle routing alien hosts.

~ Hebrews 11 Amplified Bible, Classic Edition (AMPC)

- *Faith makes you take God at His Word!*

God can not lie nor die. Faith gives you the confidence, assurance, and substance to believe:

- **His Promises:** Gods says, "I have prearranged, predestined, and planned that you possess this land!"

- **His Preparedness:** God says, "I have located, positioned and equipped you for the Promised Land."

- **His Proclamation:** God says, "Now go and possess your possession!"

Faith gives you the firm foundation for your trust in God to have hope, spunk and the backbone to Rebound. Why? Because God said it, so shall it be. It doesn't matter what it feels like, looks like, or smells like; it is over!

Faith takes you from wandering in the wilderness to possessing the Promised Land; despite the giants, you shall own your territory by force, terrifying your terrors!

> *But I have said to you, "You are to inherit and take possession of their land, and I will give it to you to possess, a land [of plenty] flowing with milk and honey." I am the Lord your God, who has separated you from the peoples (pagan nations).*
> ~ *Leviticus 20:24 Amplified Bible (AMP)*

Rebound Faith Prayer and Declaration

Lord, Hebrews 11:1 says, *"Faith is the confidence that what we hope for will happen, and it gives us assurance about the things we cannot see."*

Heavenly Father: thank You for a new day. Lord give me the measure of faith that will make me know that the next step in the journey will be safe, sure, satisfied, and secured. Thank You for remaining faithful even when I am faithless. Thank You, Lord, for Your promises to deliver and redeem me. Help me, Lord, to trust You always and to stay confident in You, even when I don't understand the process and can't seem to find You nor feel Your touch. Lord, I know the purpose is to bring You glory... So, I muscle up my mustard seed of faith... Today, I declare, decide and do it! I am coming out!

I command every mountain to move... I claim every covenant promise of God in my life. I declare a bountiful harvest to every barren area in my life... Promotion in my career; Supernatural blessings over my children, family, and household; Doors open in my Ministry; Financial breakthrough and debt cancellation; Healing, health, mental wellness, wealth, wisdom, favour, and honour; Increased income, impact, and influence to bring glory to God.

I decree and declare that I am a masterpiece, and I see myself as strong, magnificent and marvellous, with mind-blowing miracles. I have the **grit** that You are expecting in a Child of God! I shall not move from my position of victory, neither shall I be shaken from my faith in God!

I am standing in agreement with Jesus about what He said about me, *"I have come that you may have life and have it to the full. I am leaving you with a gift--peace of mind and heart. Moreover, the peace I give is a gift the world cannot give. So, don't be troubled or afraid."*

I pray that in all respects I may have peace and prosper, and be in good health just as my soul prospers. God has told me these things, so believe that I am full, complete, contented, and fulfilled; with His joy. Yes, my happiness, richness, blessings, and greatness will overflow! In Jesus mighty name, I pray, praise, and proclaim these prophetic utterances, Amen.

> *I have told you these things so that My joy and delight may be in you, and that your joy may be made full and complete and overflowing.*
>
> *~ John 15:11 Amplified Bible (AMP)*

> *So, will My word be which goes out of My mouth; It will not return to Me void (useless, without result), without accomplishing what I desire, and without succeeding in the matter for which I sent it.*
>
> *~ Isaiah 55:11 Amplified Bible (AMP)*

What is Rebound Faith? The Grit!

During the storms of 2011-2015, I attempted to define Rebound Faith several times. I knew how it renewed my mind and shifted my attitude from the problem to the Problem-Solver; giving me a strategy and solution for growth, development, and rebirth. I was confident, and it brought me peace, hope, and positivity for an expected end. It gave me grit; strengthened me in the Lord, and made me believe in my rebound that it was my time and my turn for deliverance. I experienced how it turned me to focus on the power of God instead of the pain of the process. I testified that it revealed to me who I was as a Child of God and the access I had through the Blood to go before a Holy God. I believe it emphasized my relationship with Jesus to "hook me up" through His grace with goodness, greatness, and gladness, for His glory.

Looking back at my journey, my numerous prayers and inspirational posts, and the testimony of the glory of God; I am confident in sharing with you the definition of Rebound Faith.

> ***Rebound Faith*** *is unshakeable faith in God and the fortitude to believe that despite it all, you will overcome every opposition (spiritual, mental, emotional, financial, or physical) while being victorious throughout the stages of the transformation process. You will remain fervent, confident, and strategic in your prayers, having a renewed mindset and hope for an expected end to rebound with a glorious testimony.*

Rebound Faith is faithfulness and righteousness in Christ that gives you the Grit to survive, revive and thrive from devastation and depression to deliverance!

Rebound Faith makes you bold, brave, courageous, and fearless, with resilience and tenacity; having toughness, hardiness, the strength of character, and strong-will for determination, perseverance, and endurance!

Rebound Faith, the Secret Sauce for a Paradigm Shift

We define the *secret sauce* as a unique feature, the game plan, or technique kept secret by pioneers or innovators and regarded as being the chief factor for its success.

The *paradigm shift* is that radical transformation which occurs when we replace the usual way of understanding or pursuing something with a new and different way or thinking.

We looked at the definition of Rebound and the meaning of having and plying our Faith. So, what is the *secret sauce* of Rebound Faith that will bring about a *paradigm shift* that we are seeking? Please allow me to coach you a bit by asking you to think about the revelation and information provided in the definitions, the explanations, and applications of 'Rebound' and 'Faith.'

- What if during your life challenges and changes, you renew your mind and stand, and fight in an unshakeable faith in God, declaring Christ's victory as the assurance for your rebound to chayah; to revive and 'really' live?

- What if you apply the revelation of the truth of God's Word when faced with adverse life events and circumstances?

- What would be your rebound effectiveness?

- How different would you respond to the situation, during the transition and the overall transformation?

- How would you approach the Throne of Grace for help, mercy, favour, honour, and wisdom?

- How would you view your current situation and your desired empowered future state?

- What if your approach was so radically different that from the moment you made the prayer request to God, you immediately shifted to rejoice? Pioneering a new *paradigm* in praising God in advance for the expected and favourable outcome knowing that He would give you His ultimate and utmost best.

- Wouldn't you be more peaceful, joyful, and hopeful; positively impacting you emotionally, mentally, physically, and relationally?

I guarantee you that if you choose to renew your mind, there will be a tremendous transformation in you to achieve your destiny; and as you mature in the application of Rebound Faith, you will begin to:

Dream big and have gigantic visions. God never gives you a dream that matches your resources. It is God who equips you with everything good for doing His will, which He may work in us to do what is pleasing to Him through Jesus Christ for His glory. God does not check your status, rank, title, budget, bank account, resume, and qualifications. He tests your faith! Having faith to believe the things hoped for and the evidence of things not seen.

> *Now faith is the assurance (the confirmation, the title deed) of the things [we] hope for, being the proof of things [we] do not see and the conviction of their reality [faith perceiving as real fact what is not revealed to the senses].*
>
> *~ Hebrews 11:6 Amplified Bible, Classic Edition (AMPC)*

> *But without faith, it is impossible to please and be satisfactory to Him. For whoever would come near to God must [necessarily] believe that God exists and that He is the rewarder of those who earnestly and diligently seek Him [out].*
>
> *~ Hebrews 11:6 Amplified Bible, Classic Edition (AMPC)*

Ask in faith without doubting. But let him ask in faith, nothing wavering. For he that doubt is like a wave of the sea driven with the wind and tossed (James 1:6).

> *But he must ask [for wisdom] in faith, without doubting [God's willingness to help], for the one who doubts is like a billowing surge of the sea that is blown about and tossed by the wind. For such a person ought not to think or expect that he will receive anything [at all] from the Lord, being a double-minded man, unstable and restless in all his ways [in everything he thinks, feels, or decides].*
>
> *~ James 1:6-8 Amplified Bible (AMP)*

Have the confidence that God hears your prayers and understands your needs. For this is the confidence that we have before Him: If we ask anything according to His will, He understands us. (1 John 5:14)

> *You have not chosen Me, but I have chosen you, and I have appointed and placed and purposefully planted you, so that you would go and bear fruit and keep on bearing, and that your fruit will remain and be lasting, so that whatever you ask of the Father in My name [as My representative] He may give to you.*
>
> *~ John 15:16 Amplified Bible (AMP)*

Make your requests with an eager expectation of receiving. And all things, whatsoever ye shall ask in prayer, believing, ye shall receive (Matthew 21:22).

> *Truly, truly, I tell you, whoever believes in Me will also do the works that I am doing. He will do even greater things than these because I am going to the Father. And I will do whatever you ask in My name, so that the Father may be glorified in the Son. If you ask Me anything in My name, I will do it.*
>
> *~ John 14:12-16 New International Version (NIV)*
>
> *For this reason, I am telling you, whatever things you ask for in prayer [in accordance with God's will], believe [with confident trust] that you have received them, and they will be given to you.*
>
> *~ Mark 11:24 Amplified Bible (AMP)*

Rebound Faith – It's Evolution!

Rebound Faith drives you to think positively about the outcome of your situation.

> *Our thoughts drive our behaviour, emotions, attitude, feelings, and reality; whether we choose to be reflective as a victor or reactive as a victim.*

With positive thoughts, we have a positive perspective and produce peace, positivity, and prosperity. We can journey through the storm being unaffected, resolute, and focused; with the confidence of a warranted assurance that God hears our requests and He will soon respond with His utmost and ultimately best for us.

My most profound prayer is that God will give you the revelation of Rebound Faith in your own life. For no matter where you are in the Transformative Change Process, you will pray passionately, speak prophetically and boldly proclaim your chayah; with a renewed mindset to **rejoice** at the **request** about your forthcoming testimony.

> *"Blessed [with spiritual security] is the man who believes and trusts in and relies on the Lord and whose hope and confident expectation is the Lord.*
>
> *For he will be [nourished] like a tree planted by the waters, that spreads out its roots by the river; and will not fear the heat when it comes; But its leaves will be green and moist. And it will not be anxious and concerned in a year of drought nor stop bearing fruit."*
>
> *~ Jeremiah 17:7-8 Amplified Bible (AMP)*

In 2014, (hashtag) *#ReboundFaith* started to appear in my inspirational devotions on the Nikimac Community and blogs of Nikimac webpage. At that time, no one took notice, commended nor recognized the (hashtag) *#ReboundFaith*; unlike many others, it was not a popular trend. Very few people questioned what it represented, and even fewer people reused it. It remained quiet to the mass while it shouted and celebrated my progress, my determination to triumph and discover my Purpose despite my setback and the pain of my process.

Proving that not everyone will see your vision, identify with your vow to change; neither will they understand your journey, pain, progress, nor your process of recovery; worse still, no one will even dare to believe your dreams and your destiny. They won't appreciate your calling; but that's OK, for it's not for them, it is for you. They will never understand the journey that God has asked you to take. Therefore, find something that visually represents your hope and the expected outcome, and communicate it to yourself (using various media or channels) until it resonates with you, serves your Purpose, provides the actions required for your recovery, and establishes your core value. You cannot change what happens to you, but you have control over how it impacts you. Your choice is to take the chance and let the challenge shift you to develop the character as God designed you.

The person you are becoming may initially lose friendships, finances, fortunes, and fame but gradually, you are becoming the masterpiece God designed you to be. For what good would it profit you to gain the world and lose your soul?

You were handpicked by God to fulfill the Purpose He had in mind when He created you. The battle is hot, but the fire will purify you, burn the impurities, and imperfections from you. Out of the Fire, like a phoenix, you shall arise; with all your ashes turning to beauty!

The person you are becoming will enjoy and live a joyful, beautiful, and abundant life on earth, and gain the ultimate gift of eternal life – that is the real success! You will attain, be awarded and acknowledged for a person of excellence, significance, and value. You will continuously gain the awareness, the buy-in, and accept the commitment to pursue your Purpose. Own your story - become your advocate, a cheerleader, and vow to be a Change Agent for your transformation. As you make up your mind to lead your change; the shift happens! Learn to cherish, celebrate, and cheer yourself for the advance despite the absence of the applause of the audience!

#Rebound Faith is an inward force that propels me to think positively, and pursue my vision.

#UpowerUp is the determination to empower me and others.

#Chayah is the vow to come alive, survive, revive, and thrive.

These hashtags are symbols of my vision statement, my pledge, and my core values which described my comeback while I was amid the storm. I made a vow that continues to drive my grit to box-out the opposition, to rebound to victory, and to help others along their journey of life. I am determined to come alive, survive, revive and thrive... Chayah!

•   *#ReboundFaith* materialized and continued to mature into years of Inspirational Devotions, messages/speech, motivational quotes, fervent and prophetic prayers, and media for life transformation and spiritual empowerment.

•   *#UpowerUp* manifested in the *upowerup.com*; with several empowerment events, programmes, a growing partnership network, social projects, and a compelling tagline: *Life Happens, Stay Strong!*

Some of the popular programmes offered on the upowerup.com website include:

- **Daniel Fast, 21 Days of Prayers**, God is Closing the GAP - Embracing the Change through faith and fasting.

- **Vision Board Workshop** – Gaining a new perspective of positivity towards your future to attract a positive outlook and outcome. Bringing groups and individuals together to work on their vision through visualization, declaration, and manifestation.

- **Prayed and Prepared for My Rib** – Understanding the principles of God to prepare you, your character, conduct, attributes, and actions for your relationship, marriage, family, and purpose. Share your love story to effect change as well as engage in others' real-life stories of how to experience and express love.

Therefore, the concept of Rebound Faith is more than a cute cliché but is tied to the Biblical principles of faith and works; believing and trusting in God's Word to remain positive, peaceful, and hopeful that the setback was only a setup for the comeback.

You were pulled back only to boost forward, catapult faster, propel further, and launch higher!

Rebound Faith outlines a Prophetic Prayer Strategy (5 Rs) for Life Transformation to provide you with spiritual empowerment, engagement, and encouragement; having your focus on the supernatural power of God during your Transformative Change process.

Rebound Faith ignites God's power of unexplainable peace, joy, and hope to combat the seemingly interminable, lonely and low feelings experienced during the waiting period for a Change transition; by applying the 5Rs in the Rebound Faith Prophetic Prayer approach.

During the Transformative Change Process, depression, discouragement, and hopelessness typically occur amidst the seemingly extended waiting period for the change to become the new norm. Often the affected person becomes discouraged and disheartened, and therefore, is unable to align their faith to visualize an expected, favourable end; victoriously overcome their fears and hope for the envisioned future state.

When you are going through adverse life events and the transition process, you feel lost, unloved, abandoned, and rejected as if there is no way out, no turnaround in sight, and the failure is too irreparable for recovery. You are often sad, weak, and weary. You are unable to find the strength to survive, succeed, and move forward. You are uncertain and afraid of the future, feeling frustrated, and feeling like a failure. You believe that past mistakes or current mishaps are too much to handle and you lose the confidence within yourself.

It is during the waiting period from the current situation to the future position that you need to exercise the faith to rebound, and the inspired positivity to chayah; having the grit to survive, revive, thrive and '*really*' live.

The principles of Rebound Faith will significantly encourage you, impact and influence your thought, outlook, and mindset on anything and everything that comes your way.

- You will begin to explore new opportunities and gain new insights, dream big, formulate a vision, and visualize a brighter new future.

- You will start to strengthen, fight for survival, and succeed. You will hope and have confidence that it will be OK; crawling out of denial, walking out of resistance and climbing out of the valley of despair.

- You will be encouraged to pray, declare, and speak life amidst the wilderness season; calling forth miracles, resurrection, and restoration.

- You will begin to smell success and entice a positive atmosphere to change your circle and circumstances! You begin to feel good about yourself, as moving forward looks so good on you!

- You will start to own your breakthrough and seek God's manifestation of His power in you to motivate, mature and stimulate new growth in you.

- Then suddenly, your worries will turn into worship; catapulting you to new dimensions!

Your prayers are like Psalms, shifting quickly through the 5 Rs milestones of your Rebound Faith Prophetic Prayers:

- From the Request,
- To the Revelation,
- To the Response,
- To the Receive,
- Then to the Rejoice!

It's no wonder why I am passionate about my testimony of Rebound Faith as the antidote for my depression. Rebound Faith fueled my fire, fierceness, and force that drove my transformation during my stress-filled life experience. It gave me the right backbone, moral fibre, spirit, and spunk!

My desperation drove me to pursue my deliverance deeply; I found it in God through His divine principles, practices, and the performance of the Rebound Faith Strategy and Solution which allowed me to believe, speak and manifest my deliverance and breakthrough to chayah!

God did it for me, and He will undoubtedly do it for you!

The Rebound Faith
Prophetic Prayer Strategy (5Rs)

The Strategy for Rebound Faith breakthrough prayers is to understand the five milestones (5 Rs) within the stages of praying:

- **Request**. The specific need!

- **Revelation**. The alignment and disclosure of the truth of God's Word and His promises regarding the ask.

- **Response.** The faith to believe God for the release of His promises and the activation of God's answer in the supernatural realm by standing and praying His Word.

- **Receive**. It's the manifestation of God's response in the natural domain.

- **Rejoice**. The great thanksgiving, adoration, and exaltation to God!

By exercising confidence in your prayers as you approach the Throne of Grace, knowing that God Almighty is ultimately in control; He oversees the universe. The earth is the Lord's, and everything in it. The world and its people belong to him. He holds the entire universe in His hands. He is the Beginning and the End. He has the First and the Last authority, the First and Final say. He is the Alpha and the Omega, the Creator, the God above all gods, the King of kings, the Sovereign God, the Lord, Our Shepherd... and He is your Heavenly Father, your Abba. You have got relationship and connection high up; doors, gates, channels and the heaven are open for you because He unconditionally loves you, chooses you, and grants you unlimited access to His infinite grace.

Your Heavenly Father delights to prosper and bless you. He takes pleasure in answering your prayers with the best of gifts for you, His beloved child.

> *What father among you, if his son asks for a fish, will give him a snake instead of a fish? Or if he asks for an egg, will give him a scorpion? If you, then, being evil [that is, sinful by nature], know how to give good gifts to your children, how much more will your heavenly Father give the Holy Spirit to those who ask and continue to ask Him!"*
>
> *~ Luke 11:11-13 Amplified Bible (AMP)*

As you take your prayer requests to your All-Knowing, Sovereign God, All-Loving Abba Father, He is faithful to always answer your prayers.

Sometimes, He gives you:

- **A Resounding, favourable yes!** Undoubtedly bringing God glory and aligning with His Will!

- **A Faith-building, wait, not yet!** It's not, however, the time or season in the Kingdom. Delays are not always denials; frequently, our Character needs to align with our Calling. God is using this process to mature our Godly Attributes which should drive our Actions.

- **A Merciful No!** There is something better which is in store, according to God's divine will! God is doing a new thing to bring even greater Glory to Himself and His Kingdom!

- **A Loving Silence!** When you don't understand and can't find the answers, the way seems unclear, and the wait seems too long; that's when the Lord whispers, "Trust Me!"

Trust God!

God never said become fearful, worried, anxious, or stressed out; He said, "Trust me!" During those moments when you don't understand God's answer, declare the truth of His word:

> *However, now, this is what the LORD says— He who created you, He who formed you: "Do not fear, for I have redeemed you; I have summoned you by name; you are mine. Do not let your hearts be troubled. You believe in God; trust and hope also in me. Have I not commanded you? Be strong and courageous! Do not be terrified or dismayed (intimidated), for the Lord your God is with you wherever you go. Trust in and rely confidently on the Lord with all your heart and do not rely on your insight or understanding. In all your ways know and acknowledge and recognize Him, and He will make your paths straight and smooth, removing obstacles that block your way."*
>
> *(Isaiah 43:1, John 14:1, Joshua 1:9, Proverbs 3:5-6)*

Now activate your Rebound Faith to chayah!

Lord, I'm so thankful for all the answers to my prayers which I have already received; the *"Yes!", "Not Yet!"* and *"Wait, I have something better in store!"* Your answer which I interpreted as *"No"* was painful at the time but looking back, and You were so right! The *silence* is still the hardest, but You are building my faith, and I believe that You will revive and restore me. Lord,

You always answer my prayers. You have empowered and equipped my faith to accept and activate my confidence to trust You for the responses to prayers that are yet to manifest. These are my big dreams of my even Bigger God!

O Lord of hosts, how blessed and greatly favoured is the man who trusts in you, believing in you, relying on you, and committing himself to You with confident hope and expectation. Moreover, now, O Lord God, You are God, and Your words are the truth, and You have promised this good thing to Your servant. Therefore now, may it please You to bless the house (royal dynasty) of Your servant, so that it may continue forever before You; for You, O Lord God, have spoken it, and with Your blessing may the house of Your servant be blessed forever. I have trusted and relied on and been confident in Your loving kindness and faithfulness; My heart shall rejoice and delight in Your salvation. However, as for me, I trust confidently in You and Your greatness, O Lord; I said, "You are my God. My times are in Your hands; Rescue me from the hand of my enemies and from those who pursue and persecute me." For I have trusted and relied on and been confident in Your loving kindness and faithfulness; My heart shall rejoice and delight in Your salvation. Some trust in chariots and some in horses, but I will remember and trust in the name of the Lord my God. When I am afraid, I will put my trust and faith in you. In God, whose word I praise; In God, I have put my trust; I shall not fear. What can mere man do to me?

~ Psalm 84:12 2, Samuel 7:28-29, Psalm 13:5, Psalm 31:14-15, Psalm 13:5, Psalm 20:7, Psalm 56:3-4 Amplified Bible (AMP)

You should continue to trust in the faithful God and the truth of His Word and not deceptive and lying words that are worthless (Jeremiah 7:8). You must pray earnestly and expectantly. However, ask with the right motive and purpose to bring glory to God and not to satisfy your selfish desires for evil.

- **God says you have not because you ask not!**

   You are jealous and covet [what others have] and your desires go unfulfilled; [so] you become murderers. [To hate is to murder as far as your hearts are concerned.] You burn with envy and anger and are not able to obtain [the gratification, the contentment, and the happiness that you seek], so you fight and war. You do not have, because you do not ask. [Or] you do ask [God for them] and yet fail to receive because you ask with wrong purpose and evil, selfish motives. Your intention is [when you get what you desire] to spend it in sensual pleasures.

   ~ James 4:2-3 Amplified Bible, Classic Edition (AMPC)

- **God's divine nature has given you, not some things but all things for life and righteousness.**

   For His divine power has bestowed upon you all things that are requisite and suited to life and godliness, through the full, personal knowledge of Him Who called you by and to His own glory, excellence and virtue. By means of these, He has bestowed on you His precious and exceedingly great promises, so that through them you may escape by flight from the moral decay, rottenness and corruption that is in the world because of covetousness, lust and greed, and become sharers and partakers of the divine nature.

   ~ 2 Peter 1:3-4 Amplified Bible,
   Classic Edition (AMPC)

Rebound and 'Really' Live!

Seem like every day, we faced news, situations, and circumstances that are hurtful and painful. You are in a world filled with every temptation, tribulation, trial, and trouble. You feel distressed and frustrated! Divorce is at an all-time high with broken homes, relationship and family crisis; spouses and children neglected, rejected, and abandoned. Chronic diseases, sickness, mental illness, depression, and suicidal statistics are frightening. World poverty, social, and economic marginalization is prevalent locally and globally. Crime victims, incest, and sexual violence are shocking! War, social unrest, and injustice are terrifying! Untimely deaths, for whatever the circumstances, causing great grief! Industries are facing changes driven by population, technological, financial, and sustainability crisis. Employers and entrepreneurs are dealing with productivity, performance and profitability issues; employees are fearful of redundancies, bankruptcy, joblessness, and underemployment. Individually in your own personal and professional lives, you are struggling with feelings of inadequacy, helplessness, and hopelessness. You may be experiencing relationship issues or other adverse life events, and violations that cause you emotional, mental and physical abuse which you often kept secret. So, you suffer in silence, scared of the shame and the stigma!

How can you live as an Overcomer and walk in the truth that God has deprived this world of its power to harm you and have conquered it for you? How can you arise and awake to the expectation that the whole creation, all nature, waits with eager expectation for the revealing and manifestation of God's Glory and Grace in you? You want to move forward but feel stuck, stunned and stalled; spiralled in a season of unfruitfulness and barrenness! You are often overwhelmed or intimidated; being fearful of failing and falling! At times you may ask, where is the commanding presence of God; His miracles, signs, and wonders? How am I asked to be of good cheer; being confident, calm, and courageous; when I find myself wounded, worried and wearied?

> *Jesus said, "I have told you these things, so that in me you may have perfect peace. In the world, you have tribulation and distress and suffering, but are courageous, be confident, be undaunted, be filled with joy; I have overcome the world. My conquest is accomplished, my victory abiding."*
>
> *~ John 16:33 Amplified Bible (AMP)*

The Bible warns you of this troubled world, but God also assures you that through Jesus, your victory is abiding, your success is abounding, and your life is abundant.

I encourage you to have unshakeable faith, believe and trust God for your rebound, restoration and revival; not based on the rituals of religion, but anchored on a deep loving relationship with Jesus.

> *Jesus said, "Are you tired? Worn out? Burned out on religion? Come to me. Get away with me, and you'll recover your life. I'll show you how to take a real rest. Walk with me and work with me—watch how I do it. Learn the unforced rhythms of grace. I won't lay anything heavy or ill-fitting on you. Keep Company with me, and you'll learn to live freely and lightly.*
>
> *~ Matthew 11:28-30 The Message (MSG)*

The best response to God's revelation is your obedience, humility, commitment, awe-inspired reverence in acknowledgment of your weakness, and confession of your sin. The power of His perfect love is to redeem you, His mercy, and grace for your forgiveness, inner peace, strength, and everlasting life.

Success doesn't come easy. Overcoming the barriers hindering your victory doesn't just happen; you must fight for life, to survive and to thrive. The Bible says that from years ago in history, long before my time and your time, the Kingdom of Heaven has been forcefully advancing, and violent people are attacking it; we are also experiencing these attacks. Therefore, the enemy is not just going to roll over and let you take territorial rights over your promised territory; you must conquer by force.

> *From the days of John, the Baptist until now the kingdom of heaven suffers violent assault, and violent men seize it by force [as a precious prize].*
> *~ Matthew 11:12 Amplified Bible (AMP)*

Throughout life and especially during my divorce, and now that I am going through my post-divorce life, I have learnt that to move forward and start over, you need to have confidence in God and a comprehensive plan, as both are required to empower and transform you. Moreover, it is not just having the idea but executing and managing it to achieve the goals and expected outcome. Faith without works is dead!

During my long, painful, and stressful divorce and family court battle, I discovered the Rebound Faith strategy, and I implemented it as a practical solution for my rebound. I knew that I had to get through my depressive days, my anxiety, and panic attacks as they were painful and terrifying. I had to find an anchor that was stronger than I was. The faith to believe and the discipline to act; that despite where I was on the transformation process, I would still have a victorious rebound!

What good is it, my brothers, if someone says he has faith but does not have works? Can that faith save him? If a brother or sister is poorly clothed and lacking in daily food, and one of you says to them, "Go in peace, be warmed and filled," without giving them the things needed for the body, what good is that? So also, faith by itself, if it does not have works, is dead.

But someone will say, "You have faith, and I have works." Show me your faith apart from your works, and I will show you my faith by my works. You believe that God is one; you do well. Even the demons believe—and shudder! Do you want to be shown, you, foolish person, that faith apart from works is useless? Was not Abraham our father justified by works when he offered up his son Isaac on the altar? You see that faith was active along with his works, and faith was completed by his works; and the Scripture was fulfilled that says, "Abraham believed God, and it was counted to him as righteousness"—and he was called a friend of God. You see that a person is justified by works and not by faith alone. And in the same way was not also Rahab the prostitute justified by works when she received the messengers and sent them out by another way? For as the body apart from the spirit is dead; so is faith apart from works is dead.

~ James 2:14-26 English Standard Version (ESV)

My storms taught me that despite the pain, there was a higher purpose and a power that was greater than all the forces that were attacking me. I sought the Word of God; I became transparent with where I was on the Transformation Process. I found scriptures that spoke to my rebound and empowered my future state. They gave me hope, confidence, and the trust that there was no other way through my situation without an unshakeable faith for my rebound and an action plan that would activate the strategy and solution; giving me a glimpse of my future state. I thought to myself, "If I manage Organizational and Culture Change as a Business/Digital Transformational Consultant, how do I apply these same principles to my life transformation?"

Amidst the agony of defeat, there is a point for development. I had to acknowledge my current state. I had to visualize my aspired future state. My action plan addressed the gap for me to move forward. I became "naked" in my posts; I revealed my hurt and my dependence on God to help me. I was asked to lay everything down, my career, my accomplishments, my friendships, and my net worth. I couldn't go through the eye of the needle with all these! I was emptied so God could fill me with Himself; complete me and mould me in His likeness and image. It was hard!

The (hashtag) #ReboundFaith became a source of hope and the grit that expressed my positivity, patience, and perseverance during the process, and the determination to pursue the promised and expected end. Rebound Faith provided for me a strategy and solution of both faith and works. Today, Rebound Faith remains active, productive, and practical in my ongoing life journey, testimony and ministry.

I describe Rebound Faith as a "love promise" to me by God, that His grace is sufficient therefore I can be open, naked and honest about where I am at and how I am feeling, what my fears are, where it hurts, what the symptoms are, who else is affected, and where I perceive the pain is coming from… It's like I am sitting in the lap of my Heavenly Father, who is also the Great Physician, He is Almighty God, and I got to have a personal relationship with Him through Jesus Christ. So, I tell Him everything, totally transparent, and then He conducts the diagnostics in love, mercy, grace, and forgiveness. He smiles at me and says, "It is already done, charges dropped, and the penalty of sin paid in full. All provision already made! My stripes already healed your sickness and diseases, all your wounds and broken hearts are bound up. Prosperity, success, wealth and riches belong to Me, and I also have extended access to My divine power through the Holy Spirit."

Hallelujah; What a Saviour!

Even today, Rebound Faith continuously empowers my optimism, equips my work, and strengthens me to power up; giving me hope to live, replenishing my strength, and sustaining me to succeed.

God's Word tells you that He desires and delights in your successes and it He who gives you the ability and power to gain wealth. By developing and maturing your faith, believe and trust in God to establish the works of your hands, you can be strengthened and empowered to allow Him to perform His Will in your life and impact others - This is the real deal!

I am so excited to share with you what kept me, what is keeping me, and how it can be applied in your life, no matter the circumstances might be. The Rebound Faith is a Spiritual

Empowerment and Life Transformation series providing knowledge, wisdom, and information regarding:

- ***Transformation Process*** for you to be empowered and evolved to live victoriously and achieve success. As you progress and continuously grow deeper in faith, always striving to accomplish a higher dimension in favour, fortitude, and fruitfulness.

- ***Prophetic Prayer Plan*** to encourage and empower you to live righteously; pray effectively, earnestly, and fervently. This righteous life warrants the public manifestation of God's power to bring the rewards of your persistence in private prayers as you fight for your breakthrough.

- ***Renewed Mindset*** with the passion, vision and the right attitude to lead you to the positive thoughts, emotions, actions, and outcomes.

- ***Telling your story as a Testimony of Transformation*** for encouragement, inspiration, and motivation of yourself and others to rebound and chayah! Owning, writing, and sharing your story are therapeutic to overcome physical, emotional and mental trauma.

Declare your victory! Exercise your Rebound Faith! Open your mouth and make affirmations over your life; release God's Word in the atmosphere. For no Word of God is void of power!

Rebound Faith Prayer and Declaration

I can do all things, which He has called me to do through Him who strengthens and empowers me [to fulfill His purpose—I am self-sufficient in Christ's sufficiency; I am ready for anything and equal to anything through Him who infuses me with inner strength and confident peace. (Philippians 4:13)

I take my delight in the Lord, for He will give me the desires and petitions of my heart. Let the favour of the Lord our God be upon me and establish the work of our hands upon me; yes, create the work of my hands! (Psalm 37:4, Psalm 90:17)

I shall no longer be anxious or worried or fearful about anything, but in every situation, by prayer and petition, with thanksgiving, I shall present my requests to God. (Philippians 4:6)

The LORD is with me, so I shall prosper, even if I lived in the house of the enemy. Then my enemy shall see that the LORD is with me and that the LORD has given me success in everything I do. I will find favour in God's eyes, and He shall promote me in the presence of my enemies until my cup overflows.

I have committed my works to the Lord, submitted and trusted them to Him, and my plans will succeed if I respond to His will and guidance. (Proverbs 16:3)

It is God who helps me, and therefore I shall not be afraid. I am standing on His promise: "So do not fear, for I am with you; do not be dismayed, for I am your God. I will strengthen you and help you; I will uphold you with my righteous right hand." (Isaiah 41:10)

I am like a tree planted by streams of water, which yields its fruit in season and whose leaf does not wither— whatever I do prosper. (Psalms 1:3)

My setback may have entertained my enemies and appeared to be working out for my subtraction or division, but God has already blessed me at creation with the increase, abundance, addition, and multiplication; therefore, I am confident that my impressive comeback will astonish them.

I always remember that the Lord is with me. He is here, close by my side so that nothing can defeat me. So, my heart and soul will be thrilled. Even my body will live in safety because God will not leave me in the place of death. God will not let His faithful one rot in the grave. He will teach me the right way to live. Just being with Him will bring complete happiness. Being at His right side will make me happy forever. (Psalm 16:8-11)

But I shall remember with profound respect, the Lord my God, for it is He who is giving me the power to make wealth, which He may confirm His covenant which He swore (solemnly promised) to my fathers, as it is this day. (Deuteronomy 8:18)

I shall live a full and purpose-filled life, full in the fullness of God. For those who discover these words live, 'really' live; body and soul, they're bursting with health. I shall keep vigilant watch over my heart and mind; that's where life starts. (Proverbs 4:22-23, Ephesians 3:19)

I may fall and fail to measure up to His righteousness and expectation. I wrestle against the flesh and desires of my heart. I run ahead of God, only like a sheep to get lost in the thickets; broken, bruised, and battered. For with the freedom of my wrong choices come the painful consequences. Then I cry out to God, again for His mercy. Repeatedly, He says to me, "My Child, My grace, my favour, loving-kindness, and mercy is enough for you, sufficient against any danger and enables you to bear the trouble manfully; for my strength and power are made perfect fulfilled and completed and show themselves most effective in your weakness." (2 Corinthians 12:9)

Moreover, after I have suffered a little while, the God of all grace; Who imparts all blessing and favour; Who has called me to His own eternal glory in Christ Jesus, will Himself complete and make me what I ought to be, establish and ground me securely, and strengthen, and settle me. (1 Peter 5:10)

Christ Jesus, You have carried me. You have cleansed me. You have comforted me. You have counselled me. You have corrected me. You have covered me. You have convicted me. You have cared for me. You have challenged me. You have changed me. You have conquered every condemnation. Lord, despite every circumstance; You have crowned me with Your grace and glory. You have completed me! I'm forever grateful, so thankful for my Rebound Faith to chayah!

Therefore, it is my prayer that you may apply Rebound Faith to:

Live victoriously throughout the Transformative Change Process and always identify where you are in the cycle and how to power up through the 5 Vs (from the Violation, the Venting, and Valley of depression, to the Vision, and the Vow).

Gain an understanding of the Process of Transformative Change for redemption, recovery, and restoration. At each stage in the process, you are driven by the Truth of God's Word to drown out your fears and develop your faith. You will learn, trust and believe in God's will for you, which is good and pleasing and perfect. (Romans 12:2)

Live righteously by applying the Prophetic Prayer Strategy and walking by faith with God's grace along the five milestone (5 Rs) - from the Request, Revelation, Response, Receive, and to Rejoice.

You desire to experience a righteous life that demonstrates contentment; having a sense of inner confidence based on the sufficiency of God and godliness that is the source of significant gain. God has given you all things for life and godliness. Therefore, you should consistently aim for an active, influential and intense prayer life. Always seeking, trusting and depending on God's faithfulness to experience joy and peace: - calmness, confidence, contentment, and comfort. (James 5:16, Habakkuk 2:4, 1 Timothy 6:6)

Live prosperously by having a Renewed Mindset for Mental Wellness as the new wealth which you will get by demanding, claiming, maintaining, receiving Shalom (God's divine peace).

Applying these techniques will help with the renewal of your mind. Letting God transform you into a new person by changing the way you think, your attitude, and perspective. Allow God to heal, deliver and rescue you by creating in you a clean heart, and renewing a steadfast spirit within you for positivity, peace, and prosperity. (Psalm 51:10)

Live zealously by authoring, sharing and owning your Rebound Faith Story with zeal to transform others and bring praises to God.

Sharing real testimonies of how a real God rebounds His children through real situations. We have conquered, triumphed and defeated the enemy by the Blood of the Lamb and by the word of our testimonies. (Revelation 12:11)

So today, confess that you have the grit to come alive, to survive, to revive, and to thrive!

Rebound and soar like an eagle; live as Legend and leave a Legacy of faith, so that others too can be inspired to chayah! Surrender to God and watch Him turn your pain into your gain; surrender to Him your fears and watch Him turn them to faith; give Him your worries and start your worship; surrender to God your ordinary and messed up life and watch Him turn it into a fabulous, miraculous, abundant life!

God has blessed you beyond measure; You are anointed to advance!

Be Transformed from Ordinary to Legendary

So, here's what I want you to do, God helping you: Take your everyday, ordinary life—your sleeping, eating, going-to-work, and walking-around life—and place it before God as an offering. Embracing what God does for you is the best thing you can do for Him. Don't become so well-adjusted to your culture that you fit into it without even thinking. Instead, fix your attention on God. You'll be changed from the inside out. Readily recognize what He wants from you, and quickly respond to it. Unlike the culture around you, always dragging you down to its level of immaturity, God brings the best out of you; He develops well-formed maturity in you.

~ Romans 12:1-2 The Message (MSG)

For my sisters:

> *"You are becoming the princess that*
> *God created you to be; Royalty and a daughter of the*
> *King of all kings."*

- The woman you are becoming is stronger yet gentler than the woman you are letting go. She knows who she is and to whom she belongs!

- God is amid her; she shall not be moved, fall nor fail; God will help her when morning dawns.

- Strength and dignity are her clothing, and her position is strong and secure, and she smiles at the future, knowing that she and, and her family are ready and prepared. (Proverbs 31:25)

- God dwells in this woman; God protects her from every destruction. From the very break of the day, God will guide her and secure all concerning and connecting to her.

- She is completely dependent on the Lord to fill her until she is full as well as to guide and instruct her which way to go. *"O Lord, let me hear your loving devotion in the morning, for I have put my trust in you. Teach me the way I should walk, for to You I lift up my soul."*

- She is blessed and highly favoured! She is deeply loved and honoured! She is divinely protected and supernaturally provided for every need!

- She stands with unshakable and immovable faith in the righteousness and faithfulness of God for her rebound, *"for I will be a wall of fire around her, declares the LORD, and I will be the glory within her."* (Zechariah 2:5)

Today's Affirmation

I am a Child of God... He created me for such a time as this. I am blessed, loved and favoured. I am victorious! The Lord is with me. My God personally goes before me and surrounds me with favour as a shield. This battle is for the Lord, not mine!"

> *And the angel came in unto her, and said, Hail, thou that art, highly favoured, the Lord is with thee: blessed art thou among women.*
>
> *~ Luke 1:28 King James Bible (KJV)*

For my brothers:

You are becoming the masterpiece that God has created and designed you to be!

A man of magnificence!

May the Lord continue to enable, elevate and evolve you; God has anointed you for abundance, affluence, and excellence.

You're becoming:

A man is after God's own heart. Through your obedience and righteousness, any man occupying your place in leadership, office, promotion, palace, or possession must go.

> *But now your kingdom shall not endure. The Lord has sought out for Himself a man (David) after His own heart, and the Lord has appointed him as leader and ruler over His people because you have not kept (obeyed) what the Lord commanded you."*
> *~ 1 Samuel 13:14 Amplified Bible (AMP)*

A man who is a Mighty Man of Valor, an exemplary and victorious leader; a Legend with a generational legacy of faith!

> *For just as through one man's disobedience [his failure to hear, his carelessness] the many were made sinners, so through the obedience of the one man many will be made righteous and acceptable to God, and brought into right standing with Him.*
> *~ Romans 5:19 Amplified Bible (AMP)*

A man who is blessed and fearless as you trust, believe, and rely on the Lord. For blessed is the man who has made the LORD his trust, who has not turned to the proud, nor to those who lapse into falsehood! (Psalm 40:4)

> *[Most] blessed is the man who believes in, trusts in, and relies on the Lord, and whose hope and confidence the Lord is. For he shall be like a tree planted by the waters that spread out its roots by the river, and it shall not see and fear when heat comes, but its leaf shall be green. It shall not be anxious and full of care in the year of drought, nor shall it cease yielding fruit.*
>
> *~ Jeremiah 17:7-8 Amplified Bible (AMP)*

A man worships the Lord with obedience and reverence. Therefore, you are divinely favoured and blessed by the Lord. He will protect, prosper, and provide you and your family, and your household will be happy and will flourish.

> *For you shall eat the fruit of [the labour of] your hands, you will be happy and blessed and it will be well with you. Your wife shall be like a fruitful vine within the innermost part of your house; your children will be like olive plants around your table. Behold, for so shall the man be blessed and divinely favoured who fears the Lord [and worships Him with obedience].*
>
> *~ Psalm 128:2-4 Amplified Bible (AMP)*

Beloved, God had already anointed you privately (in your mother's womb) long before He announced you publicly (His appointment of you in this world). These attacks and your adversaries are because God has appointed you for advancement. However, God has already arranged a Rock of

Escape for you and the Power of Resurrection lives in you! The same area of your affliction is the very area earmarked for your exaltation. Present your problem, the process, the people, and the pain of the purpose to the divine grace and supernatural power of God. He will empower, equip and elevate you through every situation.

Confess and declare God's truth over your life:

> *"For you formed my innermost parts; you knit me [together] in my mother's womb. I will give thanks and praise to you, for I am fearfully and wonderfully made; wonderful are Your works, and my soul knows it very well. My frame was not hidden from you when I was being formed in secret, and intricately and skillfully formed [as if embroidered with many colours] in the depths of the earth. Your eyes have seen my unformed substance; and in Your book were all written the days that were appointed for me, when as yet there was not one of them [even taking shape].*
>
> *How precious also are Your thoughts to me, O God! How vast is the sum of them! If I could count them, they would outnumber the sand. When I awake, I am still with you."*
>
> *~ Psalm 139:13-18 Amplified Bible (AMP)*

The key to your success lies in the uncovering of your Purpose in alignment with the Power and Promises of God's Word. The world is anxiously awaiting the revelation of God's Truth through you, in your attributes and actions, as well as your conduct, capacity, capabilities, and character. You are creative; created in the image and likeness of your Heavenly Father, God Almighty, with dominion, authority, and power. Everything you needed to be pretty, prosperous, and powerful was deposited in your DNA as you intricately formed in your mother's womb. You are more than enough! You are not an "oops baby" nor a mistake! You are not your past, your failures, nor the dysfunction and devastations that affect you. God uniquely created you as a masterpiece with a Purpose, a God-given identity, and God-ordained to do beautiful works as part of His divine plan. The Lord saw you before you were born. Recorded in His book is every day of your life. Laid out was every moment before a single day passed. Entirely nothing has caught God by surprise, and He has a comeback for every setback you have experienced.

For all creation is waiting eagerly for that future day when God will reveal who His children really are.
~ Romans 8:19 New Living Translation (NLT)

Place your stresses before God and receive your blessings. Place your disgrace before God and receive His Grace. Place your barrenness before God and yield your bountiful harvest. There is about to be a turning point in your situation; a shifting! A new season of uncommon favour and the manifested miracles of the Mighty God for you to chayah!

Nothing you have been through or going through, no matter how horrific or horrible it might have been and may be, shall be wasted nor have caught God by a sudden surprise; but will be used to your honour and His glory.

God said, *"In the same way I will not cause pain without allowing something new to be born. If I cause you the pain, I will not stop you from giving birth to your new nation."* (Isaiah 66:9 NCV)

The weapons are formed but shall not prosper; the enemy's plan and plot shall not prevail. When the enemy comes in like a flood, the Spirit of the Lord will lift a standard against him and put him to flight, for He will come like a rushing stream that the breath of the Lord drives out. What the enemy intended for evil was meant by God for your good and His glory, to do what He prepared and what He is doing today, the saving of many lives. (Isaiah 59:19, Genesis 50:20)

By His grace, throughout this journey of life, God holds your hand. He is ordering your steps for you to chayah, for you to live in fullness and achieve your Purpose. Boldly walk in your God-given destiny and fulfill His divine plan. Enjoy His promises of abundant and victorious life on earth and the ultimate gift of eternal life in heaven. For the LORD your God is the one who goes with you to fight for you against your enemies to give you victory. (Deuteronomy 20:4)

During hardships, remain confident of the Lord as your strength, vigour and joy. In pursuit of your purpose in life, claim your identity, heritage, inheritance, and your victory in Christ. Through every trial and test, thrive and triumph with enthusiasm and passion. For indeed there is a reward for every temptation, trouble, and tribulation which you have encountered, your hope for an expected end will not be disappointed or cut short. (Proverbs 23:18)

> *Caterpillar! Your cocooning and transformation season is over. God has even given you a new name. Beautiful Butterfly! Your wings are ready; now transformed from ashes to beauty!*

Despite It All; Chayah!

As discussed earlier, Chayah means to live, remain alive, sustain life, to recover, to be quickening to live, to be restored to life/health, as well as to live victoriously, righteously, prosperously, and vigorously.

Chayah means to come alive, survive, revive and thrive for abundant life.

'U Power Up and spring to new life!

What are your Rebound Faith expectations from God for you to chayah?

Is it to:

- Sustain you through moment-by-moment and day-by-day struggles?

- Rescue, redeem, and revive you to a new life, from pain and destruction?

- Cause you to grow amidst the troubles, trials, and tribulations of life?

- Quicken to life something in you that feels dead, dried or buried?

- Restore you to an active, abundant life of healing, health, wealth, joy, peace, and wellness?

So, wherever you find yourself today by faith, declare your Rebound Faith to Chayah! You will not die but live and will proclaim what the LORD has done. (Psalm 118:17)

You shall be rebound to live victoriously, prosperously, righteously, and zealously! Why? Because you are created, comforted, covered, counselled, cleansed, changed, crowned, and called as a Child of the King of all kings, by a God, who is the God above all gods. You are God's favourite child, the Apple of your Father's eye. Your Abba will never let you settle for less than His best!

God is always at His work. He is working in you, through you and for you! He is determined to bring restoration, revival, and new life in you with a renewed mind. The pain of the problematic process should not be confused with the assurance of God's loving-kindness, faithfulness, and goodness. There is greatness in the DNA that He has embedded in you, and opportunities predestined and ordained for you. In Christ, you are free indeed from every condemnation of your circumstances. You are a new creation! You are complete! For Christ purchased your freedom and redeemed you from the curse of the Law and its condemnation. (John 5:17, 2 Corinthians 5:17, Roman 12:2, Galatians 3:13)

God has already devised a strategy for your revival, redemption, restoration, and recovery. When the enemy plans to bring you down; God prepares to bring you up! When the enemy intends to take you out; God is ready to take you up! When the enemy plans to set you back; God prepares your comeback! When the enemy plans your disgrace; God makes His grace ready for you! When the enemy knocks you out and leaves you with a low-self-esteem; leaves you imprisoned; leaves you feeling trapped in a box, sick, and depressed; leaves you with lies that to die seems more comfortable than to live... God had already given and sent

His Only Son, who has appraised your self-value, reassessed your self-worth, taken your consequences and set you free! Christ bought you with His Blood and made you free from the punishment of the Law, bondage, curse, past, sin, mistakes, and failures.

God promises to grant to those who mourn in Zion the following:

> *To give them a turban instead of dust (on their heads), a sign of mourning], the oil of joy instead of mourning, the garment [expressive] of praise instead of a disheartened spirit. So, they will be called the trees of righteousness [strong and magnificent, distinguished for integrity, justice, and right standing with God], the planting of the Lord that He may be glorified.*
>
> *~ Isaiah 61:3 Amplified Bible (AMP)*

Rebound Faith is a Spiritual Empowerment and Life Transformation Series of teaching, revelation, and application of Biblical principles of faith to propel you through whatever life experiences or adverse life events. The four fundamental principles packaged in the Rebound Faith Strategy and Solution provides the guidance and guideline for your growth; empower you to recover, and 'really' live an abundant and joyful life.

In John 10:10 (AMP), Jesus said, *"The thief comes only to steal and kill and destroy. Jesus came so that you may have and enjoy life, and have it in abundance to the full, till it overflows."* Jesus came that you might have life abundantly! Not that you might exist and survive; but to revive, mature spiritually, develop thoroughly, and thrive.

Despite it all, 'U Power Up and Chayah! By Faith, claim your promotion, take your position and possess your possession.

Live victoriously, despite it all. Living a life that reflects your triumph in Christ; walking in His victory because His power has equipped, empowered, and enabled you. Success comes from you, O Lord. May You bless Your people to be like a Winner, Victor, a child of Valour, more than a Conqueror and an Overcomer while facing down every giant; having a sense of fearlessness, fulfilment, and favour. Jesus's birth and life, suffering and crucifixion, death and resurrection were not for us to live in anxiety or average: Just getting on by paycheque to paycheque! Not to leave you fearful, hopeless, rejected, abandoned and neglected! Never to merely exist, survive, then die and be forgotten God desires us to thrive for success, to have faith to rebound from setbacks. *For everyone born of God; is victorious and overcomes the world, and this is the victory that has conquered and overcome the world—our continuing, persistent faith in Jesus the Son of God.* (Psalm 3:8, 1 John 5:4)

Live righteously, despite it all. Live a life of righteousness by God's grace; aim to be a person of virtue and wisdom, whose conduct or character is prayerful, ethical, morally right, and justifiable. The earnest prayer of the righteous is powerful and effective. It also produces excellent results; therefore, you will genuinely have hope for the future. Being neither religious nor self-righteous but in right standing with God, being repentant, obedient, and having a genuine relationship with Jesus:

- Serve God, seek His wisdom, and keep a short account of your sins by confessing and repenting of your sins as you are convicted and turning away from your old ways.

- Gain the boldness to approach the throne of God through the Blood of Jesus and being brave through devastations, knowing with high confidence that out of destruction comes innovation.

- Live a life of righteousness in God's harvest as a tree of life in boldness, courage, and peace. (Proverbs 11:30, Proverb 28:1, Ephesians 3:12, Isaiah 32:17)

Live prosperously despite it all. Living a life of prosperity and peace; demonstrating *Shalom*! *Shalom* means peace, salvation, health, success, and well-being. We prosper as our soul prospers; having confidence in the supernatural supply and provision of a God of abundance and great quantity in harvest; more than adequate; over sufficient in every area of need. The thief comes only to steal, kill, and destroy. But Jesus came so we can have real and eternal life, living a more abundant life; a more prosperous, enriched and fulfilling life than we ever dreamed.

For Lord, You prepare a table before me in the presence of my enemies; you anoint my head with oil; my cup overflows! (Psalm 23:5)

Despite it all, remain calm, collected, and composed with a renewed mind; at peace, focused, and brave.

Mental health is a new wealth!

God says, "Be still and know, recognize and understand that I am God. I will be exalted among the nations! I will be exalted in the earth! I will fight for you while you only need to keep silent and remain calm; be still! (Psalms 46:10 AMP, Exodus, 14:14)

Live zealously, despite it all. Living a zealous life with zest so that we can refresh others when we work on ourselves; frequently, we are called to support others going through their storms while we are growing through our suffering. No matter where you are on the journey, lead while you bleed! You teach and preach a better message with your life and how you respond in faith rather than with your lips. Enjoy a life of contentment, and complete confidence that you are more than enough to seize the next opportunity. Being creative as the Creator creates us; knowing that the intensity of the Lord Almighty will accomplish this and so much more. Having an inner driving and dynamic force that inspires, influences, and ignites us to achieve our God's given destiny and purpose while remaining undaunted, undisturbed, and at peace; despite it all. Being fierce, focused, and full of fire! A life characterized by Christ's passion, love, devotion, diligence, eagerness, keenness, vigour, and energy. Becoming a legend of your time and leaving a legacy that impacts generations. The passionate commitment of the LORD of Heaven's Armies will make this happen! (Isaiah 9:17)

Rebound Faith is the antidote for devastation, depression, and defeat by developing you as an everyday hero, a Legend, an icon of Faith. You are experiencing miracles with a divine encounter with God; triumphantly walking and growing through significant challenges and overcoming obstacles in life.

Rebound Faith is building you as a Legend of victory, and you are leaving a Legacy of glory; as you empower others with your transformational stories that bring exceptional beauty and splendour to glorify God, through Christ Jesus.

> *But as for me, I will wait and hope continually and will praise You yet more and more. My mouth shall tell of Your righteousness and of Your [deeds of] salvation all day long, for their number, is more than I know.*
>
> *Psalm 71:14-15 Amplified Bible (AMP)*

REBOUND FAITH

CHAYAH!

VOLUME TWO

1st Quarter

The Five Vs of the Rebound Faith Transformative Change Process

Live Victoriously... Chayah!

Living Successfully, Triumphantly and Gloriously!

> *For you will go from strength to strength, increasing in victorious power; each of you appears before God in Zion.*
>
> *~ Psalm 84:7 Amplified Bible (AMP)*

Rebound Faith Transformative Change Process (5Vs)

Regardless of the trigger of Change whether at work, home, community, school, or life events; Change involves a process to transition the affected individual from their current state to the envisioned future stage.

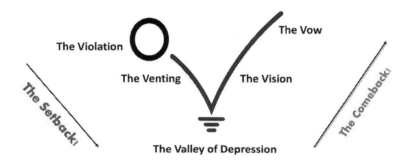

Rebound Faith Transformative Change Process (5 Vs)
Nicola McFadden, Rebound Faith: CHAYAH!

- **The Violation:** The change, adverse event, the negative experience, and the moment of devastation
- **The Venting:** The battle, resistance, negativity, self-hurt, complaints, fights, doubt, and negative utterances.
- **The Valley of Depression:** The sense of sadness, hopelessness, discouragement, and despair; the miry pit!
- **The Vision:** New hope, action, enquiry, question, exploration, acceptance, creative thinking, progress, and plan
- **The Vow:** The Grit, pledge, determination, commitment, enthusiasm, focus, advancement, growth, and resolution

Understanding where you are in the process of change is vital to the strategy for you to survive, revive, and thrive. Everyone goes through a range of emotions during a transformative change.

The key is to have faith in God who can always restore you. Keep your eyes on the prize, since your goal is to grow and develop; refuse to settle for less than you deserve or were created for, and do not entertain anything that will stunt your transformation; your rising, succeeding, and thriving!

The Setback

1. The Violation

The trigger of change often involves an act of someone (even ourselves) or something violating, breaking or disturbing our peace or comfort zone or routine of life. It could be an adverse life event, an experience or a moment of pain, torture, or discomfort. The severity varies as well as the impact on the affected individual; what might seem like a minor violation could have a significant effect on an individual.

2. The Venting

Upon the trigger of change, people go through a range of emotions and reactions. The first initial response is that this can't be happening. They face denial, feelings of numbness, and indifference or even lack of involvement or disinterest. As we face the battle – the resistance to the change, the fear of the unknown, anger, the fight to move forward, and accept the circumstances and all that comes with the change, the frustration during the waiting period, we doubt, we fear, and we worry. We vent to express a multitude of emotions whether guilt, threat, fear, sadness, anxiety, disillusion, hostility, denial, anger, complacency and release our negative energy. Often, our venting includes negative talk, complaining, and beating up on ourselves. We exercise a misguided attitude of despair and self-pity, and unwarranted doubt and fear; which disturb our peace and the assurance of our hope in God.

Jeremiah's Violation: Loneliness, Rejection, and Abandonment

Jeremiah wrestled with great loneliness, feelings of defeat, and insecurity. Also known as the weeping prophet, Jeremiah suffered from constant rejection by the people he loved and reached out to support. God had called him to preach yet forbidden him to marry and have children. He lived alone; he ministered alone, he was weak, ridiculed, and rejected by his people. Amid it, he displayed great spiritual faith and strength, and yet we also see his honesty as he wrestled with despair and a great sense of failure:

Jeremiah's venting: "Cursed is the day I was born...why did I ever come out of the womb to see trouble and sorrow and to end my days in shame?" (Jer. 20:14 -18)

Cursed be the day on which I was born; Do not bless the day on which my mother gave birth to me!

Cursed be the man who brought the news to my father, saying, "A son has been born to you!" and making him very glad and let that man be like the cities which the Lord overthrew without regret. Let him hear an outcry in the morning and a shout of alarm at noon; because he did not kill me before my birth so that my mother might have been my grave, and her womb always pregnant. Why did I come out of the womb to see trouble and sorrow, so that my days have been filled with shame?

~ Jeremiah 20:14-18 Amplified Bible (AMP)

Like Jeremiah, known as the Weeping Prophet, we lament, we vent, we forget the promises and the power of God to be the God of Vengeance against all our Violations (Jeremiah 15:19-21). Anxiety, hopelessness, and despair creep in; if we are not careful, we get tossed deep into the "miry pit!"

Jeremiah's Prayer and God's Answer

O Lord, You know and understand; remember me [thoughtfully], take notice of me, take vengeance for me on my persecutors. Do not, in view of your patience, take me away; Know that for Your sake I endure [continual] rebuke and dishonour. Your words were found, and I ate them, And Your words became a joy to me and the delight of my heart; For I have been called by Your name, O Lord God of hosts. I did not sit with the group of those who celebrate, nor did I rejoice; I sat alone because Your [powerful] hand was upon me, For You had filled me with indignation [at their sin]. Why has my pain been perpetual and my wound incurable, refusing to be healed? Will you indeed be to me like a deceptive brook with water that is unreliable?

Therefore, thus says the Lord [to Jeremiah],

"If you repent [and give up this mistaken attitude of despair and self-pity], then I will restore you [to a state of inner peace] so that you may stand before Me [as My obedient representative], and if you separate the precious from the worthless [examining yourself and cleansing your heart from unwarranted doubt concerning My faithfulness], You will become My spokesman.

Let the people turn to you [and learn to value my values] — But you, you must not turn to them [with regard for their idolatry and wickedness]."

"And I will make you to this people a fortified wall of bronze; they will fight against you, but they will not prevail over you, for I am with you [always] to save you and protect you," says the Lord.

"So, I will rescue you out of the hand of the wicked, and I will redeem you from the [grasping] palm of the terrible and ruthless [tyrant]."

~ Jeremiah 15:19-21 Amplified Bible (AMP)

3. The Valley of Depression

World Health Organization (WHO) has defined Depression.

"Depression is a common mental disorder characterized by persistent sadness and a loss of interest in activities that you usually enjoy, accompanied by an inability to carry out daily activities for at least two weeks. People with depression usually have several of the following: a loss of energy; a change in appetite; sleeping more or less; anxiety; reduced concentration; indecisiveness; restlessness; feelings of worthlessness, guilt, or hopelessness; and thoughts of self-harm or suicide."

The Valley of Depression brings hopelessness, loneliness, and darkness. You are demotivated and confused. Uncertain about your future and how you will fit, adjust or be ready for it. You have an inappropriate view of or no sense of your identity, no clear vision of the future and how to perform in it, overwhelmed by feelings of failure, fear, and sadness. The Bible describes it as a dark valley of the shadow of death (Psalm 23:4); where the feelings of despair, downcast, discouragement result in worry, weariness, and weakness which overwhelm and drench our souls with sadness. We experience a complete loss or absence of hope, fear of failure, which can lead to anguish, anxiety, and panic attacks; defeatism and severe pessimism with suicidal thoughts, where the choice to die seems more comfortable than the decision to live.

We desire to get up, but the burden seems too tremendous, and it mentally incapacitates us, making it difficult for us to move forward and see a productive outcome.

However, Psalms 23: 4 declares, *"Even when I walk through the darkest valley, I will not be afraid, for you are close beside me. Your rod and your staff protect and comfort me."*

God gives you His promise:

> *"When you go through deep waters, I will be with you. When you go through rivers of difficulty, you will not drown. When you walk through the fire of oppression, you will not be burned up; the flames will not consume you."*
>
> *~ Isaiah 43:2-3 New Living Translation (NLT)*

If you find yourself in the Valley of Depression today, know that you serve a Mighty God, a God of the Mountaintop and the Valley! (1 Kings 20:23-28)

God Almighty is right there with you. He will never leave you nor forsake you! He will never sleep nor slumber! He cannot lie nor die!

So, **do not** listen to the **lies** of the enemy who says:

- Choosing to die is more accessible than fighting to live.

- Giving up is more comfortable than holding on.

- Settling is better than starting over or moving forward.

- Failing to demand your value and claim your self-worth is safer.

- Winning the battle is either not possible or too complicated.

- God has forsaken, forgotten and not forgiven you.

- God is only with you in the mountains and not with you in the valley.

Those are strategies of the enemy to destroy you. He is the Father of Lies; but, you, my dear, you are a Child of Light!

The enemy plan is to attack you in the Valley, but the Lord is a God of the Hills and Valleys.

Now the servants of the king of Aram said to him, "Israel's god is a god of the hills; that is why they were stronger than we. But let us fight against them in the plain, and surely, we will be stronger than they. Do this: remove the [thirty-two allied] kings, each from his place, and put captains in their place, and assemble an army like the army that you have lost in battle, horse for horse and chariot for chariot. Then we will fight against them in the plain, and surely we shall be stronger than they." And he listened to their words and did so. A man of God approached and said to the king of Israel, "Thus says the Lord, 'Because the Arameans have said, "The Lord is a god of the hills, but He is not a god of the valleys," I will give this great army into your hand, and you shall know [by experience] that I am the Lord.'"

~ 1 Kings 20:23-28 Amplified Bible (AMP)

The severity of the impact of a violation or the change on the individual is affected by several factors, including, but not limited to the person's experience, perspective, culture, lifestyle, and health and wellness, as well as spiritual, social, financial, physical, psychological, emotional, and mental state. Not everyone responds to the same Change in the same way. Therefore, it is important and encouraging for you to seek professional and appropriate care for your situation when you find yourself stuck in the Valley of Depression. Often, it takes a team of practitioners working together to support you during a difficult change to achieve holistic wellness. Efficiently managing the individual and their response to the Change over this time is imperative to the affected person to transition them through the Change successfully.

The Comeback: 'U Power Up!

> *'U Power Up! Gain an immediate advantage to box-out your seemingly out-matched opponent by increasing power in your body, mind, and soul. Have the strength, stamina, and speed to overcome the fear of defeat and REBOUND to victory.*

Spiritual transformation is excellent support during a problematic change, which pulls an individual from the Valley of hopelessness to a new vision of Rebound Faith, and the vow to be different; to come alive, survive, revive and thrive!

Explore a new hope, freedom, and new possibilities of the future; transform the individual to having an outlook towards an empowered future by increasing the individual's capacity and the potential to believe an expected end. Manage and gain control over the change to understand the "what" and "why", and looking forward to successes; trust that there is a light at the end of the dark tunnel. Increase your level of self-improvement, self-confidence, self-worth, and self-esteem. There are a gradual acceptance and exploration of the promises of goodness, greatness, and glory of life. It sure feels good too! You begin to move forward and exercise more control to make things happen, and you feel better about yourself, more comfortable with the change, and the new person you are becoming. You are regaining your confidence, contentedly trusting the courage of your convictions, having faith in God, and making the right choices.

4. The Vision

As the Transformation Change process evolves and you seek the help, support, mental/spiritual health-care, and self-care, you begin to accept the change to chartering a new personal vision for the future. You should create a colossal of a concept for your aspired future. Your vision instructs your life and provides the light to lead you in new directions for a renewed future. You should write down your desires, speak life into and take actions to create your vision, and bring it into existence.

> *"A man without a vision is a man without a future. A man without a future will always return to his past."*
>
> ~ *P.K. Bernard*

The Vision:

- Acts as a bridge between your current to your future state; from where you are to where you ought to be. The Bible clearly states that we will perish or go uncontrolled and wandering without a vision.

- Establishes the compass, the charter and some core values for your life

- Provides meaning to the pain you are experiencing for the purpose, the discomfort endured, and sacrifices made to achieve the envisioned future

A dream written down becomes a Vision; A Vision broken down into manageable goals and steps with dates is now a Plan; A Plan with a Vow to act is shaping the future and changing the world!

Dream Big. Your idea should be a massive, gigantic, and extensive view of your life, because you become what you envision and believe in your life. The Vision is what you dream, declare, and decide and the way you view, interpret and relate to the concept of your future through the gracious and faithful lens of God to positively impact your attitude, outlook, and reaction to yourself, your situation, God, and others. You need to dream big and to be healthy and courageous, for the reward of your work is guaranteed. (2 Chronicles 15:7)

May God remember all your meal offerings and accept your burnt offering. May He grant you your heart's desire and fulfil all your plans. We will sing joyously over your victory, and in the name of our God we will set up our banners. May the Lord fulfil all your petitions? (Psalm 20:3-5)

Seek God for Jabez's anointing of increase, growth, expansion, extension, enlargement, boundarylessness, borderlessness, unlimited advancement, and promotion – intellectually, emotionally, mentally, globally, spiritually, financially, socially, relationally, and physically. 1 Chronicles 4:10 relates the case of

Jabez; he was the one who prayed to the God of Israel, 'Oh, that you would bless me and expand my territory! Please be with me in all that I do and keep me from all trouble and pain!' And God granted him his request!

Record the Vision. Write it down to take from the unseen realm to visualize it by bringing it to reality. Expressing the concept on paper moves the dream from your spirit (hidden world) into the physical realm where it can capture hearts, minds, and souls. A Vision Board is useful tools that will enable you visualize the concept of your future using pictures, 3D images, blueprints, models, hashtags, inspirational quotes, scriptures, stories, and testimonies of others who have overcome setbacks and were able to achieve similar dreams; as well as visits to people or places aligned with your purpose. These are all useful in depicting, capturing and creating your vision, and they empower you to communicate your vision, charter a plan, and seek support from others. You gain motivation by taking ownership of your idea. As the Lord instructs you, write down the vision, and continue to pursue the idea, even if it delays, wait patiently as undoubtedly the delay is not denial.

> *"Then the LORD answered me and said, "Write the vision and engrave it plainly on [clay] tablets so that the one who reads it will run.*
>
> *For the vision is yet for the appointed [future] time. It hurries toward the goal [of fulfillment]; it will not fail. Even though it delays, wait [patiently] for it, because it will certainly come; it will not delay.*
>
> *Look at the proud one, His soul is not right within him, but the righteous will live by his faith [in the true God]."*
>
> *- Habakkuk 2:2-5 Amplified Bible (AMP)*

Establish the Plan and Set the Goals as a Roadmap for Your Life. The vision is given to you by God to achieve your purpose; however, your responsibility is to own it and develop a plan in alignment with God to produce the desired performance, productivity, and profitability in your life.

You implement the Roadmap with manageable and measurable milestones to accomplish the overall vision. You press toward the goal for the prize of the upward call of God in Christ Jesus. You commit your work to the Lord, and your plans will be established. You seek first the kingdom of God and His righteousness, and all these things will be added to you. You delight yourself in the Lord, and He will give you the desires of your heart. (Philippians 3:14, Proverbs 16:3, Matthew 6:33, Psalm 37:4)

> *"Without consultation and wise advice, plans are frustrated, but with many counsellors, they are established and succeed."*
>
> *~ Proverbs 15:22 Amplified Bible (AMP)*

> *The plans and reflections of the heart belong to man, but the [wise] answer of the tongue is from the Lord.*
>
> *~ Proverbs 16:1 Amplified Bible (AMP)*

Take Actions. You inquire and question about new possibilities; you creatively seek small victory and quick wins which motivate us to pull up, press forward, and let go.

God's desire and delight is to take you above the normal or average life and for you to have the vision of which He is; the significant promises, extraordinary plans, and the divine purpose He has for you.

As fear meets faith, you must announce God's power, implement your plan and take actions to succeed; failure is not an option!

When God wants to develop us, He uses circumstances in our lives; when the devil wants to destroy us, he uses the details of our lives. The key is to see your situation through God's crystal-clear lens rather than the enemy's clouded and dark shades; responding with a Vision anchored on fulfilling the desire and delight of God versus the enemy.

It's OK to be scared, but you must choose not to fear, Job 3:25 says, *"For the thing which I greatly feared is come upon me, and that which I was afraid of has come unto me."*

The enemy's desires and delight are to keep you down by using fear, failure, guilt, and insecurities to keep you small with little hope of thriving for a happy, fulfilled, and abundant life. However, the steps of a man are ordered by the LORD, and God delights in his way. (Psalm 37:23)

Now, unto God, who is able to do far more abundantly than all that we ask or think, according to the power at work within us.

~ Ephesians 3:20 English Standard Version (ESV)

Now, the Lord said to Abram, "Go from your country and your kindred and your father's house to the land that I will show you. And I will make of you a great nation, and I will bless you and make your name great so that you will be a blessing. I will bless those who bless you, and him who dishonours you I will curse, and in you, all the families of the earth shall be blessed."

~ Genesis 12:1-3 English Standard Version (ESV)

You gain hope, seek healing, and take necessary actions to move forward to explore the new life, new beginning, and unique prospect with the special favour of God. You rejoice in hope, be patient in tribulation, and be constant in prayer (Romans 12:12).

God has good thoughts and very grand plans for you and your future.

> *"For I know the plans I have for you," declares the LORD, "plans to prosper you and not to harm you, plans to give you hope and a future."*
>
> *~ Jeremiah 29:11 New International Version (NIV)*

God says that you will perish without a vision, but there is a promise of prosperity when you heed the revelation and knowledge of God's word as the vision of your life.

> *Where there is no vision [no revelation of God and His word], the people are unrestrained; But happy and blessed is he who keeps the law [of God].*
>
> *~ Proverbs 29:18 Amplified Bible (AMP)*

Your lack of Vision anchored by God's revelation of His Will and purpose for your life will affect your development as an icon of faith and a legend but also negatively impact the legacy you leave for your future generations. Lord, we no longer want to be destroyed and rejected because of our lack of knowledge.

> *My people are destroyed for lack of knowledge [of My law, where I reveal My will]. Because you [the priestly nation] have rejected knowledge, I will also reject you from being My priest. Since you have forgotten the law of your God, I will also forget your children.*
>
> *~ Hosea 4:6 Amplified Bible (AMP)*

5. The Vow

A *Vow* is a solemn promise or assertion to do a specific thing.

> *If a man makes a vow to the LORD or takes an oath to bind him with a binding obligation, he shall not violate his word; he shall do according to all that proceeds out of his mouth.*
>
> ~ *Numbers 30:2 New American Standard Bible (NASB)*

Having a Vision of Rebound Faith, aligned with God's revelation and knowledge; you now make a Vow to God and an obligation unto yourself to do it!

With Christ, I, [insert your name], *Vow* to chayah, through whatever circumstances. I shall come alive, survive, revive, and thrive!

> *When you make a vow to the Lord, your God, be prompt in fulfilling whatever you promised him. For the Lord your God demands that you promptly fulfill all your vows, or you will be guilty of sin. However, it is not a sin to refrain from making a vow. But once you have voluntarily made a vow, be careful to fulfill your promise to the Lord your God.*
>
> ~ *Deuteronomy 23:21-23 New Living Translation (NLT)*

The focus is the determination and commitment to accomplish the vision. You have planned the roadmap, but now you are making a *Vow*, as a promise unto yourself to allow God to direct and establish your steps; you will be obedient, and faithful. Above all, you will trust Him for your rebound.

Step-by-step, day-by-day, hour-by-hour, and moment-by-moment, God will delight in you and grant you the desires of your heart as your decisions align with His Will, Word, and Way. He will lead you to fulfill your *Vow* and achieve your purpose.

> *"For He says, 'Precept upon precept, precept upon precept, Rule upon rule, rule upon rule, Here a little, there a little.'"*
>
> *~ Isaiah 28:10 Amplified Bible (AMP)*

When you fall, He will be there to help you up and keep your feet on the track, so you do not slip. He will go before you and clear the rough path. God will take you by the hands to lead, guide, and instruct you which way to go; whether you turn to the left or the right, you will hear a voice saying, "Walk this way!" The mind of man plans his way, but the Lord directs his steps." (Proverbs 16:9)

> *"The steps of a man are established by the Lord, and He delights in his way. When he falls, he will not be hurled headlong, because the Lord is the one who holds his hand."*
>
> *~ Psalm 37:23-24 New American Standard Bible (NASB)*

Now is the time to live, like "really" live! You make a vow to live in greatness, abundance, and excellence; to increase, multiply, and grow; unlimited advancement – spiritually, mentally, emotionally, financially, socially, relationally, professional, and personally.

Each day, we accepted the transformed and empowered future state with the right attitude, determination, the desired behaviour, buy-in, commitment, and adoption that are necessary and required to move forward.

110

My Vow

Lord, my vision is Rebound Faith! I believe that everything I am going through is what I have created and prepared for; I'm ready and able. I am determined to not only establish and achieve my vision, but I am making a vow to live out my core values and let my heart reflects You.

I vow to Chayah from whatever circumstances and live victoriously, righteously, prosperously and zealously. I pledge to come alive, survive, revive and thrive… Chayah! I vow to achieve my goals that reflect the aspiration that I have described for my life and provide the guide to accomplish my objectives in the mid-term or long-term. I am bound to follow through with my current and future actions to affect the required changes in my life and to be a source of help and support to power up others.

I decree and declare that I have the strength for all things in Christ, who empowers me. I am ready for anything and equal to anything through Him who infuses inner strength into me; I am self-sufficient in Christ's sufficiency. ~ Philippians 4:13 (AMPC)

Lord, I make this commitment to You and me,

[Insert your name].

When you make a vow to God, do not delay to fulfill it. He has no pleasure in fools; fulfill your vow. It is better not to make a vow than to make one and not fulfill it. Do not let your mouth lead you into sin. And do not protest to the temple messenger, "My vow was a mistake." Why should God be angry at what you say and destroy the work of your hands? Much dreaming and many words are meaningless. Therefore, fear God.

~ Ecclesiastes 5:4-8 New International Version (NIV)

The Lord says to Cyrus, His anointed one, whose right hand He will empower, and He is making the very same promise to you, The Lord's Chosen One:

"The Lord will go before you, and mighty kings will be paralyzed with fear, and your fortress gates will be opened, never to shut again. I will go before you and level the mountains. I will smash down gates of bronze and cut through bars of iron. Moreover, I will give you treasures hidden in the darkness— secret riches. I will do this, so you may know that I am the LORD, the God of Israel, the one who calls you by name. So why have I called you for this work? Why did I call you by name when you did not know me? It is for the sake of Jacob my servant, Israel my chosen one. I am the LORD; there is no other God. I have equipped you for battle, though you don't even know me, so all the world from east to west will know there is no other God. I am the LORD, and there is no other. I create the light and make the darkness. I send good times and bad times: I, the LORD, am the one who does these things." (Isaiah 45:1-7)

Now, you are focused on chartering a new course for your life to achieve the glory and greatness deposited in your DNA.

You are indebted to the Vow you have made to move forward. You are driven to implement your vision having the grit to survive, revive and thrive, and accomplish the envisioned future; being determined for your advancement, development, and growth.

The storm has deposited in you renewed strength, joy, hope for success and progress for you to maximize your potential and build your capacity to pursue your purpose. The Vision provides the light and sight of God; giving you the insight, hindsight, and foresight to make a vow and operate it. The Vow offers the pledge to be obedient to the promise.

The Vision in the Valley of Dry Bones

Prophesy to every dead, dying and dried bone and say, "Come Alive... Chayah!"

First, let me introduce you to your Rebound Faith Coaching Team: me, this book, your Bible, and the Holy Spirit. We are providing a creative and holistic solution as a self-help tool for you. My prayers are that you will learn and apply the precepts for your Spiritual Empowerment and Life Transformation throughout the journey of life; wherever you find yourself today, whether in the valley or on the mountaintop, God's desire is for you to become good, then better and be at your very best!

"I hear, and I forget. I see, and I remember. I do, and I understand."

~ *Confucius*

Ezekiel 37:1-14 tells the story of the Valley of Dry Bones; during a desperate situation of depression and devastation, prophet Ezekiel had a divine encounter with God. It was there, in the valley, that God gave him the vision to prophesy life to every dry and dead bone.

We will be standing on these scriptures as a guide, revelation, and evidence of manifestation; the application of the Rebound Faith strategy and solution to empower you to live victoriously.

The Lord took hold of me, and I was carried away by the Spirit of the Lord to a valley filled with bones. He led me all around among the bones that covered the valley floor. They were scattered everywhere across the ground and were completely dried out. Then he asked me, "Son of man, can these bones become living people again?"

"O Sovereign Lord," I replied, "you alone know the answer to that."

Then he said to me, "Speak a prophetic message to these bones and say, 'Dry bones, listen to the word of the Lord! This is what the Sovereign Lord says: Look! I am going to put breath into you and make you live again! I will put flesh and muscles on you and cover you with skin. I will put breath into you, and you will come to life. Then you will know that I am the Lord.'"

So, I spoke this message, just as he told me. Suddenly as I spoke, there was a rattling noise all across the valley. The bones of each body came together and attached themselves as complete skeletons. Then as I watched, muscles and flesh formed over the bones. Then skin formed to cover their bodies, but they still had no breath in them.

Then he said to me, "Speak a prophetic message to the winds, son of man. Speak a prophetic message and say, 'This is what the Sovereign Lord says: Come, O breath, from the four winds! Breathe into these dead bodies so they may live again.'"

So, I spoke the message as he commanded me, and breath came into their bodies. They all came to life and stood up on their feet—a great army.

Then he said to me, "Son of man, these bones represent the people of Israel. They are saying, 'We have become old, dry bones—all hope is gone. Our nation is finished.' Therefore, prophesy to them and say, 'This is what the Sovereign Lord says: O my people, I will open your graves of exile and cause you to rise again. Then I will bring you back to the land of Israel. When this happens, O my people, you will know that I am the Lord. I will put my Spirit in you, and you will live again and return home to your own land. Then you will know that I, the Lord, have spoken, and I have done what I said. Yes, the Lord has spoken!'"

~ Ezekiel 37:1-14 New Living Translation (NLT)

1. **Acknowledge the violation.** Identify your current situation. Present your impossible request before God as He challenges you to believe that nothing is impossible with him. *"Can these dead, dying and dried bones live?"*

And He said to me, "Son of man, can these bones live?" And I answered, "O Lord God, You know."

~ Ezekiel 37:3 Amplified Bible (AMP)

2. **Stop venting and start praying, praising, and prophesying!** Stop the complaints and foolish negative talks! Utter worthy, not worthless words! Stop reciting the problem over and over. Choose to let go! The more you focus on the issue, the more you magnify the situation. Start counting your blessings and stop the stressing! It's OK to have a temper tantrum and a pity party, but don't make a bed there and dwell there. Exercise your Rebound Faith and prophesy to these bones!

> *Again, He said to me, "Prophesy to these bones and say to them, 'O dry bones, hear the word of the Lord."*
> *~ Ezekiel 37:4 Amplified Bible (AMP)*

Stop venting; start prophesying!

Venting prepares sympathy; prophesying produces Strength!

Venting focuses on your fears; prophesying focuses your Faith!

Venting enables your negativity; prophesying equips you with positivity!

Venting emphasizes the pain; prophesying embraces the Purpose!

Venting concentrates on the problem; prophesying centres on the Problem-Solver!

3. **Right there in the Valley of Depression; your venture is to live and not die!** Make a positive declaration over your situation. Declare your victory! Introduce the problem to the Dunamis power of God (His strength, might, ability, miraculous divine nature, excellence, and influence). Almighty Sovereign

God, the Creator, The Resurrection and Life, He will make breath enter you.

> *Thus, says the Lord God to these bones, 'Behold, I will make breath enter you so that you may come to life.'*
>
> ~ *Ezekiel 37:5 Amplified Bible (AMP)*

4. **Create a Vision.** Uncover the desired or envisioned future state. Believe, receive, and activate the manifestation of the Word of God and declare Christ – the Breath of Life for you to revive and be quicken to life. Speak with power, authority and dominion: "*O, breathe, Breath of Life!*"

John 20:22 (AMP) says, "And when He said this, He breathed on them and said to them, "Receive the Holy Spirit."

Genesis 2:7 (AMP) says, "Then the Lord God formed [that is, created the body of] man from the dust of the ground and breathed into his nostrils the breath of life; and the man became a living being [an individual complete in body and spirit]."

> *Then He said to me, "Prophesy to the breath, son of man and say to the breath, 'Thus says the Lord God, "Come from the four winds, O breath, and breathe on these slain bones, that they may live."'*
>
> ~ *Ezekiel 37:9 Amplified Bible (AMP)*

5. **Make a Vow.** Enter into a Contract with God, by making a *Vow*. A contract is 2-way; it is an agreement by both parties for the fulfilment of its terms and conditions. Your responsibility is to seek, trust and obey God; while His commitment is to honour and perform His Word in accordance to His Will in your life.

Declare with confidence your Rebound Faith, *"My God will make me come up and bring me back... I shall revive and 'really' live! I shall chayah!"*

> *Therefore, prophesy and say to them, 'Thus says the Lord God, "Behold, I will open your graves and make you come up out of your graves, my people; and I will bring you [back home] to the land of Israel.*
>
> *~ Ezekiel 37:12 Amplified Bible (AMP)*

Receive God's promises as His terms and conditions of the contract; God will make you come to life and chayah!

> *"Then you will know [with confidence] that I am the Lord, when I have opened your graves and made you come up out of your graves, My people. I will put My Spirit in you, and you will come to life, and I will place you in your own land. Then you will know that I the Lord have spoken, and fulfilled it," says the Lord.'"*
>
> *~ Ezekiel 37:13-14 Amplified Bible (AMP)*

His Grace Is Sufficient
and Always Available to You!

As you travel along life's journey, you need the Grace of God to engage, empower, equip and elevate you through your failures, mistakes, weaknesses, temptations, and troubles.

Recently, while in the middle of writing this book, which should be a season of empowerment for me, I felt daunted, drained, and disappointed; and I was beating up on myself...

> *However, God said to me, "My Child, My grace is sufficient for you. My lovingkindness and My mercy are more than enough—always available—regardless of the situation; for My power is being perfected and is completed and shows itself most effectively in your weakness.*
>
> *Therefore, as a Child of God, I will all the more gladly boast in my weaknesses, so that the power of Christ may completely enfold me and may dwell in me.*
>
> *~ 2 Corinthians 12:9 Amplified Bible (AMP)*

Thank you, Jesus, for Your grace! Immediately, the energy shifted, and I felt totally and completely free, and at rest. *O LORD, You will establish peace for us, for, indeed, all that we have accomplished, You have done for us.* (Isaiah 26:12)

As I share my testimony and stories, I chose to be open and naked to you, so you know that I am not perfect... I fall, I fail, and I rise, but always thriving through every transformative change. Therefore, most gladly I will rather boast in my infirmities, that the power of Christ may rest upon me.

Jesus is right here travelling this journey of life with you. Not in an empty seat but right there in your cluttered heart is where He dwells; emptying you of yourself and filling you with His Grace!

Less of me and More of You, O Lord!

O what unmerited favour, mercy, perfect love, the most effective and complete power to escape what we truly deserve... Thank you, Jesus!

Hallelujah! O what a Savior!

Transformative Change

> *So be strong and courageous! Do not be afraid and do not panic before them. For the Lord, your God will personally go ahead of you. He will neither fail you nor abandon you.*
>
> *~ Deuteronomy 31:6 New Living Translation (NLT)*

No one changes during his or her moments of comfort and convenience. Challenges and hardship, though uncomfortable and painful, drive us to transformative change. Transformative Changes position us for Purpose, so, we must go through the Process to receive the Promise.

Transformative Change is not an event, but a process.

The violation or disaster may be an experience, a moment or a life event (the divorce, abuse, sexual molestation, unemployment, family crisis, relationship issues, financial troubles, betrayal, false accusation, and other life circumstances) that triggered the transformation journey. The change is, however, a process that happens over time.

Transformative Change is painful and difficult.

You need the energy to accept and process the information regarding the situation. Your perception of the case that is your ability to think, see, hear, or speak positively and become aware of the truth of God's Word concerning your situation, triggers your emotions. The perceived difference between your perception and the reality sends signals that register as pain in your brain. The revelation of this knowledge should help you to shift your focus from the shock to the purpose; develop the strength to show empathy, compassion, and kindness to yourself and others.

Transformative Change must be structured and managed to yield a successful outcome.

There is the Current State, which is where you are in the process today. The Future State your envisioned or desired empowered state; the Gap is the difference between the current state and the future state.

The perceived gap drives your reaction towards the acceptance and adoption of the change.

- **Your Perception vs. the Reality**

The more significant the difference between your opinion of the deficit and the reality of the change is the higher the fear, stress, and anxiety to face the future.

- **Take the chance to choose to focus on Faith, not the Facts**

The gap is viewed either by considering the truth of God's Word (faith) or considering the perception of the facts by what we see. However, you should walk by faith and not by sight; it is that confidence and hope that comes from hearing and hearing through the word of Christ (Romans 10:17).

Faith	Fact
The complete trust or confidence or belief in God based on the spiritual revelation of who God is rather than proof or evidence.	The reality or actuality of how it appears in the natural realm. Examples: doctor's diagnosis, credit score, reports, or that thing that is evident, that is the case.

Attitudes Shape the Reality of the Change

Whatever you think, you achieve! You magnify what you give focus! You attract what you expect! When your brain expects something, it shapes your reality and visualization of your outlook and outcome. That's why it is critical in developing a vision of your future state, declaration of your expected and empowered end; and the certainty of the only Wise God, who holds, knows, predestines, and ordains a prosperous future.

Ask yourself whether you are facing the unknown future with your Great Physician, Great Protector, Great Provider, and even your Greater God.

The knowledge of this should help with changing your perspective, approach, and outlook to become more optimistic and positive.

Change your attitude; Change your altitude!

- **Your attitude drives your action**

You measure, manage, and monitor your situation according to the truths of God's Word to shape your expectation of the outcome and influence your attitude. Your attitude then drives your words, emotions, and actions. Make the declarations of God's promises over your situation which will reduce your despair, anxiety, and fear to cope with the stress of life.

During the transformative change triggered by stressful life events or experiences, do you focus on the facts or the Truth of our Faith?

Respond to the Change with Rebound Faith to Chayah! Reinvent yourself; a renewed mindset for new results!

The Waiting Period for the Transformative Change Is Painful!

Change is hard and painful! Move forward with the assurance that

- God is your rear guard,
- God is your present help and
- Faith says, before you get there, He will have already been there.

Initially, the Transformative Change Process may seem like destruction; however, during the delays and sporadic growth, wait patiently; for suddenly come exponential enlargement, expansion, vigorous growth, and abundant harvest.

> *"For a seed to achieve its greatest expression, it must come completely undone. The shell cracks, its insides come out, and everything changes. To someone who doesn't understand growth, it would look like complete destruction."*
>
> — *Cynthia Occelli*

Transformative changes lead to paradigm shifts, radical progress and vigorous growth; though painful and scary but are excellent mechanisms for our elevation, expansion, and evolution. Moreover, God is faithful, dependable, reliable, trustworthy and can be trusted to adjust, adapt, and advance us.

> *"And now, Master God, being the God you are, speaking sure words as you do, and having just said this wonderful thing to me, please, just one more thing: Bless my family; keep your eye on them always. You've already as much as said that you would, Master God! Oh, may your blessing be on my family permanently!"."*
>
> ~ *2 Samuel 7:28-29 The Message (MSG)*

Faith has that Confident Hope in God throughout the Transformative Change Process!

For you are my hope, O Lord, God, You are my trust and the source of my confidence from my youth. Now, Lord, for what do I wait? My hope is in you. For blessed is the man who trusts in the LORD, whose confidence in Him. Moreover, I have believed in your mercy; my heart shall rejoice in your salvation. I pray that God, the source of hope, will fill me completely with joy and peace because I trust in Him. Then I will overflow with confident hope through the power of the Holy Spirit to rebound me into who I am as a child of God and I shall Chayah! (Psalm 71:5, Psalm 39:7, Jeremiah 17:7, Psalm 13:5)

Created in the image and likeness of God; wherever you have lowered your anchor, it's time to reclaim your position and possess your possession. No more shrinking back in your dominion and authority, no more lukewarm commitment to God, and indeed no more average or mediocrity living and settling for less than you deserve, worth, or created to be.

You are not ordinary; you are legendary! No longer being limited by the natural realm; you are calling forth God's supernatural anointing. Arise and be awakened! Be equipped, empowered and elevated in every area of your life - mentally, emotionally, physically, personally, professionally, and financially! Today is a new day! It is a transformation time! God has given you power, authority, and dominion to walk into your greatness.

> *You need the energy to accept and process the information regarding the situation. So, God created man in His own image, in the image and likeness of God He created him; male and female He created them. And God blessed them [granting them certain authority] and said to them, "Be fruitful, multiply, and fill the earth, and subjugate it [putting it under your power]; and rule over (dominate) the fish of the sea, the birds of the air, and every living thing that moves upon the earth."*
>
> *~ Genesis 1:27-28 Amplified Bible (AMP)*

Listen carefully: I have given you authority [that you now possess] to tread on serpents and scorpions, and [the ability to exercise authority] over all the power of the enemy (Satan), and nothing will [in any way] harm you.

~ Luke 10:19 Amplified Bible (AMP)

Rebound Faith Affirmation

It's a new day! This day brings new beginnings, fresh anointing, and new starts. You let go of yesterday, liberated of your past mistakes, failures, and disappointment. Today, embrace a new attitude, a new outlook, a new perspective; a renewed mindset with an untainted view of today; and hope for a tomorrow with fabulous opportunities, new possibilities, and the opening of new doors in your future. You can move forward from the past, and free yourself from your failures and disappointments. This day brings moments to celebrate, to love, to laugh, to live, to learn, to leap forward, to be a light, and to make peace with every situation. It's a choice to make this the best day of your life creating exciting memories to be kind, happy, joyful, and forgiving. The day that the Lord has made and saved you, so be glad and rejoice in it. So, keep up your courage, believe in God, and have complete confidence in Him that it will turn out exactly as you have been told. (Act 27:25) So, rebound yourself from the "disgrace" of yesterday to the grace that this new day brings:

Rebound from valley to victory!

Rebound from mess to miracles!

Rebound from test to testimony!

Rebound from worry to worship!

Rebound from stressing to blessings!

Rebound from your pain to His power!

Rebound from wandering to possessing!

Rebound from breakdown to breakthrough!

Rebound from hopelessness to hopefulness!

Rebound from faithlessness to faithfulness!

Rebound from being fearful to being fearless!

Rebound from being overlooked to being overbooked!

2nd Quarter

Live Righteously... Chayah!

Living Virtuously, Rightly and Justly!

> *And may the Lord our God show you His approval and make your efforts successful. Yes, make your efforts successful! May God equip you with all you need for doing His will; May He produce in you through the power of Jesus Christ, every good thing that is pleasing to Him; All glory to Him forever and ever! Amen.*
>
> *~ Psalm 90:1, Hebrews 13:21*

Living a righteous life indicates living your life with a real personal relationship with God. So, just like the time you spend communicating with your family and friends to establish a connection and build intimacy; so, does it take the time to involve, invest, pray, and mature in your relationship with God. Create, connect, challenge, and change you to trust Him. Have the confidence of God's character, His conduct, attributes, and actions. Know His love, His faithfulness, goodness, greatness, and awesomeness as revealed as you spend time in His presence, praying, praising, and practising His Word. Living a righteous life is pleasing to God, and it requires you to live in right standing with God, receiving the gift of Salvation, accepting Jesus as your personal Lord and Saviour. When you have a relationship with someone, you can call upon them with confidence and courage. When you are in trouble, distress, or even in success, you can call the name of Jesus with power and authority, because you have established a stable relationship with Him. You thrive to live righteously, having a vibrant, joyful, faithful, and exciting life while continuously developing your relationship with Jesus. You were created and designed with spiritual hunger and thirst; the void and emptiness that can only be satisfied by God; driving us to experience Him and to live a purpose-driven, meaningful, and righteous life. Many times, we have tried to soothe this spiritual longing and desire with ungodly earthly things, sinful actions, and toxic relationships.

Living a righteous life involves tremendous blessings from the Lord. You activate these blessings through:

- Longing, living and loving the presence of God
- Praying, listening, worshipping, and seeking the encounter of God
- Gaining strength, revelation, and strategies for victory in the experience of His power
- Receiving the gift of Salvation, Jesus Christ, as your personal Lord and Saviour, to be reconciled to God, Your Heavenly Father. God has made provisions that through the gift of His Only Begotten Son, Jesus, His life, death, and resurrection; we can live in a right relationship with Him, and, also have good relationships with others.
- Obeying God, committing to His Way, confessing and repenting of your sins; dwelling in the presence of God.

How lovely are your dwelling places, O Lord of hosts! My soul (my life, my inner self) longs for and greatly desires the courts of the Lord; My heart and my flesh sing for joy to the living God.

The bird has found a house, and the swallow a nest for herself, where she may lay her young— Even Your altars, O Lord of hosts, My King, and My God.

Blessed and greatly favoured are those who dwell in Your house and Your presence; They will be singing Your praises all the day long.

Blessed and greatly favoured is the man whose strength is in you, in whose heart is the highways to Zion. Passing through the Valley of Weeping (Baca), they make it a place of springs; the early rain also covers it with blessings. They go from strength to strength [increasing in victorious power]; each of them appears before God in Zion. O Lord God of hosts, hear my prayer; Listen, O God of Jacob!

See our shield, O God, and look at the face of your anointed [the king as your representative]. For a day in your courts is better than a thousand [anywhere else]; I would rather stand [as a doorkeeper] at the threshold of the house of my God than to live [at ease] in the tents of wickedness.

For the Lord God is a sun and shield; The Lord bestows grace and favour; No good thing will He withhold from those who walk uprightly.

O Lord of hosts, how blessed and greatly favoured is the man who trusts in you [believing in you, relying on You, and committing himself to You with confident hope and expectation].

~ Psalm 84 Amplified Bible (AMP)

There are earthy and eternal benefits, rewards and promises from God for you to live righteously, and in right standing with Him, receiving Jesus as your Personal Lord and Savior; for God in His divine power has bestowed on us absolutely everything necessary for dynamic spiritual life and godliness, through accurate and personal knowledge of Jesus who called us onto Himself through His glory and excellence. (2 Peter 1:3)

However, even as believers, Children of Righteousness, we encounter cycles of attacks in life where the sudden feeling of excitement, thrill, pleasure, and delight in the victory of the Lord is replaced so quickly by the extreme physical, emotional or mental suffering, negative emotions, attitudes, and fear from the anguish of defeat. Therefore, confidently trusting in God requires our constant spiritual maturity in righteousness to focus our thoughts, hearing, and speech on the truth of the Word of God. For the righteous shall live by faith! By faith, we are encouraged and empowered for our rebound. We will have a successful, victorious and favourable outcome; it shall end well. The latter shall be greater, better, more substantial, significant, and abundant than the former!

For in the gospel, the righteousness of God is revealed, both springing from faith and leading to faith [disclosed in a way that awakens more faith]. As it is written and forever remains written, "The just and upright shall live by faith."

~ Romans 1:17 Amplified Bible (AMP)

Rebound Faith is being courageous in your trust in God, gaining Hope in who God is as the Great I Am, what He has already done for you through the sacrificial death of Jesus Christ, and what He has spoken over your life and had in store for your future.

Rebound Faith is confidence in the faith of who you are, your identity, inheritance, and heritage as a Child of God, ignited with power, dominion, and authority to overcome the every and even sudden feelings of despair.

Rebound Faith knows that despite the appearance of defeat, the attacks of the enemy, the agony of the battles, the accusations of our haters, the apparent strength of our giants; as Children of Righteousness, you are walking by faith, not by sight for an overwhelming victory is already yours.

Life circumstances and adverse life events can leave you broken, bruised, and burdened. However, we have the choice to mope around becoming bitter, better, or blessed. During these problematic challenges, whatever you believe in on the inside is what manifests itself on the outside. Your belief in God in alignment with what you think about yourself is what drives your Rebound Faith - impacting your attitude, behaviour, thoughts, actions, choices, and your relationships. Throughout your battles, you can learn attributes of sacrifice, selflessness, service, and strength which are instrumental to your rebound, you are arising as a Legend, shattering glass ceilings; while leaving a Legacy of Faith and Glory for future generations.

1 Kings 19 gives us an account of Elijah's cave experience at Horeb.

Now Ahab told Jezebel everything Elijah had done and how he had killed all the prophets with the sword. So, Jezebel sent a messenger to Elijah to say, "May the gods deal with me, be it ever so severely if by this time tomorrow I do not make your life like that of one of them." Elijah was afraid and ran for his life. When he came to Beersheba in Judah, he left his servant there, while he himself went a day's journey into the wilderness. He came to a broom bush, sat down under it and prayed that he might die. "I have had enough, LORD," he said. "Take my life; I am no better than my ancestors." Then he lies down under the bush and fell asleep. All at once an angel touched him and said, "Get up and eat." He looked around, and there by his head was some bread baked over hot coals and a jar of water. He ate and drank and then lay down again. The angel of the LORD came back a second time and touched him and said, "Get up and eat, for the journey is too much for you." So, he got up and ate and drank.

Strengthened by that food, he travelled forty days and forty nights until he reached Horeb, the mountain of God. There he came to a cave and spent the night in it; and behold, the word of the Lord came to him, and He said to him, "What are you doing here, Elijah?" He said, "I have been very zealous (impassioned) for the Lord God of hosts (armies) [proclaiming what is rightfully and uniquely His]; for the sons of Israel have abandoned (broken) your covenant, torn down your altars, and killed Your prophets with the sword. Moreover, I, only I, am left; and they seek to take away my life."

So, He said, "Go out and stand on the mountain before the Lord." And behold, the Lord was passing by, and a great and powerful wind was tearing out the mountains and breaking the rocks in pieces before the Lord, but the Lord was not in the wind. And after the wind, [there was] an earthquake, but the Lord was not in the earthquake. After the earthquake, [there was] a fire, but the Lord was not in the fire; and after the fire, [there was] the sound of a gentle blowing. When Elijah heard the sound, he wrapped his face in his

133

mantle (cloak) and went out and stood in the entrance of the cave. And behold, a voice came to him and said, "What are you doing here, Elijah?" He said, "I have been very zealous for the Lord God of hosts (armies) because the sons of Israel have abandoned (broken) Your covenant, torn down Your altars and killed Your prophets with the sword. And I, only I, am left; and they seek to take away my life."

~ 1 Kings 19 Amplified Bible (AMP)

Like Elijah, you can experience victory in one moment and then the sudden devastation and hardship of life. For me, during my divorce, I was at the pinnacle of my career in a global corporation, living in a million-dollar home in one of the best executive neighbourhoods in Toronto, both boys in a Christian private school, a believer and married to a Christian man, small weekly group held at my home, and worked in Children Church every Sunday. I was enjoying a season of success; then suddenly, the agony of defeat stepped in.

Elijah experienced God answering Him by Fire on Mount Carmel in a great moment of triumph and then faced the threats of Jezebel which caused trouble in his life. Elijah found himself violated, venting to the Lord and hiding in a cave, depressed, defeated. and dejected; thrown in the valley of despair.

Elijah's Transformative Change Process

- **Elijah's Violation:** From great victory to the victim due to a threat of death by his enemy

- **Elijah's Venting:** Fear, negativity, complaints

- **Elijah's Valley of Depression:** Dejection, feelings of fear and failure, suicidal thoughts

"I have had enough Lord, he said. Take my life; I am not better than my ancestors." (1 Kings 19:4)

Elijah was discouraged, weary, suicidal, and afraid. Unlike many others, Elijah didn't recite this exhausted prayer after an adverse life event. However, after an amazing and impressive victory where God displayed him as the splendour of His glory – working a miracle nationally. However, in only short order of a day, Elijah crumbled from his spiritual height to the point of running fearfully from a wicked queen. He felt afraid and alone.

Frequently, we also feel discouraged in the journey of life, in leadership (spiritual or secular), business, and the household. Sudden threats and attacks, from the enemy, usually physically, mentally and emotionally drain and weary us. So, following the dominant spiritual victory over the prophets of Baal, this mighty man of God feared and ran for his life, far away from the threats of Jezebel. So, there in the desert, he sat down and cried; depressed, worried, and worn-out.

> *But he himself travelled a day's journey into the wilderness, and he came and sat down under a juniper tree and asked [God] that he might die. He said, "It is enough; now, O Lord, take my life, for I am no better than my fathers."*
>
> *~ 1 Kings 19:4 Amplified Bible (AMP)*

God responded to Elijah's cry by first caring for his necessities - food, water, proper rest; giving him the strength to power up. God mentored Elijah by asking him a critical question to think, reflect, change his attitude and regain Rebound Faith; amid his depression, discouragement, and despair –

"What are you doing here, Elijah?"

God reminded Elijah that the Greater One was with him; therefore, he was never alone. 7,000 others did not bow to Baal. God revealed His glory to Elijah.

This story reminds us that Rebound Faith means that we know that there is a spiritual as well as a practical approach to overcoming devastation or depression. There are faith and works! There are prayer and a plan. There are a strategy and a solution; a Prophetic Prayer Strategy and a Transformative Change Process for you to develop a *Vision* (in alignment with God's revelation and your Purpose) and make a *Vow* (to be steadfast with your progress and obedient to God).

There is help available to care, treat, and support you during your depression. You show self-care by receiving spiritual empowerment, as well as physical treatment and mental health care, which includes meeting your basic needs of food, water, rest, and proper medication (if required); as well as life transformation strategies, counselling or mentoring and support which are all available, all working in alignment with the power and presence of God. This strategy gives you a new perspective of your current situation and the faith to challenge yourself to believe that victory abounds in the future.

Moreover, how did God respond to Elijah's venting and Elijah's place in the valley? God repeatedly asked, *"What are you doing here, Elijah?"*

Today, God is asking you, the same question: *"As a Child of Righteousness, what are you doing here, [insert your name]?"*

That's a fully loaded question, so let's unpack it through the lens of Rebound Faith.

- **The truth of who God is to anchor your hope.** Do you know who I am as the Almighty, Sovereign, and All-Powerful God? Your Heavenly Father, Abba? The Great I AM? Your Lord and Saviour? Your Redeemer? Your Helper? Your Healer? Your Provider? Your Protector? The God of Miracle, Wonders, and Power? The King of the Universe, who holds your tomorrow?

- **The truth of who you are.** Do you know who you are as a Child of God? Your identity? Your inheritance? Your heritage? Your future? Your power, authority, and dominion in the presence of God?

- **The power of your belief in God's promises for you.** Do you believe God's covenant promises? That God has already gone ahead of you and prepared a path for your prosperity, protection, and provision? That greater is He who lives within you? That the enemies you see today, you will never see again? Will God fight your battles? Are you more than a conqueror? In this circumstance, overwhelming victory is yours through Christ! Do you believe?

- **Your claimed position with Christ.** Have you chosen to receive My gift of Salvation, accepting Jesus Christ as your Personal Lord and Savior, whose all-sufficient Grace has fully paid the price of all your sins, mistakes, and failure?

- **The expected good outcome of God's performance in your situation.** Do you know the rewards of your commitment and obedience as you have chosen to seek me, pursue me, and live righteously?

This challenge was to drive, push, force and propel your change.

"These mountains that you are carrying, you were only supposed to climb."

— *Najwa Zebian*

If so, what are you doing here, violated, venting, and in the valley of depression when overwhelming victory is already yours? Why not claim the vision to be manifested at the appointed time and make a vow to endure and enjoy the expected good outcome?

Like an arrow, you were pulled backward, to be launched and catapulted forward!

God is saying, "My Child, I have already given you my Son and My Word as My promise that if you choose life; choosing to live righteously and seek Me; you will have the power to be prosperous and victorious, to be undefeated and unharmed in every battle."

We have entrusted with the very Words of God; wherever you find yourself, exercise Rebound Faith and choose life. Change your perspective, starting with a new vision to bring into operation the power of God in the process, your problem, and your pain. God remains faithful even we are faithless; He is faithful, for He cannot deny Himself. (Deuteronomy 30:15-20, 2 Timothy 2:13)

You may ask, "But what if some did not believe and were unfaithful to God? Would their lack of belief nullify and make invalid the faithfulness of God and His word?" Absolutely and certainly not! Let God be found true as He will be, though every person is found a liar, just as it is written [in Scripture], "That You may be justified in Your words, and prevail when You are judged by sinful men." (Romans 3:2-4)

God has allocated to you a measure of faith to live righteously and rebound victoriously through the 5Vs of the Transformative Change Process; overcoming the Violation, Venting, and Valley of depression, and then 'U Power Up to experience an impressive comeback and achieve your Vision. God has already given you His Word as a Vow to assure you of making an affirmative declaration of faith over your life and the confidence to win.

Write the vision down, surrender it to God through prayers, though the vision tarry, it shall not delay. (Habakkuk 2:2-4)

Delay is not denial, the righteous shall live by their faith in the true God, and your hope shall not be disappointed. God is making all things new, breaking, and destroying evil foundations and raising up a godly foundation; breaking limitations and revoking curses; you are propelling further and faster! You are on a trajectory to catapult forward!

Application of the Rebound Faith Prophetic Prayer Strategy (5 Rs)

Request: You present your pain to God's power in prayers, "Plead my case and bring the success of my desired future vision, Oh Lord!"

For me, my prayer request presented to God:

1. No more spousal support payments
2. Custody of my children
3. Healing from depression
4. Financial breakthrough to be able to start over (post-divorce)
5. Restoration, revival, and recovery in my life and the lives of my children

Revelation: God reveals to us His Word in alignment with our requests.

When God gives you His word, don't ever let go of it! No more doubt, fear and looking at your limited abilities as Gideon, Sarah, and Mary did.

With God, all things are possible!

God is saying, "Take heart, My Child. You are fighting from a position of victory. You are an Overcomer, a Victorious Warrior. The hotter the battle, the sweeter the victory! Like seriously; bring it on!"

"For the LORD your God is the one who goes with you to fight for you against your enemies to give you victory. They will fight against you, but they will not overcome you, for I am with you to deliver you," declares the Lord. (John 16:33, Jeremiah 1:19)

Response: Yes, and Amen! I believe! I receive it! I claim it! I activate the manifestation in my life!

Make a decree, declare and decide: *"My story will end in victory!"* Read the end of their stories. Gideon defeated the enemies. Sarah, the barren old woman, gave birth to Isaac. Mary, the virgin, became pregnant and gave birth to Jesus. Expect your miracle!

"Pardon me, my Lord," Gideon replied, "But how can I save Israel? My clan is the weakest in Manasseh, and I am the least in my family." (Judges 6:15)

So, she laughed silently to herself and said, "How could a worn-out woman like me enjoy such pleasure, especially when my master--my husband--is also so old?" (Gen 18:13)

"How will this be," Mary asked the angel, "since I am a virgin?" (Luke 1:34)

Jesus looked at them and said, "With man this is impossible, but with God all things are possible." (Matt 19:26)

Beloved, we take God at His Word and move forward; forgetting what is behind and straining toward what is ahead, we press on toward the goal to win the prize for which God has called us heavenward in Christ. (Phil 3: 13-14)

Receive: Claim the manifestation of your miracle, breakthrough, deliverance, and restoration in the physical realm. Wait upon the Lord for His display and deliverance; trusting in Him always. Write your new vision and make a vow for your new beginning; develop a renewed mind. Share your story!

Rejoice: Give all Glory to God! Thanking Him, showing exaltation, adoration, admiration, praises, thanksgiving, and glorifying His name.

Sing to the LORD, all the earth; proclaim his salvation day after day. Declare his glory among the nations, his marvellous deeds among all peoples. For great is the LORD and most worthy of praise; He is to be feared above all gods. For all the gods of the nations are idols, but the LORD made the heavens? Splendour and majesty are before him; strength and joy in his dwelling place. Ascribe to the LORD, O families of nations, ascribe to the LORD glory and strength and ascribe to the LORD the glory due to His name. Bring an offering and come before him; worship the LORD in the splendour of his holiness. Tremble before him, all the earth! The world is firmly established; it cannot be moved. Let the heavens rejoice, let the earth be glad; let them say among the nations, "The LORD reigns!"

~ 1 Chronicles 16:23-31 New Living Translations (NLT)

Serve the LORD with gladness! Come into His presence with singing! Worship Jesus with gratefulness, boldness, and faithfulness! (Ps 100:2)

Many times, we approach our battles in our physical strength, limited knowledge, and finite earthly resources. Saul wanted David to fight Goliath in his armor; but David refused! (1 Sam 17:38-40)

So, David took them off and instead put on the Armor of God, being strong in the Lord and His mighty power. (Ephesians 6:10-18)

As you mature in your faith in Jesus Christ, you should put on the Armour of God and pray for His mighty power, supreme wisdom, and countless supernatural miracles. Trust Him to fight and win your battles, stand on His word to rule your world and defeat the enemy; leading to victory every time! David did kill Goliath!

Then Saul dressed David in his own tunic. He put a coat of armour on him and a bronze helmet on his head. David fastened on his sword over the tunic and tried walking around because he was not used to them. "I cannot go in this armour," he said to Saul, "because I am not used to them." (1 Sam 17:38-40)

God will reveal to you the right strategy to deliver you from your storm. He will direct your steps! Listen to His voice. Read His Word. Hold on to His promises. Be obedient to His direction. Prophesy blessings and strength in every dry area or season in your life. Then testify of His Glory!

Beloved, welcome to a new day, with fresh anointing, a brand-new beginning!

God's Word tells us that immediately the presence of God was established, David took the stronghold of the Philistines.

Moreover, the Lord gave victory to David wherever he went. (2 Samuel 8:6)

In the name of Jesus, as you dwell in the presence of God, you will take hold of that which is leading you, and instead of being driven, you will lead forth in God's purposes. The Lord shall give you supernatural victory in everything you do and everywhere He leads you, through the remaining of this year. I declare that you shall finish this year strong and start the New Year even stronger, in Jesus mighty name!

God may ask you to lay down the things of this world and become the masterpiece which He created and designed you to be. You shall not miss the purpose of going and growing through the eye of the needle!

Jesus answered him, "If you would be perfect [that is, have that spiritual maturity which accompanies self-sacrificing character], go and sell what you have and give to the poor, and you will have riches in heaven; and come, be my disciple [side with my party and follow me]." But when the young man heard this, he went away sad (grieved and in much distress), for he had great possessions. And Jesus said to His disciples, truly I say to you, it will be difficult for a rich man to get into the kingdom of heaven. Again, I tell you, it is easier for a camel to go through the eye of a needle than for a rich man to go into the kingdom of heaven. When the disciples heard this, they were utterly puzzled (astonished, bewildered), saying, "Who then can be saved [from eternal death]?" But Jesus looked at them and said, "With men this is impossible, but all things are possible with God." (Matthew 19:21-29)

I declare: *"Less of me and more of You, O Lord!"*

You must lie down; lie so low that Christ may rise higher in you. He must increase, become more significant, more excellent and more magnificent in you; however, you must decrease, become less! (John 3:30)

All things are working together for your good. Nothing you go through is going to be a waste. God will never cause pain unless He wants to give birth to a new nation.

Today, you shall focus on the purpose and not the pain of the process. We know that for those who love God, all things work together for good, for those called according to His purpose (Romans 8:28). The enemy intended to harm you, but God meant it for your good, His glory and to accomplish what is now happening, the saving of many lives. (Gen 50:20)

REBOUND FAITH PRAYER AND DECLARATION

Heavenly Father, my Abba, I commit this day, this week, this month to You. I pray for Your divine intervention, divine protection, divine security, and divine victory.

Lord, I ask You to increase my faith to believe that I will bounce back even higher, faster and better than expected despite the setbacks and the missed opportunities. Jesus take lordship over my thoughts, actions, and words; let them reflect Your character. Renew Your Spirit within me, restore my strength, revive me; the joy of the Lord is my strength. I shall praise the Lord while I wait for my deliverance as my Hope is standing on the Truth of God's Word. Jesus is the anchor of my soul and the Horn of my Salvation. He is sure, steadfast, and present with me. I recall and rejoice in God's faithfulness and His work in my past... How the Lord came through for me and rescued me. How He provided for me. How He delivered me. How I recovered, received above and beyond, and was thrilled with the victory, the spoils and plunders of the battle... My many past testimonies of the superabundant supply, deliverance, provision, and blessings of the Lord's breakthroughs... Better yet, how the

LORD saved and continued to transform me. He gave me a new life, made me a new creature. He blessed me with His gift of Salvation, Shalom, Chayah, and Glory. Thank you, Lord Jesus! O Lord, You reminded me that I still had these gifts and all their benefits because I continued to put and have my Faith in You."

LORD, forgive me for looking for you in the same familiar places when You are promoting me to new realms and new dimensions. However, O Lord, I must confess, the walk on this new path of the journey is a bit uncomfortable, and the fears are real. You challenge my faith as I face the Red Sea before me, the sounds of Pharaoh and His chariots are in hot pursuit, chasing after me. Lord, I can't wait to see how you will bring Glory out of this current test. I confess that there are times I wonder, where my Father is? Why I can't see Him, hear Him, feel His touch? Know these are the moments, I have allowed my fears to overwhelm me. Sadly, there are times that I let my worries, anxieties, fears, and concerns to override my faith. These are the times; I have taken my eyes off my Lord and magnified my troubles, trials, and tribulations. However, God, you are BIGGER! These are the moments, I have less of Christ, and so I feel restless, helpless, hopeless, and faithless. However, even when we are faithless, God remains faithful—for He cannot deny Himself. O Lord, I confess and repent as of the conviction of my sin, my weakness, my unbelief, my spiritual immaturity, and my ignorance.

I am awakening, by Your revelation, the knowledge of who I am as a Child of God - my identity, heritage, inheritance, relationship, purpose, destiny, assignment, mission, resources, times and season, and my legacy as a Child of God.

They say that every new level comes with new devils! I rebuke Satan and his demons, and I reject his oppositions and his lies, in the name of Jesus. I declare that I am not a victim, but a threat to the enemy! With so many past and future victories under Christ's belt, knowing who I am in Christ, there are more with me than against me. These trials are here only to make me stronger. The setbacks are setups for my comeback! An arrow is pulled back to shot, launch and catapult me forward, further, and faster. When life difficulties are pulling me behind, I am being prepared to move ahead! I stay focused, and I keep aiming... I know I shall arise, shine and give God Glory, for His Son has risen to set me free.

Today, I stand in unshakeable faith and silent my voices of confusion, my chaos, and my condemnations. I confirm and confess God's Word in my current condition. What shall we say about such wonderful things as these? If God is for us, who can ever be against us? He did not spare even His Own Son but gave Him up for us all, won't He also give us everything else? Who dares accuse those who God has chosen? No one for God Himself has given us right standing with Himself. Who then will condemn us? No one—for Christ Jesus died for us and was raised to life for us, and He is sitting in the place of honour at God's right hand, pleading for us. Can anything ever separate us from Christ's love? Does it mean He no longer loves us if we have trouble or calamity, or are persecuted, or hungry, or destitute, or in danger, or threatened with death? (As the Scriptures say, "For your sake we are killed every day; we are being slaughtered like sheep." No, despite all these things, overwhelming victory is ours through Christ, who loves us. And I am convinced that nothing can ever separate us from God's love. Neither death nor life, neither angels nor demons, neither our fears for today nor our worries about tomorrow—not even the powers of hell can separate us from God's love. No power in the sky above or in the earth below—indeed, nothing in all creation will ever be able to separate us from the love of God that is revealed in Christ Jesus, our Lord. *(Romans 8:31-39)*

In the name of Jesus, I break free and break forth to take hold of God's steadfast love, grace, and greatness, which is sufficient for me and makes strong in my weakness. I stand unshakably on God's Word that He will never leave me, forsake me, forget me, nor fail me. In Jesus' mighty and matchless name, I pray, praise and make these prophetic utterances, AMEN!

Biblical Principles of Rebound Faith Prophetic Prayer Strategy

The Rebound Faith Prophetic Prayer Strategy provides a Biblical approach for you to remain faithful, thankful, and unbothered; despite the roller coaster of life. As you live righteously, you will stay in peace whether walking on the mountain of a tremendous spiritual victory in a season of real success; or arrested by defeat with evil forces trying to drive you downcast and disheartened or tossing you in the valley of despair, suddenly from one moment to the other. You must develop your faith by:

Walking in the righteousness; being undaunted and undisturbed, knowing that even your failures are tools of restoration for your fortunes. As the righteous and devoted person's life results in peace, quietness and confident trust in God for their ability, wisdom, and justice to inherit wealth, true riches and filled treasures.

> *"I, [Wisdom, continuously] walk in the way of righteousness, In the midst of the paths of justice, That I may cause those who love me to inherit wealth and true riches, and that I may fill their treasures. The Lord created and possessed me at the beginning of His way before His works of old [were accomplished]."*
>
> *~ Proverbs 8:20-22 Amplified Bible (AMP)*

And the effect of righteousness will be peace, and the result of righteousness will be quietness, and the confident trust forever.

~ Isaiah 32:17 Amplified Bible (AMP)

Praying effectively and earnestly with a sincere and intense prayer for the righteous person's prayers have high power and produce beautiful results. Refuse to be limited by any evil power of darkness, indebtedness, sickness, unfruitfulness, sadness, hopelessness; come against the demonic powers with Light, Force, Fire, and Blood in Jesus name, and you will see every stronghold, failure, setback annulated.

Is anyone among you suffering? He must pray. Is anyone joyful? He is to sing praises [to God]. Is anyone among you sick? He must call for the elders (spiritual leaders) of the church, and they are to pray over him, anointing him with oil in the name of the Lord; and the prayer of faith will restore the one who is sick, and the Lord will raise him up; and if he has committed sins, he will be forgiven. Therefore, confess your sins to one another [your false steps, your offences], and pray for one another, that you may be healed and restored. The heartfelt and persistent prayer of a righteous man (believer) can accomplish much [when putting into action and made effective by God—it is dynamic and can have tremendous power].

~ James 5:13-16 Amplified Bible (AMP)

Taking risks and acting innovatively with increased capacity, capability, and creativity. The righteous man is as bold as a lion for righteousness produces boldness. He is therefore courageous and has confident access to God through faith in Jesus Christ.

The wicked flee when no one pursues them, but the righteous are as bold as a lion.

~ *Proverbs 28:1 Amplified Bible (AMP)*

In whom we have boldness and confident access through faith in Him [that is, our faith gives us sufficient courage to freely and openly approach God through Christ].

~ *Ephesians 3:12 Amplified Bible (AMP)*

Believing, trusting and knowing that the Lord wholeheartedly approves the way of the righteous.

For the Lord knows and fully approves the way of the righteous, but the way of the wicked shall perish.

~ *Psalm 1:6 Amplified Bible (AMP)*

Expecting a multiplication and an increase in fruitfulness; flourishing and harvesting in the seasons of life. The righteous man bears abundantly, prosperously, victoriously and lives zealously, and rewarded with Godly blessings.

The fruit of the [consistently] righteous is a tree of life and he who is wise captures and wins souls [for God— he gathers them for eternity; if the righteous will be rewarded on the earth [with godly blessings]. How much more [will] the wicked and the sinner [be repaid with punishment]!

~ *Proverbs 11:30-31 Amplified Bible (AMP)*

Jesus' Demonstration of Rebound Faith

Therefore, I say to you, whatever things you ask when you pray, believe that you receive them, and you will have them.

~ Mark 11:24 New King James Version (NKJV)

As you journey through life and seek to live righteously, you should desire like Jesus to grow in wisdom, stature and favour with God and all the people; as well as pursue growth in the grace and knowledge of our Lord and Savior, Jesus Christ. (Luke 2:52, 2 Peter 3:18)

Life challenges, though difficult and painful, are the processes that God uses to develop, grow, and transform us. Through life's challenges, we have a divine encounter with God, and we experience the empowerment and transformation of the divine nature of God to intervene, redeem, and restore us. We marvel at how God can take total devastation and turn it into a complete victory. We mature in our faith like Jesus, the epitome of believing and trusting in God, the Father, to perform His promises and prophecies, and answer seemingly impossible and challenging prayers.

And whatever things you ask in prayer, believing, you will receive."

~ Matthew 21:22 New King James Version (NKJV)

I will answer them before they even call to me. While they are still talking about their needs, I will go ahead and answer their prayers!

~ *Isaiah 65:24 New Living Translation (NLT)*

One of the most memorable and profound expressions of Rebound Faith Prophetic Prayer Strategy was demonstrated by Jesus in John 11:41. Lazarus was dead and buried, and Jesus had delayed His arrival when He was requested to be there to perform a miracle of healing; now the situation was more severe. Lazarus was dead! Jesus asked that they remove the stone from the tomb and He prayed; one of the most significant demonstrations of Rebound Faith. Jesus confirmed His confidence in God to hear and perform, to do the impossible - resurrect the dead to life and bring glory to His name.

So, they took away the stone. And Jesus raised His eyes [toward heaven] and said, "Father, I thank You that You have heard Me. I knew that You always hear Me and listen to Me; but I have said this because of the people standing around, so that they may believe that You have sent Me [and that You have made Me Your representative]." When He had said this, He shouted with a loud voice, "Lazarus, come out!" Out came the man who had been dead, his hands and feet tightly wrapped in burial cloths (linen strips), and with a [burial] cloth wrapped around his face. Jesus said to them, "Unwrap him and release him."

~ *John 11:41-43 Amplified Bible (AMP)*

How did Jesus begin when He asked of Abba Father, God to do the impossible? At His **Request**, He **Rejoices!** *Jesus said, "Father, I thank you that You have heard me..."*

Rebound Faith Prophetic Prayer Strategy challenges you today:

- What is the confidence do you have when you pray?

- Do you pray for the impossible with such assurance knowing that God is able and absolutely nothing is impossible for Him to do for you, in you and through you?

In this story, Lazarus was dead, completely dead, like he was dead for four days. (John 11:17)

The circumstance through man's perspective seems hopeless, the family was discouraged, the help seemed to have delayed, the restoration denied, and a favourable outcome was impossible; but when God stepped in, miracles happened! Jesus was confident that God was more than able, and this was neither difficult nor impossible with God. Jesus modelled Rebound Faith, He requested and immediately rejoiced; giving God thanks that He heard His prayer and it predestined and already answered. Today, we all know that the dead Lazarus did come forth from the grave alive!

In growing up, you have been trained to say thank you after you receive that which you have requested. However, Jesus did not wait until He saw the physical manifestation of His impossible request to praise God; He rejoiced in advance, at the asking!

The application of Rebound Faith in our circumstances ensures us to be confident that God can do the impossible. So, you thank God for hearing your request. You muscle the measure of the mustard seed sized faith allotted to you to shift your gears through revelation, and response, and then receive and rejoice in advance.

Our confidence in God will result in the tricky, challenging and seemingly impossible being accomplished, performed, and so, produce a favourable outcome.

- So, go ahead and make bold **Request** to God,
- Confident of His **Revelation** as revealed in His Word
- Manage your **Response** as you believe the performance of His Word to release His best to you
- Activate the manifestation of His Word to **Receive**
- Moreover, like Jesus, immediately give thanks and **Rejoice!**

When we Request of the Lord, He reveals His Revelation to us in many ways. So, don't ignore and disobey; instead, your Response should be to Receive and Rejoice!

Request to Revelation

Do not be anxious or worried about anything, but in everything [every circumstance and situation] by prayer and petition with thanksgiving, continue to make your [specific] requests known to God.

Philippians 4:6 Amplified Bible (AMP)

G od encourages us to **ask**, and He promises to reward our faith as we trust in Him. When we **pray**, we need **patience** during the process to be comforted, contented, and confident that God is still working during the Wait.

Ask and keep on asking and it will be given to you; seek and keep on seeking and you will find; knock and keep on knocking and the door will be opened to you.

~ Matthew 7:7 Amplified Bible (AMP)

1. Make your request, your big, bold, gigantic ask of your God; He is more prominent than every need you have – health, healing, finances, family, employment, household, business, ministry, relationship, depression, fear of failure, loneliness, or whatever the situation you are facing might be.

   And I will do whatever you ask in my name [as my representative], this I will do, so that the Father may be glorified and celebrated in the Son. If you ask me anything in my name [as My representative], I will do it.

   ~ John 14:13 Amplified Bible (AMP)

2. Establish your relationship with God through prayers. Call Him, Abba! Pray in the mighty and matchless name of Jesus!

> *Pray, then, in this way: 'Our Father, who is in heaven, Hallowed be your name. Your Kingdom come, Your will be done on earth as it is in heaven. Give us this day our daily bread. And forgive us our debts, as we have forgiven our debtors [letting go of both the wrong and the resentment]. And do not lead us into temptation but deliver us from evil. For yours is the kingdom and the power and the glory forever. Amen.'*
>
> *~ Matthew 6:9-13 Amplified Bible (AMP)*

3. Approach the Throne of Grace with Humility, Repentance, and Reverence to your Holy God. Call upon God for your forgiveness, mercy, and grace. Gain access to your redemption by receiving the Gift of Salvation to bring light to every darkness, the Blood of Jesus to wash away every infirmity, and the Fire of the Holy Spirit to burn away every impurity of sin.

Prayer: O Lord, be merciful and gracious to me, a sinner. I am taking the accountability for my actions and consequences. Lord, I am honest, open, and transparent with you; humbling myself before you. Lord, I repent of my sins and all the mistakes from my past; acknowledging my need, Your grace, mercy, and help. Lord, please forgive me. Please, help me. Please, take me as your child. I receive your love and the price Jesus paid on the cross for my sins. I discontinue that old life and seek a new life with you. Lord, set me free from all captivity; grant me deliverance, breakthroughs, and miracles. Abba Father, Sovereign God,

You promised that You would hear and answer my prayer; save me, in Jesus name. AMEN!

> *But the tax collector, standing at a distance, would not even raise his eyes toward heaven, but was striking his chest [in humility and repentance], saying, 'God, be merciful and gracious to me, the [especially wicked] sinner [that I am]!' I tell you, this man went to his home justified [forgiven of the guilt of sin and placed in right standing with God] rather than the other man; for everyone who exalts himself will be humbled, but he who humbles himself [forsaking self-righteous pride] will be exalted."*
>
> *~ Luke 18:13-14 Amplified Bible (AMP)*

4. Examine your hearts and deeds for sin, sinful desires, and ungodly influences. You are approaching and expecting a Holy God to hear your prayers. Therefore, you must not be continuously dwelling in sin and seek His mercy. You draw close to His throne of Grace through the Blood of Christ.

> *"If I regard to sin and baseness in my heart [that is, if I know it is there and do nothing about it], the Lord will not hear [me]. But certainly, God has heard [me]. He has given heed to the voice of my prayer. Blessed be God, Who has not turned away my prayer or His lovingkindness from me."*
>
> *~ Psalm 66:18-20 Amplified Bible (AMP)*

5. God is getting ready for you everything that you are praying for according to His will. What you are going through is preparing and positioning you for that which you have requested, everything you asked for in yours. When you are

in a right relationship with God, He not only listens to your prayers, but He is excited about meeting your needs.

"The eyes of the Lord are toward the righteous [those with moral courage and spiritual integrity] and His ears are open to their cry. The face of the Lord is against those who do evil, to cut off the memory of them from the earth. When the righteous cry [for help], the Lord hears and rescues them from all their distress and troubles."

~ Psalm 34:15-17 Amplified Bible (AMP)

6. God is listening to your prayer requests. He sees your despair and desperation. He is delighted to respond because of His love, mercy, and compassion towards you; not because of your goodness but His grace.

O my God, incline Your ear and hear; open Your eyes and look at our desolations and the city which is called by Your name; for we are not presenting our supplications before You because of our own merits and righteousness, but because of Your great mercy and compassion. O Lord, hear! O Lord, forgive! O Lord, listen and take action! Do not delay, for your own sake, O my God, because your city and Your people are called by Your name."

~ Daniel 9:18-20 Amplified Bible (AMP)

7. As you keep yourself from sin, make your request before the Lord. Keep praying, excitedly and eagerly waiting! Watch God divinely intervenes, avenges on your behalf, to rescue you, to restore what you lost, to fight for you and box-out the opponent, and rebound you to victory. You remain

diligent and steadfast; every morning anticipates God to work mightily on your behalf to destroy evil and power of darkness.

> *In the morning, O Lord, You will hear my voice; in the morning I will prepare [a prayer and a sacrifice] for you and watch and wait [for you to speak to my heart]. For you are not a God who takes pleasure in wickedness; No evil [person] dwells with you. The boastful and the arrogant will not stand in your sight; you hate all who do evil.*
>
> *~ Psalm 5:3-5 Amplified Bible (AMP)*

8. Have the confidence in God to hear every request and reveal His answer. He answers every prayer by His will. As nothing (past, present, or future) is unknown by God; He knows the motive behind the request, reason, and purpose or if the demand is good or bad for you.

> *"And we are confident that He hears us whenever we ask for anything that pleases him. And since we know He hears us when we make our requests, we also know that He will give us what we ask for."*
>
> *~ 1 John 5:14-15 New Living Translation (NLT)*

> *"And even when you ask, you don't get it because your motives are all wrong—you want only what will give you pleasure."*
>
> *~ James 4:3 New Living Translation (NLT)*

9. Make your request and tell God of your fears. Cry out to God about the violation. He can take your venting. Tell Him that the battle is too much for you, the enemies are stronger

than you, and you are feeling overwhelmed, worried, scared, and tired. Don't be afraid to pour out your heart to God. Knowing that you are not the first to ask Him to make the cup of bitterness and pain slip and pass away. Then wait and watch how His presence divinely intervenes, changes your perspective, and grants you His peace!

> *He went away a second time and prayed, saying, "My Father, if this cannot pass away unless I drink it, your will be done." Again, He came and found them sleeping, for their eyes were heavy. So, leaving them again, He went away and prayed for the third time, saying the same words once more.*
>
> *~ Matthew 26:42-44 Amplified Bible (AMP)*

During my divorce and family court battle, I recall muscling up all the courage and strength I had, which was not much to return to work. My short-term disability had run out, and I was now on no-pay leave of absence. The court had passed a motion for spousal allowance. I was in several months' worth of spousal support debts as I had no income. My reported taxable annual income (T4) was too high for food banks, so a friend I met at Nick's football game would go and share the food received with my boys and me. I had no money to take care of my children, and though I was still unwell, I forced myself to return to work. Upon my arrival, only to be informed by Payroll that FRO (Family Responsibility Office) had garnished my salary for spousal support payments and arrears. Broken and burdened! I rushed to the restroom to cry but broke down in tears before I got there.

I just wept! I cried out to God, "O Lord if this cup could pass!" I can't do this anymore; all my strength left. I thought this was punishment for my progress of growing in my career. I felt I was being taken advantage of, and though it was the law, I felt unloved, uncared for, misunderstood, and abused. I was fearful for my future. I was worried about my present situation. I was broke, indebted and broken; but God, He reminded me that I was indeed loved and blessed. He brought me comfort as other ladies came to the restroom and consoled me, though they had no idea the reason for my drama.

Within a few weeks after returning, my manager called me in for a meeting. I was so fearful and reluctant. She calmly told me that I was not able to lead my team as I was not focused, and I should go home and take care of myself. I left work confused, "Lord, what was happening to me, my career, my children; our future?" In a few months, the insurance company then approved my long-term disability. We don't know what our future holds, but we know who holds our future. This assurance in God makes us hope and surrender our will to God's will, having complete confidence and courage that He is in complete and ultimate control, what is under His power can never be out-of-control. Entirely nothing is impossible for Him, and He knows what is best, and He will make a way, even when there seems to be no way.

Jesus, our perfect role model, modelled for us the act of surrendering, being in obedience and acting in submission to the Father's Will. He faced the agony of the cross; He cried out to the Father to spare Him the burden of crucifixion - sin, shame, suffering and ultimate death on the cross. He could have given up, but He let go of His will and said nevertheless, not my will, but Your will be done! Thank you, Lord Jesus, You did not give up! We are the reason He gave His life, and the reason He suffered, sacrificed, shamed, and died. He provides us with the right to live, to have hope, never to give up!

We should still make our request to God, even if we have doubts, fear, and insecurity regarding the facts – We see the credit score; we know what the doctor's reports say; we know the spouse is cheating. There are chaos and confusion in the home! There are more bills than income! They fired us and walked us out of a job! We honestly confess that Lord; we can't possibly see how you will make good out of all this mess. However, declare, *"I trust, You, Lord! O Lord, I do believe you, help me overcome my unbelief. Lord, even when I am faithless, you are faithful as you cannot deny yourself. Jesus, be Lordship, over my circumstance and give me a second chance. O Lord, You reign!"*

We make our request with trembling in fear with mustard-seed-sized faith and believing that is more than enough to our opponents. God will do it because it is not the size of our faith but the size of our God that counts.

> *Immediately the father of the boy cried out [with a desperate, piercing cry], saying, "I do believe; help me to overcome my unbelief."*
> *~ Mark 9:24 Amplified Bible (AMP)*

10. As a believer, you are in right standing with God; your prayers are powerful and effective. You can boldly approach the Throne of Grace, persistently with big, impossible, and ridiculous requests. You must stop putting limits on a limitless God. You commit your day and situation to God. You command your day to bring success, peace, freedom, and prosperity.

Look at Elijah; He prayed that it might not rain, and it didn't rain for 3 ½ years. (James 5:16-18)

Joshua prayed that the sun and moon shall stand still until he defeated his enemies. (Joshua 10:11-13)

Jabez prayed for enlargement and territorial rights. (1 Chronicles 4:10)

Moreover, God granted all these requests!

> *Therefore, confess your sins to one another [your false steps, your offences], and pray for one another, that you may be healed and restored. The heartfelt and persistent prayer of a righteous man (believer) can accomplish much [when putting into action and made effective by God—it is dynamic and can have tremendous power]. Elijah was a man with a nature like ours [with the same physical, mental, and spiritual limitations and shortcomings], and he prayed intensely for it not to rain, and it did not rain on the earth for three years and six months. Then he prayed again, and the sky gave rain and the land produced its crops [as usual].*
>
> *~ James 5:16-18 Amplified Bible (AMP)*

So, approach Your Abba Father with your request as if today is your birthday and ask for a big request.

> *Let me tell you what God said next. He said, "You're my son, and today is your birthday. What do you want? Name it: Nations as a present? Continents as a prize? You can command them all to dance for you or throw them out with tomorrow's trash."*
>
> *~ Psalm 2:7-9 The Message (MSG)*

Revelation to Response

But he did not doubt or waver in unbelief concerning the promise of God, but he grew strong and empowered by faith, giving glory to God.

Romans 4:20 Amplified Bible (AMP)

The right and accurate response to the revelation of God is your belief in Who He is, the truth of His word, His Ways, and His Will. The acknowledgement of the awesomeness of God, the confession of your sins, your humility and repentance in desperation for His mercy, forgiveness, goodness, peace, joy, and eternal life. For concerning the promise of God, you should not waver in unbelief but grow strong in faith, giving glory to God For absolutely nothing will be impossible with God.

Revelation is defined as the divine or supernatural disclosure of the unseen world to humans by bringing something relating to the human into existence or the seen world or reality.

A **response** is your reaction to something.

During my divorce and family court battle, I went through four different lawyers, representing my arguments. Eventually, I ran out of money for legal fees. My case was over a four-year duration, and I had numerous court appearances and a huge file. To hire a new attorney required them going through the history of my record, and therefore there was a request for a considerable retainer, but I was broke!

I continued to pray and seek the Lord for strategies to overcome, then one day in Summer 2014, I got a Word from the Lord in 2 Kings 8:6 says, *"And when the king asked the woman, she told him. So, the king appointed an official for her, saying, 'Restore all that was hers, together with all the produce of the fields from the day that she left the land until now.'"*

I was confident that the Lord was asking me to take the case out of the court and He would appoint an Official (a Mediator and an Arbitrator) to my situation. So, against all the odds, I obeyed!

As the mediation proceeded, there seemed to be no agreement; hence the matter went into arbitration. I was still struggling with my depression and was self-represented as there were no funds to retain a lawyer. Frequently, I felt defeated entirely; I cried out to the Lord.

A few weeks later, one morning, after dropping my boys at school, I sat in my truck; prayed earnestly and just wept. In desperation, I prayed an eleventh-hour cry, *"God, if you could please send me a lawyer to navigate the complexity, confusion, and condemnation of the mediation and arbitration sessions. O Lord, even Archangel Michael!"*

Instantaneously, God heard my request and my cry for help; He responded!

No lie! Before I could finish praying, I got a WhatsApp message and from a Christian gentleman who reported to me when I was a Director. He was seeking a reference for a new role. He asked how I was doing. I told him that I needed a family lawyer but had no money to retain one. He said, *"A friend of mine, he is a lawyer, and he recently arrived in Canada. I will contact him and do not worry about the money. You were an exceptional manager and are extremely helpful to me in my career growth. So, I will speak with him on your behalf."*

That same evening, the lawyer called me and introduced himself. He said, *"Good evening, Nicola! My name is Michael!"* I started to cry in awe-inspired reverence to an Amazingly Awesome God! The Lord heard my mourning and groaning in my prayers and responded to my request. Michael asked for no retainer. He is a Christian, zealous for the Lord; smart, knowledgeable, strategic, compassionate, caring, calm, yet firm.

That first night when Michael called, he asked me if I could sing. I said, "I can make a joyful noise (smile)." He said, "Can I sing with you?" I whispered, "Yes!" So, he began singing the popular hymn:

> *"God will make a way! Where it seems to be no way... He works in ways we cannot see... He will make a way for me... He will be my guide... Hold me closely to His side... With love and strength for each new day, He will make a way... He will make a way!"*

I just wept! I felt the presence of God's loving and everlasting arms wrapping around me, promising, protecting and providing for me. Michael mentored and prayed with me throughout the remaining part of my case until it was over, without a financial reward. I spoke to him almost daily for the next few months in 2014 as he supported me legally and spiritually, but I never met him until after the case was closed in early 2015. Indeed, God made His Way for me! God says in Isaiah 43:18, *"Behold, I am doing a new thing; now it springs forth. Do you not perceive it? I will make a way in the wilderness and rivers in the desert."*

Therefore, you should learn, depend, and trust the revelation of God's Word and scriptures regarding every prayer request and need. For faith comes from hearing, what is told in the Word of God, and what is heard comes by the preaching of the message concerning Christ. For all the promises of God in Him are yes, and in Him Amen, to the glory of God through us. He is the same unchangeable God! (Romans 10:17, 2 Corinthians 1:20)

> *In the beginning was the Word, and the Word was with God, and the Word was God. The same was at the beginning with God.*
>
> ~ *John 1:1-2 King James Version (KJV)*

> *"I will worship toward thy holy temple and praise thy name for thy loving-kindness and for thy truth: for thou hast magnified thy Word above thy entire name."*
>
> ~ *Psalm 138:2 King James Version (KJV)*

Search through the Bible and gain the wisdom of God's Word regarding your specific request. Believe and pray as revealed in the Word of God. Pray for His response to the expected outcome not just reciting your troubles. Hold God accountable for His Word!

> *Your beliefs affect your realization. What you affirm and accept will activate your physical reality!*

What are you seeking of God for you?

Discover what God's Word says about your situation, the revelation, and application of His covenant promises to you. With the technological era, it makes finding these scriptures and messages so much more comfortable and at your fingertips. Digital Technology, the internet, social media, and various Bible reference websites such as https://biblehub.com/ are to your advantage. Use them to research and equip you to declare your

Rebound Faith in the atmosphere, the highways, and byways, globally and locally, generations and nations.

Study and reflect on the scriptures and testimonies of God's truth and make the relevant application in your life and your current situation.

What does the truth of God's Word say about your promised future? State the beauty of living your experiences with the same unchangeable faithful God.

• *Financial Breakthrough* – God's provision, debt cancellation prosperity, wealth, successes, riches, breaking the curses of poverty, tithing, economic restoration, and Shalom (mental wellness).

- *The Miracle of Multiplication:* Read the story of the Widow and the Oil in 2 Kings 4. She was fearful of losing her two sons into slavery due to the death of her husband and their indebtedness. The story revealed that the miracle of multiplication manifested in her life as she trusted, relied upon, and obeyed God to turn her 'little oil' into 'plenty' filling and overflowing every vessel they found.

> *Otherwise, you may say in your heart, 'My power and the strength of my hand made me this wealth.' But you shall remember [with profound respect] the Lord your God, for it is He who is giving you the power to make wealth, that He may confirm His covenant which He swore (solemnly promised) to your fathers, as it is this day.*
>
> *~ Deuteronomy 8:17-18 Amplified Bible (AMP)*

• **Promotion** – Read stories of Bible Heroes; Esther, Joseph, Daniel, the 3 Hebrew boys, to name a few.

For promotion cometh neither from the east, nor from the west nor from the south. But God is the judge: He putteth down one and setteth up another.

~ Psalm 75:6-7 King James Version (KJV)

• **Employment, career and business advancement** – Claim Jabez' anointing for an increase, multiplication, expansion, growth, creativity, and innovation.

Jabez was more honourable than his brothers; but his mother named him Jabez, saying, "Because I gave birth to him in pain." Jabez cried out to the God of Israel, saying, "Oh that You would indeed bless me and enlarge my border [property], and that Your hand would be with me, and You would keep me from evil so that it does not hurt me!" And God granted his request.

~ 1 Chronicles 4:9-10 Amplified Bible (AMP)

• **Needing the God of the Second, even third, fourth and many chances.** Examine the Second Chance testimonies for Women of spotty reputation and experiences – Rahab, Ruth, Bathsheba, the Woman at the Well, the Woman with the issue of the Blood, the Woman caught in Adultery, to name a few.

- **Rahab, the prostitute**, lineage of the generation of Jesus. She is the wife of Salmon, one of the spies from the tribe of Judah, and Boaz was her son. Rahab was saved (chayah) from the devastation that came upon Jericho. (Joshua 6:25)

- **Ruth, the Moabite**, a single woman in a strange land. She found love and became the wife of Boaz. One day, she was gleaning on the field; then the next day, she owned the field. Ruth is also listed in the lineage of the generation of Jesus.

- **Bathsheba, wife of Uriah**, a beautiful "sexy" woman who had an adulterous encounter with King David. He saw her bathing, desired her, requested her, made love to her and impregnated her, then killed her husband as a cover-up. Their son conceived during the adulterous encounter later died. David later married her, and they gave birth to Solomon, the King, David's successor. Bathsheba is also, the lineage of the generation of Jesus. Let me introduce you to a Queen and the Mother of a King!

- **The Woman at the Well with a situation**, several failed relationships, multiple partners, and currently a "side chick." One day, she met a new man, Jesus with unconditional love for her and a man who died to set her free. She became an Evangelist with a new vision and a new life; she chayah!

- **The Woman with the issue of the blood**, an outcast and sick for over 12 years. Healed, restored and rebound with a "stolen touch" from the hem of Jesus' garment. Immediately, she chayah!

- **The Woman caught in adultery,** who had her sins overlooked, forgiven and set free by Jesus Himself in the front of her accusers! They brought the woman caught in adultery, had her standing naked and exposed in front of the crowd.

However, look at the revelation of the God of Second Chance revealed in Jesus' response. His grace, mercy, and forgiveness to the woman; accused, shamed, ridiculed, humiliated, guilty, and exposed to her sins publicly! She rebound to 'really' live... Chayah!

"Teacher," they said to Jesus, "this woman was caught in the act of adultery. The law of Moses says to stone her. What do you say?"

They were trying to trap him into saying something they could use against him, but Jesus stooped down and wrote in the dust with his finger. They kept demanding an answer, so he stood up again and said, "All right, but let the one who has never sinned throw the first stone!" Then He stooped down again and wrote in the dust.

When the accusers heard this, they slipped away one by one, beginning with the oldest, until only Jesus was left in the middle of the crowd with the woman. Then Jesus stood up again and said to the woman, "Where are your accusers? Didn't even one of them condemn you?"

"No, Lord," she said.

And Jesus said, "Neither do I. Go and sin no more."

~ John 8:1-11 New Living Translation (NLT)

• **Desperate for health, healing, wellness from every disease, sickness and illness (physical, mental, emotional, spiritual, even financial.)** Search for scriptures of healing, recovery, and extension of life, resurrection from death (Lazarus) and so many testimonies of the miracles of healing performed by Jesus. God glorifies Himself by healing us! You shall not die but live to declare the glory of the Lord.

When Jesus heard this, He said, "This sickness will not end in death; but [on the contrary, it is] for the glory and honour of God, so that the Son of God may be glorified by it."

~ John 11:4 Amplified Bible (AMP)

But He was wounded for our transgressions, he was bruised for our iniquities: the chastisement of our peace was upon Him, and with his stripes, we are healed. All we like sheep have gone astray; we have turned everyone to His own way, and the Lord hath laid on Him the iniquity of us all.

~ Isaiah 53:5-6 King James Version (KJV)

Bless and affectionately praise the Lord, O my soul, and do not forget any of His benefits; Who forgives all your sins, Who heals all your diseases; Who redeems your life from the pit, Who crowns you [lavishly] with loving-kindness and tender mercy;

~ Psalm 103:2-4 Amplified Bible (AMP)

• **Healing of the broken hearted and brokenness from every shattered promise, broken trust and toxic relationship.** God heals the brokenhearted and binds up their wounds. (Psalm 147:3)

"For I will restore health to you, and I will heal your wounds,' says the Lord, 'Because they have called you an outcast, saying:

'This is Zion; no one seeks her, and no one cares for her.'"

~ Jeremiah 30:17 Amplified Bible (AMP)

• **Deliverance from captivity, depression, and addiction (spiritual, mental, emotional, social, financial, and physical bondage)** – Promoting you from a slave to a son's inheritance, identity, heritage; freedom from all sins, curses of the law, generational curses, breaking of chains; The Rock of Escape,

Redemption, Restoration, Recovery, and acceptance of the prodigal son.

> *Jesus answered them, "Most assuredly, I say to you, whoever commits sin is a slave of sin. And a slave does not abide in the house forever, but a son endures forever. Therefore, if the Son makes you free, you shall be free indeed.*
>
> *~ John 8:34-36 New King James Version (NKJV)*

• **Restoration of Life, Relationships, Family, and Household** – Find testimonies in the Bible of Household salvation (Rehab, Jailer); Marriage, divorce, and adultery (Hosea and Gomer), Husband and Wife, First Family – Adam and Eve, Finding a wife for Isaac; marriage, character building and relationship development. Children and Siblings Relationships: Return of missing, runaway, wayward children - Prodigal son; siblings' jealousy (Cain and Abel); Joseph and his brothers; David as a teenager and his brothers, and so many more stories; read Proverbs 31 and Ephesian 25.

• **Spiritual Warfare, evil pronunciation, and breaking of generational curses**: *We wrestle not against flesh and blood. We put on the full Armour of God and fight. For the weapons of our warfare are not of the flesh but have divine power to destroy strongholds. Weapons are formed but not prospered.* (Isaiah 54:17, Ephesians 6:10-18, 2 Corinthians 10:4-6)

> *"No weapon that is formed against you will succeed, and every tongue that rises against you in judgment you will condemn. This [peace, righteousness, security, and triumph over opposition] is the heritage of the*

servants of the Lord, and this is their vindication from
Me," says the Lord.

~ Isaiah 54:17 Amplified Bible (AMP)

Listen carefully: I have given you authority [that you
now possess] to tread on serpents and scorpions, and
[the ability to exercise authority] over all the power of
the enemy (Satan), and nothing will [in any way] harm
you.

~ Luke 10:1 Amplified Bible (AMP)

• **Healing of barrenness and unfruitfulness in the
reproduction of the womb** – See the testimonies of Sarah,
Hannah, Elizabeth, Rebekah, Leah, Rachel, to name a few. God
makes the barren woman abide in the house as a joyful mother
of children. Praise the LORD! (Psalm 113:9)

Isaac pleaded with the LORD on behalf of his wife,
because she was unable to have children. The LORD
answered Isaac's prayer, and Rebekah became
pregnant with twins.

~ Genesis 25:12 New Living Translation (NLT)

Isaiah said, "Rejoice, O, childless woman, you who
have never given birth! Break into a joyful shout, you
who have never been in labor! For the desolate
woman now has more children than the woman who
lives with her husband!

~ Galatians 4:27 New Living Translation (NLT)

• The miraculous healing of spiritual and physical blindness and
restoration of vision to men: Check out Jesus Healing of the
Man Born Blind; The recovery of sight (vision, wisdom and

173

insight) in the physical, emotional, mental and spiritual blindness. (John 9:1-12)

> *'In the last days,' God says, 'I will pour out my Spirit upon all people. Your sons and daughters will prophesy. Your young men will see visions, and your old men will dream dreams.'*
>
> *~ Acts 2:17 New Living Translation (NLT)*

• **God as your Comforter** when you are grieving the loss of loved ones, lost years, in affliction or troubles.

> *He comforts us in all our troubles so that we can comfort others. When they are troubled, we will be able to give them the same comfort God has given us.*
>
> *~ 2 Corinthians 1:4 New Living Translation (NLT)*

• **Needing a family for your Loneliness and singleness** – Overcoming rejection, abandonment, homelessness, and neglect.

> *God places the lonely in families; He sets the prisoners free and gives them joy. But he makes the rebellious live in a sun-scorched land*
>
> *~ Psalm 68:6 New Living Translation (NLT)*

• **The promise of Restoration** of time, losses, wasted years, and everything the enemy has killed, stolen or destroyed. God will restore your peace, joy, happiness, fortunes, family, finances, and your future.

> *And I will restore or replace for you the years that the locust has eaten—the hopping locust, the stripping*

locust, and the crawling locust, My great army which I sent among you. And you shall eat in plenty and be satisfied and praise the name of the Lord, your God, Who has dealt wondrously with you. And My people shall never be put to shame. And you shall know, understand, and realize that I am in the midst of Israel and that I the Lord am your God and there is none else. My people shall never be put to shame.

~ Joel 2:25-27 Amplified Bible, Classic Edition (AMPC)

God, your God, will restore everything you lost; he'll have compassion on you; he'll come back and pick up the pieces from all the places where you were scattered. No matter how far away you end up, God, your God, will get you out of there and bring you back to the land your ancestors once possessed. It will be yours again. He will give you a good life and make you more numerous than your ancestors. God, your God, will cut away the thick calluses on your heart and your children's hearts, freeing you to love God, your God, with your whole heart and soul and live, really live. God, your God, will put all these curses on your enemies who hated you and were out to get you. And you will make a new start, listening obediently to God, keeping all his commandments that I'm commanding you today. God, your God, will outdo himself in making things go well for you: you'll have babies, get calves, grow crops, and enjoy an all-around good life. Yes, God will start enjoying you again, making things go well for you just as he enjoyed doing it for your ancestors, but only if you listen obediently to God, your God, and keep the commandments and regulations written in this Book of Revelation. Nothing half-hearted here; you must return to God, your God, totally, heart and soul, holding nothing back. This commandment that I'm commanding you today isn't too much for you; it's not out of your reach. It's not on a high mountain - you don't have to get mountaineers to climb the peak and bring it down to your level and explain it before you can live it. And it's not across the ocean - you don't have to send sailors out to get it, bring it back, and then explain it before you can live it.

~ Deuteronomy 30:3-13 The Message (MSG)

• **Blessing and Anointing for Visionary leadership,** the insight and wisdom for your Ministry, Mission, and Marketplace. Ask Bible Heroes: Solomon, Joseph, Peter, Paul, Moses, Daniel, to name a few.

Let's look at Solomon's request for wisdom, the revelation of God, and the divine manifestation of knowledge, plus wealth, intelligence, affluence and influence.

Solomon's Prayer for Wisdom

That night God appeared to Solomon and said, "Ask, and I will give it to you!"

Solomon replied to God: "You have shown great and loving devotion to my father David, and You have made me king in his place. Now, O LORD God, let Your promise to my father David be fulfilled. For, You have made me king over people as numerous as the dust of the earth. Now grant me wisdom and knowledge, so that I may lead these people. For who is able to govern these great people of Yours?"

God said to Solomon, "Since this was in your heart and you have not requested riches or wealth or glory or the death of your enemies—and since you have not even requested long life but have asked for wisdom and knowledge to govern My people over whom I have made you king—therefore wisdom and knowledge have been granted to you. honour and I will also give you riches and wealth and honour unlike anything given to the kings before you or after you."

(1 Kings 3:4-15, 2 Chronicles 1:7-13)

What does God's Word reveal about your specific request? Have you asked, claimed, believed, received and activated God's Word regarding your situation, giving you hope, courage, confidence, and a renewed mind for mental wellness (Shalom) to have a new outlook on your life with prayer, positivity, patience, persistence, and perseverance? Have you deliberately decreed, declared, and decided on God's Word over your situation? If any of you lacks wisdom, you should ask God, who gives generously to all without finding fault, and it will be given to you. (James 1:5)

Stop the negativity; start believing and speaking positivity and manifest prosperity!

Let every stone thrown at you be used to build the bridges to climb out of the valley of depression. Start visualizing, verbalizing and venturing into your Vision. Make a Vow in your heart to be empowered and transformed; to achieve your Purpose.

Write out your Rebound Faith Prophetic Prayers, inspirational quotes, scriptures, and begin to pray, declare, speak, share, post, repeat, decree, proclaim and prophesy your deliverance! Utter them in the atmosphere. Shift the energy and attract positivity! God has given you authority and dominion. Ask for the impossible! Pray from a position of victory. Believe that God has already accomplished; He won, fixed, healed, reversed,

177

rescued, and restored it! Speak it into being! God said it, and so shall it be! Tell the devil the truth of God's Word, and what the devil is saying, that's a lie!

The Violation, Venting & the Valley, maybe saying –	But, align your Vision and Vow to manifest God's Word
• You can't work it out! • You are too weary and weak! • This is impossible, and there is no way out! • You are unlovable! • You are unforgivable! • You are forgotten! • You are forsaken! • You are worthless! • You are not smart! • You are not able! • You can't do this! • You must give up! • You can't manage! • You are not enough! • You are afraid and	• God will order your steps (Proverb 3:5-6) • God will give you rest (Matthew 11:28-30) • With God, all things are possible (Luke 18:27) • God loves you with an everlasting love and beneath you are his eternal arms (John 3:16) • God forgives you (Romans 1:8) • It is worth it, and you are worthy of it (Roman 8:28) • God gives wisdom (James 1:5) • God is able (2 Cor 9:8) • God's grace is sufficient (Phil 4:13) • God will supply all you need (Phil 4:19) • With God, you can do all things (Phil 4:13 • God has not given you a spirit of fear (2 Tim 1:17) • God will never leave you nor

The Violation, Venting & the Valley, maybe saying –	But, align your Vision and Vow to manifest God's Word
fearful! • You are alone!	forsake you (Deut 31:6) • God will always remember you, and He is with you forever (Psalm 16:8)

Now, begin to war for your aspired future and take your possession and the Promise back by force! Renew your mind! Take back your inner peace! Take your seeds back! Take your power back! Be so angry with the devil that you have a driving force that is indescribable and unspeakable compared to your defeat. Power up the strength for your rebound, make a massive comeback, and 'really' live; Chayah!

And it shall come to pass, that before they call, I will answer; and while they are yet speaking, I will hear.

~ Isaiah 65:24 King James Version (KJV)

Confess your faults one to another, and pray one for another, that ye may be healed. The effectual fervent prayer of a righteous man availeth much.

~ James 5:16 King James Version (KJV)

At the beginning of your supplications, the command [to give you an answer] was issued, and I have come to tell you, for you are highly regarded and greatly beloved. Therefore, consider the message and begin to understand the [meaning of the] vision.

~ Daniel 9:23 Amplified Bible (AMP)

Now, choose your response which demands you to stand on something.

Will you be anchored by *faith* or angered by *fear*, as either requires of you to believe that which has not yet seen?

I pray that you will choose to *respond* with Rebound Faith!

Response to Receive

So, will My word be which goes out of My mouth; It will not return to Me void (useless, without result), Without accomplishing what I desire, and without succeeding in the matter for which I sent it.

~ Isaiah 55:11-13 Amplified Bible (AMP)

S o, you have been praying and fasting; you have fervently made your prayer requests, you are standing on the Word of God regarding your situation, and you are eagerly waiting for the release from God in accordance to His Will and in His time. Waiting for the promises of God is hard work, for it is during the waiting period that God nurtures your faith the most. It is during the waiting period that the devil tempts and tests your faith the most. You are maturing your Rebound Faith; the grit, your endurance and trust to hold God by His Word with the confidence and belief to rebound!

You must stand unshakeably on the Word of God!

God is not a man that He should lay; neither the son of man that He should repent: hath He said, and shall He not do it? Or hath He spoken, and shall He not make it good?

~ Numbers 23:19 King James Version (KJV)

"Lest Satan should take advantage of us; for we are not ignorant of his devices."

~ 2 Corinthians 2:11 New King James Version (NKJV)

"What shall we then say to these things? If God is here for us, who can be against us?"

~ Romans 8:31 King James Version (KJV)

"Praise the Lord who has given rest to his people Israel, just as he promised. Not one word has failed of all the wonderful promises he gave through his servant Moses."

~ 1 Kings 8:56 New Living Translation (NLT)

It is the same with my word. I send it out, and it always produces fruit. It will accomplish all I want it to, and it will prosper everywhere I send it."

~ Isaiah 55:11 New Living Translation (NLT)

The Lord said to Joshua, "Do not fear them, because I have given them into your hand; not one of them shall stand before you."

~ Joshua 10:8 Amplified Bible (AMP)

Then he said, "Don't be afraid, Daniel. Since the first day you began to pray for understanding and to humble yourself before your God, your request has been heard in heaven. I have come in answer to your prayer.

~ Daniel 10:12 New Living Translation (NLT)

So, whatever you have been praying for, apply your Rebound Faith to believe you are a winner; victoriously accomplished. Jesus already has the victory! God will fight for you! We are on the team, Jesus; therefore, we too are on the Champion's Team. Whatever opponents have come up against you in defence, tackles and attack, in the name of Jesus, I command that thing to be aligned and hear the unfailing Word of God. We are standing on what the Bible says about our situations. We are confident that God has the final authority and final say, as only His Word is eternal; all other words, opinions, and programs have an expiration and a termination date! We call forth the termination date of every plan of the enemy, as we are stepping by faith, not by sight. We block-out every opponent and outrebound them, in Jesus mighty name.

Your response to God's revelation is to activate the manifestation of God's word in your life, believe that God said it, and therefore, it is already taken care of and provided for, and you shall receive it, in Jesus mighty name.

You should hold tightly without wavering to the hope that you affirm, for God can be trusted to keep His promise. Also, you should think of ways to motivate one another to acts of love and good works. We should not neglect to meet, help and encourage each other with the same hope and grace that we have experienced. Our troubles reveal and confirm that indeed God is faithful and a very present help in time of need; He is the Lifter of our heads, source of strength, our Peace and Provider.

Let us seize and hold tightly the confession of our hope without wavering, for He who promised is reliable and trustworthy and faithful [to His word]; and let us consider [thoughtfully] how we may encourage one another to love and to do good deeds.

Hebrews 10:23-24 Amplified Bible (AMP)

Receive to Rejoice

I will exalt you, my God and King, and praise your name forever and ever. I will praise you every day; yes, I will praise you forever. Great is the Lord! He is most worthy of praise! No one can measure his greatness. Let each generation tell its children of your mighty acts; let them proclaim your power. I will meditate on your majestic, glorious splendor and your wonderful miracles. Your awe-inspiring deeds will be on every tongue; I will proclaim your greatness. Everyone will share the story of your wonderful goodness; they will sing with joy about your righteousness.

~ Psalm 145:1-7 New Living Translations (NLT)

You need faith to rejoice at the request, even before you have received the victory, making a prophetic declaration in confidence based on the attributes, actions, character, and conduct of God. Prophesy your breakthrough, praise God for Who He is, share your testimonies and bring God Glory for your deliverance. Sometimes, the opponent attacks you with shame, then society attached a stigma to your past, and this stops you from declaring God's goodness, but your God shall deliver you from ashes to beauty! Remember the enemy attacks you in the same area of your anointing, as He is afraid of your advancement. You are not a victim of your past nor present. Your breakthrough is a significant threat to inflict pain and damage on the enemy and his destructive plans!

So, upon your Request; **Rejoice!**

"Do not fret or have any anxiety about anything, but in every circumstance and in everything, by prayer and petition (definite requests), with thanksgiving, continue to make your wants known to God."

~ Philippians 4:6 Amplified Bible, Classic Edition (AMPC)

Moreover, when you Receive; **Rejoice!**

"Blessed be the Lord because He has heard the voice of my supplications! The Lord is my strength and my shield; My heart trusted in Him, and I am helped; Therefore, my heart greatly rejoices, and with my song, I will praise Him.

~ Psalm 28:6-7 New King James Version (NKJV)

Throughout the Psalms, David celebrates! He exalts God for his expected as well as actual receipt of his answered prayers – even today, we are recipients of the benefits David and many other Bible heroes' testimonies and praises. *Lord, You are holy, O You who are enthroned in the sacred place where your people offer their praises.* (Psalm 22:3)

Mary rejoices! Luke 1:46-51 says, *"Oh, how my soul praises the Lord. How my spirit rejoices in God my Saviour; For He took notice of his lowly servant girl, and from now on all generations will call me blessed. For the Mighty One is holy, and He has done great things for me. He shows mercy from generation to generation to all who fear Him. His mighty arm has done tremendous things!"*

Hannah rejoices! 1 Samuel 2:1 says, *"At that time Hannah prayed, 'My heart rejoices in the Lord! The Lord has made me strong. Now I have an answer for my enemies; I rejoice because you have rescued me!'"*

Lord, we pray and praise you! We seek your divine intervention to help us during life's trials and tribulations. As we mature our faith for the assurance of a high expected Rebound, we box-out every opposition, and gain the victory; even taking it by force and bringing great exaltation, adoration, and glorious praises to your name.

> *"O Lord, Almighty God, King of the Universe, Abba Father won't You revive us again so that your people can rejoice in you?"*
>
> *Psalm 85:6 New Living Translations (NLT)*

God response:

> *"You don't have enough faith," Jesus told them. "I tell you the truth, if you had faith even as small as a mustard seed, you could say to this mountain, 'Move from here to there,' and it would move. Nothing would be impossible."*
>
> *~ Matthew 17:20 New Living Translation (NLT)*

> *And the Lord said, "If you have [confident, abiding] faith in God [even as small] as a mustard seed, you could say to this mulberry tree [which has very strong roots], 'Be pulled up by the roots and be planted in the sea'; and [if the request was in agreement with the will of God] it would have obeyed you."*
>
> *~ Luke 17:6 Amplified Bible (AMP)*

I decree and declare that Psalm 26 shall be your testimony. Rejoice for your Restoration is coming... Chayah!

When the Lord restored the fortunes of Zion, it was as if we were dreaming. Then our mouths were filled with laughter and our tongues with joyful songs. Then the nations said, "The Lord has done spectacular things for them." The Lord has done spectacular things for us. We are overjoyed! Restore our fortunes, O Lord, as you restore streams to dry riverbeds in the Negev. Those who cry while they plant will joyfully sing while they harvest. The person who goes out weeping, carrying his bag of seed, will come home singing, carrying his bundles of grain.

~ Psalm 126 God's Word Translation (GWT)

The Lord is merciful and compassionate, slow to get angry and filled with unfailing love. The Lord is good to everyone. He showers compassion on all His creation. All of your works will thank you, Lord, and your faithful followers will praise you. They will speak of the glory of your kingdom; they will give examples of your power. They will tell about your mighty deeds and about the majesty and glory of your reign. For your kingdom is an everlasting kingdom. You rule throughout all generations.

The Lord always keeps his promises; he is gracious in all he does. The Lord helps the fallen and lifts those bent beneath their loads. The eyes of all look to you in hope; you give them their food as they need it. When you open your hand, you satisfy the hunger and thirst of every living thing.

The Lord is righteous in everything he does; He is filled with kindness. The Lord is close to all who call on Him, yes, to all who call on Him in truth. He grants the desires of those who fear Him; He hears their cries for help and rescues them. The Lord protects all those who love Him, but he destroys the wicked. I will praise the Lord and may everyone on earth bless His holy name forever and ever. (Psalm 145:8-21)

Praises Prevent the Pain during the Process!

> *"A smooth sea never made a skilled sailor."*
> — *Franklin D. Roosevelt.*

Pain and problems are often drivers with transformative changes. Rebound Faith is about having the strength to let go, and the courage to not give up; remain in hope, trust, and faith in God. We continue to pray and praise God during our afflictions with the confidence that the pain, no matter how great, cannot compare to the greater glory, the plan, and the purpose that God has in store for you.

> *For I consider [from the standpoint of faith] that the sufferings of the present life are not worthy to be compared with the glory that is about to be revealed to us and in us!*
>
> *~ Romans 8:18 Amplified Bible (AMP)*

We are patient, and we persevere during the pain of the process, and that produce increased faith, hope, and trust in God; as our problems are excellent teachers with practical experiences. When you surrender to the Lord, you will experience His love, His unchangeable character, and His divine nature.

You examine and explore His very great plan, glorious promises, His divine power and His predestined purpose for you to experience miracles and the manifestation of His Word, in your life; to deliver, heal, restore and to bring glory to His name.

Jeremiah 29:11-13 (NLT) says, *"For I know the plans I have for you. They are plans for good and not for disaster, to give you a future and a hope. In those days when you pray, I will listen. If you look for me wholeheartedly, you will find me."*

2 Corinthians 12:10 (AMP) says, *"So, I am well pleased with weaknesses, with insults, with distresses, with persecutions, and with difficulties, for the sake of Christ; for when I am weak [in human strength], then I am strong, truly able, truly powerful, truly drawing from God's strength."*

> And not only this, but [with joy] let us exult in our sufferings and rejoice in our hardships, knowing that hardship (distress, pressure, trouble) produces patient endurance; and endurance, proven character (spiritual maturity); and proven character, hope and confident assurance [of eternal salvation]. Such hope [in God's promises] never disappoints us, because God's love has been abundantly poured out within our hearts through the Holy Spirit who was given to us.
>
> ~ Romans 5:3-5 Amplified Bible (AMP)

In 2 Corinthians 11:24-27, Paul describes his sufferings and service for Christ:

Five times I received from the Jews thirty-nine lashes. Three times I was beaten with rods, once I was stoned; three times I was shipwrecked, a night and a day I have spent in the deep. I have been on frequent journeys, in dangers from rivers, dangers from robbers, dangers from my countrymen, dangers from the Gentiles, dangers in the city, dangers in the wilderness, dangers on the sea, dangers among false brethren; I have been in labor and hardship, through many sleepless nights, in hunger, and thirst, often without food, in cold and exposure.

Wow! Imagine how we murmur and complain about our trials, troubles, and tribulations as we suffer and serve God. Thanks, are given to God, for not testing us beyond what we can bear. Though during the process of the trial, the pain is often seeming unbearable and unending. But God!

> *"No temptation [regardless of its source] has overtaken or enticed you that is not common to human experience [nor is any temptation unusual or beyond human resistance], but God is faithful [to His word—He is compassionate and trustworthy], and He will not let you be tempted beyond your ability [to resist], but along with the temptation He [has in the past and is now and] will [always] provide the way out as well, so that you will be able to endure it [without yielding, and will overcome temptation with joy]."*
>
> *~ 1 Corinthians 10:13 Amplified Bible (AMP)*

My light and momentary troubles, though, I considered them painful at the time, are mild when compared to Paul's, and possibly yours and exponentially, infinitely miniature when compared to Jesus; His sacrificial death and suffering for our sins, shame, and sorrows.

However, Jesus' Rebound Story to Chayah, His resurrection to life has rekindled and re-ignited our Rebound Faith that one day, we too shall Chayah!

Rebound Faith Prayer and Declaration

Heavenly Father, Lord, once again here I am, I give you my all, I surrender everything to you. Father, as I continue this journey of life, I am learning to depend on your faithfulness, rely upon Your steadfast love and trust Your heart. Lord, rekindle my faith and ignite Your fire in me, which have dampened with the current storms or even successes in life. Lord, help me when I can't see nor feel Your touch when I don't understand where Your hands are leading me, and I don't seem to hear Your voice to trust Your heart. Being confident of who I am in You and who You are as my God, Your Character, Your Conduct, Your Attributes, and Your Activities as the GREAT I AM.

Holy Spirit; help me, strengthen me, and increase my faith to rebound, as I believe and trust in you during the stages: from the request to the revelation, from the disclosure to the response, from the answer to the reception, and indeed to the state of rejoicing.

I declare, *"I am gaining Rebound Faith, the Grit, my unshakeable faith in Jesus Christ to gain resilience, perseverance, endurance, and persistent trust in God and power me through for victory to Chayah!"*

Lord, it is during the wait periods when my faith is challenged and tested. When fears grip me, the devil and his demons taunt, toss and tell me lies. "God, didn't say that? Are you still trusting God? He won't come through. God has let you down!"

God, I am holding on to you and your promises, even when my enemies, friends, and sometimes even my family laugh and mock me saying, "Ah... Still believing; Still waiting? Haven't given up yet? God has forgotten and forsaken you."

During Job's calamity and affliction, his friends condemned him, and even his wife told him to give up, curse God and succumb to his sufferings.

Then his wife said to him, "Do you still cling to your integrity [and your faith and trust in God, without blaming Him]? Curse God and die!"

~ Job 2:9 Amplified Bible (AMP)

During these critical waiting times is when the discouragement, hopelessness, and depression creep in, and I get thrown into the Valley of Despair. However, I must stay connected to The Lord (The Vine) and keep my eyes on Him as my Rock, Refuge, and my Anchor - immovable, unshakeable, bigger, and stronger than the current situation.

I will always remember that God is good; He can't be anything other than good. His character is good! He was right in the past, He is unchanging, and therefore, He will remain good! When I can't see His hands, I let go, but not give up, and trust His heart, His timing, His goodness, His thoughts, His will, His ways.... and indeed, His Words!

This is the unshakeable and impenetrable faith that I am praying for today. Lord, grant me Rebound Faith to believe in You and trust You to rebound me during these waiting times, with great testimonies. I must refuse to be chased around, and driven into discouragement, hopelessness, anxiety, panic attacks, depression, and suicidal thoughts by life's tribulations and the temptations of Satan.

"Rejoice in the Lord always [delight, take pleasure in Him]; again, I will say, rejoice! Let your gentle spirit [your graciousness, unselfishness, mercy, tolerance, and patience] be known to all people. The Lord is near. Do not be anxious or worried about anything, but in everything [every circumstance and situation] by prayer and petition with thanksgiving, continue to

make your [specific] requests known to God. And the peace of God [that peace which reassures the heart, that peace], which transcends all understanding, [that peace which] stands guard over your hearts and your minds in Christ Jesus [is yours]."

~ Philippians 4:4-7 Amplified Bible (AMP)

I thank you, Lord Jesus, for the peace that You have given me and the faith to rebound and chayah! I believe that I will gain overwhelming victory as an Overcomer, in Jesus name.

Jesus looked at them intently and said, *"Humanly speaking, it is impossible. However, with God, everything is possible."* (Matthew 19:26)

I claim the revelation that absolutely nothing is impossible with the Lord.

We define *strength* as the quality or state of being strong, the capacity for exertion or endurance. It means power, vigour, might, energy, and fervency. Also means having the ability because of influence, authority, or resources.

God's Word causes a new strength to come upon me, which renews my faith, giving me righteousness, boldness, confidence, and assurance to testify in advance of my deliverance. To call forth my victory and to declare my breakthrough despite what we see or feel! I will sing of the mercies of the Lord forever; with my mouth will I make known your faithfulness to all generations. For I have said, "Mercy shall be built up forever; your faithfulness You shall establish in the very heavens." (Psalm 89:2)

LORD, You have a mighty arm; Strong is Your hand, and high is Your right hand. Righteousness and justice are the foundation of Your throne; Mercy and truth go before Your face. Blessed are the people who know the joyful sound! They walk, O Lord, in the light of Your countenance. In Your name, they rejoice all day long, and in Your righteousness, they are exalted; for You are the glory of their strength, and in Your favour our horn is exalted; for our shield belongs to the Lord and our king to the Holy One of Israel. Then, the Lord spoke in a vision to His holy one and said: "I have given help to one who is mighty; I have exalted one chosen from the people. I have found my servant [insert your name]; with my holy oil, I have anointed you, with whom my hand shall be established. My arm shall strengthen you! The enemy shall not outwit you, nor does the son of wickedness afflict you. God will beat down your foes before your face, and plague those who hate you." (Psalm 89:13-23)

In the name of Jesus, I declare that God anoints me with fresh oil for strength, energy, ability, and power to increase the capacity and strategies of global and generational breakthroughs; exploiting emerging possibilities of excellence and expansion. I claim my advantage and advancement with the manifestation of covenant promises and inheritance as a Child of God. I am positioned, strengthened, favoured, honoured, and empowered with significant influence, authority, and resources equipped for every opportunity. I have the strength, power, and mighty force to resist the enemy, withstand, reverse, and boomerang every attack. O Lord, build a protective wall of fire to surround me, go before me and be my rearguard now. I have faith to boldly ask the Lord for the impossible, invincible, invisible, and indescribable under God's Will. Holy Spirit, strengthen me so that I overcome, win, master and lead; making me indestructible, unconquerable, unbeatable, unstoppable, and unassailable against every enemy, forces of darkness, diabolic scheme, evil power, strategy, curse, and weapon and plot of the enemy in Jesus name.

O God Almighty, is anything too complicated or too beautiful for You? In the name of Jesus, I declare that the appointed time of my breakout seasons has come in my life, my children, my household, family, health, finances, and work of our hands. The divine blessings, deliverance, breakthroughs, mind-blowing miracles, steadfast love, and victory shall suddenly come upon us; not a trickle but a tidal wave, a mighty explosion of God's goodness, greatness, grace, and glory. We shall finish this season strong and start the new season even stronger. We shall chayah, in Jesus name; AMEN!

REBOUND FAITH

CHAYAH!

VOLUME THREE

3rd Quarter

Renewed Mindset for Mental Wellness (Shalom)

Live Prosperously... Chayah!

Living Healthily, Wealthily, Affluently and Richly!

"Beloved, I pray that in every way you may succeed and prosper and be in good health [physically], just as [I know] your soul prospers [spiritually]."

3 John 2:2 Amplified Bible (AMP)

Rebound Faith Antidote for Depression

Every day, we encounter people who are at different stages in the journey of life. Many are in the valley of depression; unhappy, hurting, lonely, and overwhelmed with fear and pain triggered by various circumstances and conditions. Unfortunately, often, we are so preoccupied with updating our social media (*Instagram. Facebook, Linkedin, SnapChat*) status, news feed, and stories. We become too busy in pursuit of success to stop and notice, to be gentle, to show kindness, and to care; bringing hope and happiness to them. Sometimes, we hurt ourselves or become too busy, or begin covering up and masking our despair to stop, look, and listen. Mental illness such as depression can affect anyone – rich or poor, saved or unsaved, old or young, man or woman; their creed or status notwithstanding.

Mental health is a state of well-being!

The World Health Organization, WHO defines Mental Health as

"A state of well-being in which every individual realizes his or her potential can cope with the normal stresses of life can work productively and fruitfully and can contribute to her or his community."

The encouraging standpoint of Mental Health is as described in WHO's constitution: *"Health is a state of complete physical, mental, and social well-being and not merely the absence of disease or infirmity."*

- Mental health is beyond the absence of mental disorders or disabilities
- Mental health is a vital contributor to health; indeed, there is no health without mental health.
- Prolonged physical health can negatively affect our mental health
- Mental health determinants include a range of socioeconomic, biological and environmental factors
- Cost-effective public health and intersectional strategies and interventions exist to promote, protect, and restore mental health

Mental health is imperative to us as human - as an individual or within groups (family, home, school) - to think, interact with each other, earn a living, contribute to society and enjoy life.

As such, to disrupt the stigma of mental illness, as a Believer and a Transformational Consultant, I am taking the positive perspective on mental health. I prefer the reference of *mental wellness* as having inner security and rest of mind, body, and soul which is the inward sense of peace defined in the Hebrew word Shalom.

The definition of Shalom *is the completeness, fullness, greatness, wholeness, health, Salvation, peace, prosperity, favour, success, and all goodness in life.*

Therefore, I aim to become an Advocate for *mental wellness*. I seek to encourage, empower, and support our well-being as the divine blessing of Shalom. Hence, the promotion, protection, and provision of mental wellness is an essential aspect for all individuals, communities, churches, corporations, and societies; globally and generationally.

The journey of Rebound Faith to Chayah is imperative to our mental wellness:

- *Surviving life experiences or events*
- *Reviving from every devastation or depression*
- *Thriving for shalom (peace) to chayah (to rebound and 'really' live)*

Often, the trigger of depression can be a combination of life experience or event or heredity or chemical imbalances. Studies indicate, and my expertise testifies that the most effective recovery process is a combination treatment of antidepressant medication and psychotherapy (with spiritual empowerment for life transformation).

There is no reason to be ashamed of your mental illness. Many people experience depression, anxiety, and other mental health disorders. People should feel pleased to seek mental health care, no different than the healthcare for other medical complications including heart disease, cancer, diabetes, or high blood pressure.

Depression is a common but very treatable mental disorder and, the good news is that medication, psychotherapy, and spiritual empowerment are effective recovery strategies for those who do seek treatment; gaining the faith to rebound to live prosperously!

Mental Wellness is indeed the new Wealth!

You have a choice to decide how you respond; do you hold on to the hurt and bitterness, or offer forgiveness and free ourselves? Do you let go and take hold of the opened door to explore new beginnings, opportunities, and possibilities? It would be healthy if you respond showing peace that surpasses all understanding, that instead of focusing on your problems, you shift your thoughts to focus on – *Positivity, Perseverance, Praise, Prophecy, and Prayers.*

Don't let the past capture the crown of your future. It is imperative that you learn, love, listen, let go, laugh, be light and leap forward to live; come alive, survive, revive, and thrive... Chayah!

Jesus, Himself warned you that you would encounter troubles in the journey of life, but He also encouraged you to have perfect peace. He has already rebounded the enemy and overcoming the world; gaining permanent, eternal and overwhelming victory. (John 16:33, James 1:2-4)

> *"I have told you these things, so that in Me you may have [perfect] peace. In the world, you have tribulation and distress and suffering, but be*

201

courageous [be confident, be undaunted, be filled with joy]; I have overcome the world." [My conquest is accomplished, my victory abiding.]"

-- *John 16:33 (Amplified Bible (AMP)*

"Consider it nothing but joy, my brothers and sisters, whenever you fall into various trials. Be assured that the testing of your faith [through experience] produces endurance [leading to spiritual maturity, and inner peace]. And let endurance have its perfect result and do a thorough work, so that you may be perfect and completely developed [in your faith], lacking in nothing."

-- *James 1:2-4 Amplified Bible (AMP)*

However, during the storms, challenges, and difficulties in life, how can we have the seeming impossible peace and joy that John 16:33 and James 1:2-4 spoke of, and so many other scriptures in the Bible promised?

Many people become overwhelmed with these life challenges (such as unemployment, divorce, financial struggle, family crisis, relationship issues, health problems, grief, tragedy, addiction, and other psychological trauma) leading to depression and negatively impacting the person's life, family, and relationships. Depression can result in increased stress, dysfunctional behaviours, and adversely affecting the person's mental health.

The World Health Organization (WHO) emphasizes that Mental Wellness is a factor of our well-being, where we recognize our potential to manage and adjust to the ups and downs and the normal stresses of life, contributing effectively and successfully to life, work, school, home, or the community.

The World Health Organization (WHO) website, research, and reports confirm that depression worldwide is increasing as a common illness impacting millions of people of all ages. Depression is among the highest cause of disability worldwide and is a significant contributor to the overall global burden of disease. Depression is not merely mood swings or temporary emotional reactions to everyday life challenges. Depression is moderate or severe feelings of sadness, hopelessness, and failure; impacting the affected person's performance at work, at home, at school, and in relationships. More and more women are affected by depression than men. There are serious health concerns as depression can lead to suicide. Unfortunately, WHO stated that there are thousands of suicidal deaths annually and suicide is the second leading cause of death in 15-29-year-olds.

Since recently, depression has become a hot topic in the modern society, but the Bible has numerous stories of people experiencing and overcoming depression. There are many testimonies of both influential man of God and women of faith who suffered the shame, pain, and struggles of hopelessness and despair. The Bible often describes the symptoms of depression as weary, downcast, mourning, agonizing, despairing, troubled, broken-hearted, anguished, miserable, anxious. However, with God, these bible heroes suffered and struggled, but survived, revived, and thrived. Throughout the Rebound Faith book series, we will look at some of these stories, the source, and symptoms of depression, support for healing, and coping strategies, as well as supernatural recovery process to their rebound.

As we said before, depression is a prevalent mental disorder, but a very curable illness. Many people recover and restore to experience an abundant life. Unfortunately, still, others suffer in silence and loneliness due to the stigma and the shame.

Recently, the news captured many reports of suicides of famous people that hidden beneath the smile is a deep sadness; beyond the fame and fortune, hidden is the fear of failure and hopelessness; where the choice to die seems more comfortable than the fight to live. That's a lie from the enemy! If you are ever in such despair, run to God; call on the name of JESUS! *Cast all your cares, anxiety and worries on Him because He cares for you* (1 Peter 5:7). He is the Light in the darkness and the Life over death.

The long and brutal divorce, family court battles, and other traumatic life circumstances triggered my despair; diagnosed with situational depression. I experienced some significant losses – the death of my father, my broken marriage, the loss of the family home, financial crisis, the adverse effects on my career, and the fear of losing my children; all contributed factors and sources of negatively impacting my mental wellness.

Initially isolated, I suffered alone; tortured by the multiple court encounters, the low self-esteem, and disappointment as I felt a sense of frustration to my children and the loss of the promised commitment of my marriage and the fear of my future. I lost many friends and even experienced withdrawal from some family members; not wanting to get caught in the mess or dragging their children through my troubles or picking sides.

Then, I reached out for help. God gave me a team of people to support me:

- **Family:** My mother visited from Jamaica, stayed and took care of my boys and me. Unfortunately, she had a fall in Niagara Falls and became ill.
- **Health Care:** My family doctor, Dr. Alina Nuica, provided me with exceptional holistic health care.
- **Therapy:** My therapist, Dr. Wendy H. Hofman, Ph.D., who is also a believer, offered counselling, treatment, and spiritual empowerment.

- **Church and Community:** Multiple pastors provided pastoral care, motivation and prayers. They took me under their Pastoral wings and pastored for me. They were firm, yet loving, their faith was strong, and they prayed earnestly, counselled, supported, and guided me. Senior Pastor of Acts Community Worship Center, Hamilton, ON, Apostle Sceon Leslie, even accompanied me to my trial management and case court appearances. Each day, she encouraged me to draw my strength, hope, and courage from the Lord. We attended conferences and retreats together. She also facilitated her Chayil Small Group, an engaged support group of believers, met weekly in my home as led by my Pastor.

God provided numerous ways to support me financially, emotionally, mentally, physically, and spiritually.

Research, as well as my experience, has claimed evidence that the most effective recovery process is a combined treatment of antidepressant medication (depending on the severity of the mental disorder), psychotherapy balanced with spiritual empowerment support for life transformation, as well as providing the physical and social support to sustain and improve the situation. I agree!

My greatest desire is to see the corporations, community and the church working with the clinicians to create innovative therapies that integrate faith and social responsibility.

Rebound Faith is a Spiritual Empowerment and Life Transformation approach that is deeply grounded in God's providence, prayers, and positivity to gain increase faith, hope and trust in the power of God for the rebound to victory. This approach can combine traditional therapies including:

- **Cognitive Behavioural Therapy** (CBT) to manage and monitor as well as control and change unwanted thoughts and behaviours.

- **Interpersonal Treatment** to improve patients to experience more effective relationships with others.

Rebound Faith acknowledges and embodies the holistic wellness

- Physical indicating the external triggers of the Change such as an adverse life event or life experience

- Psychological reporting the effects of the mind impacting the mental and emotional state of a person

- Psychosocial indicating the interrelation of social factors and, individual thought and behaviour

- Spiritual meaning the impact to the human spirit or soul as opposed to material or physical aspects of depression is imperative.

Moreover, God has given us Jesus, The Gift of Peace for every mental disorder, including depression.

Jesus Himself fore-warned us that living in this world is hard, but He also imparted great Words of Comfort and Hope for us in John 16:33. In Jesus, we will have perfect peace and confidence despite the tribulation, trials, distress, and frustration we could face in this world. We can be of good cheer, courageous, confident, satisfied, and fearless; for Jesus has already overcome the world. Jesus has deprived the enemy of his power to harm you and has conquered him and this world for you. Believe, as this is the strategy to chayah, to live, revive, survive and thrive to an abundant life!

This promise of peace and joy during trials are only possible through faith to believe that your rebound to victory is warranted and guaranteed through Jesus, despite the adverse life events. As believers, we have favour with God because of who we are in Christ. Having a positive attitude and thoughts are not only preventative but also corrective measures, reducing worry, anxiety, stress, and depression. Having rest in our minds, the surety that it shall be well is the beginning for our recovery and restoration and real prosperity. Mental Wellness is vital for you to enjoy a peaceful, prosperous, healthy and wealthy life!

Mental Wellness is the Mind-Blowing Wealth!

"Behold, I will restore you. I will bring you to health and healing, and I will heal you. I will reveal to you an abundance of peace (prosperity, security, stability) and truth. I will restore your fortunes and will rebuild you as I have created you at first, in authority, dominion, and power to be fruitful and multiply. I will cleanse you from all your wickedness (guilt) by which you have sinned against Me, and I will pardon (forgive) all your sins by which you rebelled against Me. You will be to Me a name of joy, praise and glory before all the nations of the earth which will hear of all the good that I do for you, and they shall fear and tremble because of all the good and all the peace (prosperity, security, stability) that I provide for you."

Says God (Jeremiah 33:6-10)

This word is God's promise of tranquillity and rest of mind for you today, as written in Jeremiah 33:6-9. His peace brings you prosperity, security, stability, and success. Wherever you find yourself today, claim your Rebound Faith, believe, and declare:

"For the LORD is my Peace through every turmoil!"

Life is a great teacher, and every lesson learned from your experience is intended to elevate your purpose, providence and prominence. The story of Gideon is a testimony of God's peace, promotion to prosperity amidst what seemed like defeat.

Gideon was very depressed, disheartened, and disappointed with God. He was hiding; feeling forgotten by God, frustrated by the enemies, and fearful for his survival. His family has suffered severe losses from their oppressors, the Midianites. In the valley of depression, He had a divine encounter with God, who lovingly reminded him to be at Peace and not be afraid for he will not die, but live; chayah!

> *The Lord said to him, "Peace to you, do not be afraid; you shall not die." Then Gideon built an altar there to the Lord and named it "The Lord is Peace."*
>
> *~ Judges 6:23-24*

God in His encounter provided reassurance of the rebound to live; giving promise of strength, new hope, victory, and peace.

Strength: The joy of the Lord is your strength. The name of the LORD is a reliable, strong and mighty tower; the righteous man runs into it and is safe, secure, and set on high, far above evil (Proverbs 18:10). You find strength when you are encouraged in the Lord. Gideon's God-Moment provided him with empowerment from God, Himself, *"The LORD is with you, mighty warrior."* (Judges 6:12) Though Gideon felt more like a victim at the time than Valor, the motivational declarations from the Word of God empowered and strengthened him for the battle, to believe that, indeed, God created, designed, and developed Gideon to be a mighty warrior.

Hope: Trust God for a favourable outcome, a more secure and purposeful future to equip you to fight, to quicken you to life from depression, devastation, and oppression; hope that gives birth to new life, miracles, and expectation. *"You are not going to die!"*

Victory: No Word of God shall return void and unfulfilled. Therefore, Gideon became that which the Lord has spoken over him. The Lord is actively watching over His word ready to perform it. God said you are a mighty warrior, a Valor! You are more than a conqueror, an overcomer! You shall win and be victorious over every oppressor, opponent, hindrance, hater, the accuser, and the enemy! The enemy you see today, you shall see them no more! You shall save your family from the enemy and become a great leader.

Peace: The Lord revealed Himself to Gideon when their oppressors were ravishing he and his family; hiding their food for survival. He was disturbed, frustrated, fearful, and confused in his mind. During their unrest and no peace; he heard the declaration, *"The Lord is Peace!"* You will not die but live prosperously because the Lord is your peace; *Shalom*!

Embrace God, Encounter His Presence; Experience Shalom; Enjoy Mental Wellness!

The Hebrew word **Shalom** explains the divine peace that God promises; that peace of God which reassures the heart; that peace which transcends all understanding; that peace which stands guard over your hearts and your minds in Christ Jesus, is yours – entirely yours! (Philippians 4:7)

Shalom means to be at rest in your mind, body, and soul. It defines salvation, your inner completeness, and tranquillity; every goodness of life, wholeness, fullness and well-being; peace, health, and prosperity.

The Lord, He rescues people from many troubles. The same unchangeable God, He is still in the business of setting captives free today from mental, physical, emotional, and financial bondage.

The storm and the struggles were there for you to stumble upon your strength. During the storm, in those days when you feel that you can't go on any further, as you have been there long enough, and the pain is too high to bear any longer, let God intervene with His peace!

In those moments when the fragility of your heart and the fears, failures, and frustration overwhelm you, that's when you encourage yourself in the Lord, find your strength in the Lord, and exercise Rebound Faith to declare,

> *"The joy of the Lord is my strength! His grace is sufficient for me. Lord, you are My Strength, My Strong Tower, My Hiding Place, My Safe Refuge, My Protector, My Provider, My Deliverer, My Way-Maker. My Everything! You are the Consuming Fire in the fiery furnace! The Lion of Judah in the lion's den! The Mighty Warrior! The Great I AM, and I am yours! Completely yours! I'm the apple of Your eyes! Thank You, Lord!"*

God responds,

> *"I will personally go with you. My presence will go with you, and I will give you rest. It is I who go before you; I will be with you. I will not fail you or abandon you. Do not fear or be dismayed."*
>
> *(Exodus 33:1, Deuteronomy 31:28)*

211

Wherever you are going (future), wherever you are (present), and wherever you have been (past), God has already been there. He has already paved the way for you!

> *The Lord is near to all who call on Him to all who call on Him in truth (without guile). He will fulfill the desire of those who fear and worship Him [with awe-inspired reverence and obedience]; He also will hear their cry and will save them.*
>
> *~ Psalm 145: 18-19 Amplified Bible (AMP)*

Stand on God's promises as you kneel in His presence!

> *"Do not fear, for I have redeemed you [from captivity]; I have called you by name; you are Mine! When you pass through the waters, I will be with you; And through the rivers, they will not overwhelm you. When you walk through fire, you will not be scorched, nor will the flame burn you."*
>
> *~ Isaiah 43:1-3 Amplified Bible (AMP)*

> *God is our refuge and strength [mighty and impenetrable], a very present and well-proved help in trouble. Therefore, we will not fear, though the earth should change and though the mountains are shaken and slip into the heart of the seas, though its waters roar and foam, though the mountains tremble at its roaring.*
>
> *~ Psalm 46:1-3 Amplified Bible (AMP)*

Stop being worried, anxious, and fearful! Find your Peace in God. Claim all the grand plans and glamorous promises He has for you.

Don't fret or worry. Instead of worrying, pray. Let petitions and praises shape your worries into prayers, letting God know your concerns. Before you know it, a sense of God's wholeness, everything coming together for good, will come and settle you down. It's wonderful what happens when Christ displaces worry at the center of your life.

~ Philippians 4:6-7 The Message (MSG)

You are empowered and equipped with power, might, faith, love, dominion, and self-control.

For God did not give us a spirit of timidity, cowardice or fear; but [He has given us a spirit] of power and of love and of sound judgment and personal discipline [abilities that result in a calm, well-balanced mind and self-control].

~ 2 Timothy 1:7 Amplified Bible (AMP)

Own your moment! Be thankful! Share your story and continue to trust God. Seek His help, care, and support. Glorify God as you testify in advance of your victory.

I sought the Lord [on the authority of His word], and He answered me and delivered me from all my fears.

~ Psalm 34:4 Amplified Bible (AMP)

"Behold, God, my salvation! I will trust and not be afraid, For the Lord God is my strength and song; Yes,

He has become my salvation. Therefore, with joy, you will draw water from the springs of salvation."

~ Isaiah 12:2-3 Amplified Bible (AMP)

Let's disrupt the stigma!

We confess the entire scriptures of Psalm 107; praising the God who delivers us from devastation and depression.

O give thanks to the Lord, for He is good; For His compassion and loving-kindness endures forever! Let the redeemed of the Lord say so, whom He has redeemed from the hand of the adversary, and gathered them from the lands, from the east and from the west, from the north and from the south. They wandered in the wilderness in a [solitary] desert region and did not find a way to an inhabited city. Hungry and thirsty, they fainted. Then, they cried out to the Lord in their trouble, and He rescued them from their distresses. He led them by the straightway, to an inhabited city [where they could establish their homes]. Let them give thanks to the Lord for His loving kindness or His wonderful acts to the children of men!

For He satisfies the parched throat and fills the hungry appetite with what is good, some dwelt in darkness and in the deep (deathly) darkness, Prisoners [bound] in misery and chains, because they had rebelled against the precepts of God and spurned the counsel of the Most High. Therefore, He humbled their heart with hard labour; they stumbled, and there was no one to help. Then they cried out to the Lord in their trouble, and He saved them from their distresses. He brought them out of the darkness; the deep (deathly) darkness and broke their bonds apart. Let them give thanks to the Lord for His loving-kindness, and for His wonderful acts to the children of men for He has shattered the gates of bronze and cut the bars of iron apart.

Fools, because of their rebellious way and because of their sins, were afflicted. They detested all kinds of food, and they drew near to the gates of death. Then they cried out to the Lord in their trouble, and He saved them from their distresses.

He sent His word and healed them and rescued them from their destruction. Let them give thanks to the Lord for His loving-kindness, and for His wonderful acts to the children of men! And let them offer the sacrifices of thanksgiving and speak of His deeds with shouts of joy! Those who go down to the sea in ships, who do business on great waters; they have seen the works of the Lord, and His wonders in the deep; for He spoke and raised up a stormy wind, which lifted up the waves of the sea. They went up toward the heavens [on the crest of the wave], they went down again to the depths [of the watery trough]; their courage melted away in their misery. They staggered and trembled like a drunken man and were at their wits' end [all their wisdom was useless]. Then they cried out to the Lord in their trouble, and He brought them out of their distresses. He hushed the storm to a gentle whisper so that the waves of the sea were still. Then they were glad because of the calm, and He guided them to their desired haven (harbour). Let them give thanks to the Lord for His loving-kindness, and for His wonderful acts to the children of men! Let them exalt Him also in the congregation of the people and praise Him at the seat of the elders.

He turns rivers into a wilderness, and springs of water into a thirsty ground; A productive land into a [barren] salt waste, Because of the wickedness of those who dwell in it. He turns a wilderness into a pool of water and a dry land into springs of water; and there He has the hungry dwell, so that they may establish an inhabited city, and sow fields and plant vineyards, and produce an abundant harvest. Also, He blesses them so that they multiply greatly, and He does not let [the number of] their cattle decrease. When they are diminished and bowed down (humbled) through oppression, misery, and sorrow, He pours contempt on princes and makes them wander in a pathless wasteland. Yet He sets the needy securely on high, away from affliction, and makes their families like a flock. The upright sees it and rejoice, but all unrighteousness shuts its mouth. Who is wise? Let him observe and heed these things; [thoughtfully] consider the loving-kindness of the Lord. **(Psalm 107 AMP)**

Today, I pray for your peace of mind and release a blessing of peace (Shalom) over you.

> *May you prosper, you who love the Lord; may peace be within your walls and prosperity within your palaces; for the sake of my brothers and my friends, I will now say, "May peace be within you."*

> *The Lord blesses you, and keeps you, protect you, sustain you, and guard you. The Lord makes His face shines upon you with favour and is gracious to you surrounding you with loving-kindness. The Lord lifts up His countenance (face) upon you with divine approval, and gives you peace, a tranquil heart, and life.*
>
> *~ Numbers 6:23-27 Amplified Bible (AMP)*

Renewed Mind for Mental Wellness (Shalom)

So, how do you consistently live out God's promise of unexplainable **peace** in this roller coast journey called Life? You put on your new nature, with a renewed mind, as you learn to know your Creator and become like Him. (Colossians 3:10) For when you are unable to change circumstances, you are challenged to transform yourself by the renewing of your mind! I boldly testify that my greatest transformation came when I had a renewed mindset to perceive my situation differently, through the truth of God's Word. I will share with you the winning strategies for continual restoration.

> *...that, regarding your previous way of life, you put off your old self [completely discard your former nature], which is being corrupted through deceitful desires, and be continually renewed in the spirit of your mind [having a fresh, untarnished mental and spiritual attitude], and put on the new self [the regenerated and renewed nature], created in God's image, [godlike] in the righteousness and holiness of the truth [living in a way that expresses to God your gratitude for your salvation].*
>
> *Ephesians 4:23-25 Amplified Bible (AMP)*

Allow the truth of God's Word to transform your life by the renewing of your mind. Introduce your thoughts, actions and behaviour to God's divine peace and His power; knowing that you are already a winner and a world changer!

Your brain believes anything you tell it; speak life! The acceptance of defeat is a state of mind. So, declare that despite it all, you are a victorious Champion, an Overcomer and more than a Conqueror through Christ! Redefine the way, you think, decide and act!

For that significant setback was only a setup for a colossal comeback!

Apply the Word of God for consecration, detoxification, purification and regeneration of your mind. Purge your thoughts of the lies of the enemy, others and even yourself.

And do not be conformed to this world [any longer with its superficial values and customs], but be transformed and progressively changed [as you mature spiritually] by the renewing of your mind [focusing on godly values and ethical attitudes], so that you may prove [for yourselves] what the will of God is, that which is good and acceptable and perfect [in His plan and purpose for you].
~ Romans 12:2 Amplified Bible (AMP)

You are in rigorous training to renew your mind and transform your life by changing your thoughts, attitude, and your emotions. Being driven, disciplined, determined and diligent; undaunted by the distractions, and passionate to rebound and chayah!

It starts with you! It's time to level up with a renewed mindset for emotional and mental wellness. Know that the light inside you consumes and extinguishes the fire that surrounds you. You must not conform to this world but be transformed by the power of the Holy Spirit from the inside out. You are turning the trajectory of your life by the renewing of your mind! You are building grit; your Rebound Faith, the strength of character, moral fiber, fortitude, virtue, courage, backbone, resilience, confidence, and endurance. You approach your battles with a new perspective and hope in Christ. You are pursuing your purpose as the fulfillment of God's divine plan. Be at peace! Indeed, God is faithful; He is working all things together for your good and His glory. Despite all that is happening, continue to pursue God's will for your life with Positivity, Perseverance, Praise, Prophecy, and Prayers.

Positivity - Having a positive attitude, emotion and excellent thoughts. Even in seemingly adverse situations remain positive! The battle is not yours, and you can't handle it by yourself, so hand it over to the Lord and rejoice in the celebration of your victory! Speak life and think positive thoughts! *Whatever is true, whatever is honourable and worthy of respect, whatever is right and confirmed by God's word, whatever is pure and wholesome, whatever is lovely and brings peace, whatever is admirable and of good repute; if there is any excellence, if there is anything worthy of praise, think continually on these things, center your mind on them, and implant them in your heart.* (Phil 4:8)

Perseverance is the commitment, patience, determination, resoluteness, and steadfastness in doing something despite difficulty or delay or seemingly denial in achieving success. Showing persistence, tolerance, and endurance, despite the pain of the process; actively waiting for the turnaround! You must not become weary in doing well, for at the proper time you will reap a harvest if you do not give up. (Galatians 6:9)

God will give you a new life as the victor's crown and you shall chayah! Revelation 2:10 says,

> *"Fear nothing that you are about to suffer. Be aware that the devil is about to throw some of you into prison, that you may be tested in your faith, and for ten days you will have tribulation. Be faithful to the point of death, if you must die for your faith, and I will give you the crown consisting of life."*

God desires you to persevere despite everything that is happening; having the grit to overcome every trial, tribulation, temptation, obstacles, troubles and difficulties, to encounter God's presence, experience God's power and testify of your victory in Christ.

> *"Because you have obeyed my command to persevere, I will protect you from the great time of testing that will come upon the whole world to test those who belong to this world."*
>
> *~ Revelation 3:10 New Living Translation (NLT)*

Praise - Being grateful, joyful and thankful to God; bring adoration, admiration to His namesake. You praise the great name of the Lord, for His name alone is exalted; His majesty, splendour, and glory are above earth and heaven. (Psalm 148:13)

Rejoice and proclaim His exaltation with songs of joy, deliverance and thanksgiving. Your praises confuse the enemy! Praise preludes the victory! So instead of worry start worshipping! *"I have got to be dreaming, but I got a feeling everything's going to be all right! Thank you, Lord for your favour, mercies, grace, miracles… O Lord, My God, I bless you.*

My soul praises you, I celebrate you, Lord! I worship you. I glorify your name. You're worthy!"

Prophecy – Seek and speak to the future in alignment with the revelation of God's predestined promises in His Word. Demonstrate unshakeable faith regardless of the facts or fears; proclaim life, prophesy miracles, signs, and wonders; call forth the strength, success, healing, freedom, and Salvation in Christ Jesus.

> *Above all, you must realize that no prophecy in Scripture ever came from the prophet's own understanding, or from human initiative. No, those profits were moved by the Holy Spirit, and they spoke from God.*
>
> *2 Peter 1:20-21 New Living Translation (NLT)*

Prayers – Be persistent and pressing in your prayers for deliverance, breakthroughs and miracles. Be joyful in hope, patient in affliction, and faithful in prayer.

> *Continually rejoicing in hope because of our confidence in Christ, steadfast and patient in distress, devoted to prayer, continually seeking wisdom, guidance, and strength.*
>
> *~ Romans 12:12 Amplified Bible (AMP)*

Seek God for His care, Self-care and Mind-care!

Romans 1:28 says, *"And since they did not see fit to acknowledge God, God gave them up to a debased mind to do what ought not to be done."* O Lord, we do not want a corrupted mind, we acknowledge You and ask You, Lord, to renew our minds.

The battle is for your mind! Guard your heart! Fight for your soul! The defeat or victory first happens in your mind – you choose! It's your choice: Stop making excuses; Begin making progress! Conduct a mindset spring cleaning and identify everything that negatively impacts your emotion, attitude and behaviour; check your associations and thoughts. Eliminate sins as well as rid yourself of toxic relationships and negativity.

A calm mind is the best combat against every challenge!

Strengthen your mind to be more potent than your emotions; don't let your emotions control you or else you will lose yourself, your relationships, your future, and even your soul. So, don't allow situations to pull the strings of your emotions like a puppet. Always remember, nothing is permanent; everything has an expiration date. Stop stressing yourself out, for no matter how bad, or long it seems; it's only temporary and will eventually change.

You should nurture and nourish your mind with prayers, positivity, praises, perseverance and prophecy. Prophesy over your life, situations, thoughts, and dreams. Meditate on God's promises. Show forgiveness, gratitude and thankfulness; being kind to yourself and others. Practice mindfulness for mind-care and self-care to minimize stress.

The mind processes and programs everything you feed it. Cultivate your mind with truth. Nourish it with faith. Cherish it with love. Encourage it with hope and trust. Foster it with calmness, kindness and thankfulness. Feed the mind with purity and virtue. Develop it with praises. Flourish it with goodness, graciousness and gladness. Seek God to teach, train, and tailor your mind with the truth of His Word to be wise in your thinking, decisions and actions.

Since they thought it foolish to acknowledge God, he abandoned them to their foolish thinking and let them do things that should never be done.

Romans 1:28 New Living Translation (NLT)

Lord, I choose to think, speak, act, and live by the Holy Spirit with a renewed mindset. As I am living by the power of the Holy Spirit, I am continually putting to death the sinful deeds of the body, so that I will 'really' live forever and chayah. For when I allow the Spirit of God to lead me, I am accepting my identity as a child of God; claiming my inheritance and heritage.

So, don't you see that we don't owe this old do-it-yourself life one red cent? There's nothing in it for us, nothing at all. The best thing to do is give it a decent burial and get on with your new life. God's Spirit beckons. There are things to do and places to go! This resurrection life you received from God is not a timid, grave-tending life. It's adventurously expectant, greeting God with a childlike "What's next, Papa?"

God's Spirit touches our spirits and confirms who we really are. We know who he is, and we know who we are: Father and children. And we know we are going to get what's coming to us - an unbelievable inheritance! We go through exactly what Christ goes through. If we go through the hard times with him, then we're certainly going to go through the good times with him!

That's why I don't think there's any comparison between the present hard times and the coming good times. The created world itself can hardly wait for what's coming next. Everything in creation is being more or less held back. God reins it in until both creation and all the creatures are ready and can be released at the same moment into the glorious times ahead. Meanwhile, the joyful anticipation deepens. All around us we observe a pregnant creation. The difficult times of pain throughout the world are simply birth pangs. But it's not only around us; it's within us. The Spirit of God is arousing us within. We're also feeling the birth pangs. These sterile and barren bodies of ours are yearning for full deliverance. That is why waiting does not diminish us; any more than waiting diminishes a pregnant mother. We are enlarged in the waiting. We, of course, don't see what is enlarging us. But the longer we wait, the larger we become, and the more joyful our expectancy. Meanwhile, the moment we get tired in the waiting, God's Spirit is right alongside helping us along; if we don't know how or what to pray, it doesn't matter. He does our praying in and for us, making prayer out of our wordless sighs, our aching groans. He knows us far better than we know ourselves, knows our pregnant condition, and keeps us present before God. That's why we can be so sure that every detail in our lives of love for God is worked into something good.

Romans 8:12-28 The Message (MSG)

Speak Life – Positivity produces Prosperity!

"You will also decide and decree a thing, and it will be established for you, and the light of God's favour will shine upon your ways."

~ Job 22:28 Amplified Bible (AMP)

Each day is inspired to decree positivity over your life! You must speak hopefulness and thankfulness, prophetically into your life; changing your attitude, demonstrating gratitude, seeking to forgive, gaining a new perspective, and putting your faith in Christ. These primary rules will equip you with a Renewed Mindset for your rebound; despite any setback!

To overcome the situational depression caused by the trauma of my brutal divorce and horrendous family court battle, I started a daily routine by speaking life around **3 Cs**: *Commanding, Committing and Conversing.*

1. **Commanding** my day with 5 AM prayer: Day speaks; so, decree joy, prosperity, peace, and protection to my day. (Psalm 19:2-3)

> *Day unto day utters speech and night unto night sheet knowledge. There is no speech nor language, where their voice is not heard.*
>
> *~ Psalm 19:2-3 King James Version (KJV)*

2. **Committing** my life, my children, my household, my family, our relationships, our finances, dreams, projects, academics, careers, callings, days, and future to the Lord. I surrender to Jesus to be Lordship, over every thought, action, mind, body and soul. I am very confident in God, in whom, I have believed and persuaded that He can keep that which I have committed unto Him against that day. (2 Timothy 1:12)

> *This is why I suffer as I do. Still, I am not ashamed; for I know Him [and I am personally acquainted with Him] whom I have believed [with absolute trust and confidence in Him and in the truth of His deity], and I am persuaded [beyond any doubt] that He is able to*

guard that which I have entrusted to Him until that
day [when I stand before Him].

~ 2 Timothy 1:12 Amplified Bible (AMP)

3. **Conversing** with myself (self-talk) by repeating positive affirmations over my life; repeating them until I accept them. I call into being that which does not exist! Let the weak say that I am strong! (Joel 3:10)

Whatever you tell yourself, you will believe, so speak positivity with uplifting, empowering, motivating, and inspiring thoughts and talks!

As it is written, I have made you the father of many
nations. [He was appointed our father] in the sight of
God in Whom he believed, Who gives life to the dead
and speaks of the nonexistent things that [He has
foretold and promised] as if they [already] existed.

~ Joel 3:10 King James Version (KJV)

In the name of Jesus, I am condemning every negative tongue that revolt against me. I demolish every argument of limitation, self-destruction, and negative utterance over my life. Jesus takes Lordship over my mind. I allow only empowering, motivational, and inspirational thoughts reflecting the truth of God's Word, His covenants promise, plans and thoughts over my life. Jesus replaces every curse with His blessings.

In the name of Jesus, I *'speak life'* for the power of life and death are within the tongue. I express things that are not as though they already are. I talk to every mountains, situations, and sickness; I commend them to move, fail and dry up at the roots.

By Rebound Faith, you must believe, receive and activate with confidence and courage that the desired changes have already happened. God is already there! You shall have positive thoughts, attitude, and emotions despite the circumstances and therefore you reverse negativity, speak life to fulfill and attract the positive experiences and opportunities in your day and future.

You will succeed in whatever you choose to do, and God's light will shine on the road ahead on you. (Job 22:28 NLT)

I know that there is an excellent calling over my life as well as your life. They say thieves don't break into empty houses. The devil knows the greatness and treasures embedded in us. He fears us and our future; he attacks us to get us out. We are worn-out, wearied-out and worried-out so that we give up. Most times, with the anointing upon our lives, the devil can't even kill us, he resorts to strategies, such as depression, divorce, drama, debts, diseases, and other devastations, and then he tempts us to take out ourselves. The devil comes to kill steal and destroy, but Jesus came to give life, life in its abundance!

So, we got to rise each day, rebuke the devil, and he will flee, say,

Devil, you are a liar, the father of lies – I am a Child of Light... You can't take me out before my time, as my God, He has the key to life and death. My time and seasons are in His hands. You are a thief, and I demand a seven-fold payback for everything you have stolen from me - my peace, joy, strength, happiness, health, character, children, family, friends, career, creativity, conduct, relationships, determination, self-control, self-esteem, and my power. In the name of Jesus, I receive full restitution, the restoration of everything lost or stolen to me, the proper and rightful owner, and complete recompense, repayment, and reimbursement for my all loss, injury, damages and suffering. I shall recover it all, big and small, in Jesus name, Amen!

1 Samuel 30:8 (NLT) says, *"Then David asked the LORD, 'Should I chase after this band of raiders? Will I catch them?' And the LORD told him, 'Yes, go after them. You will surely recover everything that was taken from you!'"*

Do not be afraid! You must believe, decide, and act! Your decision will be carried out and established for you. You must have the confident assurance that whatever you need, God is more than able to provide it and resolve it. The devil will do everything in his limited powers to make you question and doubt the presence and existence of the limitless God, but God wants you to put your faith in Him to believe for your rebound. Everything the Devil has stolen, he must pay you back sevenfold. It is crucial that we continue to praise God despite our feelings; praise Him for who is and what He has already done for us.

> *People do not despise a thief if he steals to satisfy himself when he is hungry; But when he is found, he must repay seven times [what he stole]; He must give all the property of his house [if necessary to meet his fine].*
>
> *~ Proverbs 6:30-31 Amplified Bible (AMP)*

Each day until this, I write and post an inspirational devotion to turn my worry into worship, to encourage myself, and empower others; then I get up, get dressed and take a few selfies (Diva for Jesus). The writing was very therapeutic for me; it allowed me to express what I couldn't say and gave me hope and assurance of an expected end. It also provided engagement, empowerment, and elevation to me and others. It continues to be a useful tool for me to let go as I tell God everything; my feelings, fears, and failure; I express my gratitude and seek His wisdom... I love the verses that mention, *'...thus says the Lord.'*

Many times, I posted photographs, and I glorify God, of My Story behind my smile; reflecting that my ashes are turning to beauty. A routine practice of my self-care, self-love, and self-assurance to rebuild my self-esteem reposition my crown that shifted during the fall. *"For my God, He is more excellent than every struggle, insecurities, and fears. For the Lord is my Strength in my Highs and Lows!"*

You are your greatest fan and cheerleader! So even if no one told me that day, my first conversation was to speak positive affirmations about myself and capturing every thought, belief, and emotion with positivity. Look at yourself and say:

> *"O my love, you are altogether beautiful and fair. There is no flaw or blemish in you!"*
> ~ *Song of Solomon 4:7 Amplified Bible (AMP)*

You are gorgeous; fearfully and wonderfully made! You are calm! You are confident! You are courageous! You are more than enough, complete and whole! You are loved! You are powerful! You are not alone; neither forsaken nor abandoned. You are unstoppable! You are accepted! You are needed! You are talented, smart, and gifted! You are fearless, fierce, and full of Fire! You are a masterpiece. You are creative. You are unique and special. You are an anointed Child of God, the King of All Kings. You are going to get through this. It is only a temporary affliction and won't last very long. The pain you are feeling cannot compare to the glorious triumph that is imminent. You are grateful, generous and great! You are forgiven, favoured, and fruitful. You are strong! Choose to forgive everyone that has hurt you and caused you pain. Let go but never give up!

You serve a God of Second Chances and when you think your chances have run out, in step His grace and mercy; absolutely nothing can separate you from His love. I am glad that you are alive. God has forgiven you; now you will show grace and choose to accept the apologies that you never got. I am proud of you. I am committing you to excellence and abundance. You are alive, arisen and awaken to see this new day! Today is full of possibilities. A day that the Lord has made, this is the day the Lord has saved you, and you will rejoice and be glad in it. You are in control of your attitude, thoughts and your actions! Make today so awesome; yesterday is envious!

No matter what, these big dreams or strong enemies can't match your BIGGER and MIGHTIER GOD... While waiting, God is working! No matter what comes your way today, remain focused, undisturbed, and unaffected. Declare, today is the day of peaceful, confident, and praiseworthy thoughts and deeds. Peace of mind is new wealth. You shall become 'rotten rich' in your mental wellness! God has called you by your name, and He will make you are a beautiful display of the splendour of His glory! You are His! *You're loved!*

Practice your positive self-talks by repeating daily affirmations; the power of life and death are in your tongue! So, choose to speak life!

"Today and every day of this year, it shall be my best day ever. I am unashamed to share that God is first in my life and I love Jesus Christ! I believe that I am His Beloved and every covenant promises in the Bible belongs to me. I am beautiful! I am brilliant! I am brave! I am as bold as a lion. I am beyond ordinary; I'm fabulous and highly favoured! I shall achieve

better than expected; exceedingly, abundantly, and immeasurably more outcomes. I shall blaze new trails with creative and innovative ideas and solutions. Every barren area in my life, family, business, and ministry shall bloom and bear this season. I have big visions. I shall have billion of dollars as my net worth. I shall author best-selling books. I shall experience breakthrough upon breakthroughs. I shall receive bonuses and benefits for my labor and giving. I am blessed to be a blessing to others, a financial pillar to nations, to set captives free and share the gospel globally. I believe and receive the everlasting and unconditional love from my Heavenly Father to His Beloved child."

Signed: [Insert your name]

Manifest your Vision: Dream. Declare. Decide. Do

Where there is no vision, the people perish: but he that kept the law, happy is he.

~ Proverbs 29:18 King James Version (KJV)

As discussed earlier, creating a vision is critical during the Transformative Change Process. Do you have a personal vision statement? If not, you should create one; God's Word says without a vision people perish.

You bring your 'unseen' God-ordained Vision to be visible in the 'seen' world by activating it with your voice, re-focusing your thoughts, renewing your mind, and declaring positivity and creativity. These positive experiences are then inspired and manifested in your life – health, wealth, wellness, affluence, influence, and excellence in your relationships.

My Self-Talk – "Nicola, you are a beautiful and loving parent of victorious and miraculous children. You are a Proverbs 31 woman and wife; being prepared for an Ephesians 5:25-33 husband! Greatness and creativity are in your DNA; passed on also to your children and future generations. Your offspring will be mighty in the land enjoying the generational blessing. You are building and leaving a legacy that outlives and outlasts you. You are not ordinary, and you are extraordinary, a Legendary, a Pioneer, a Visionary, an Innovator! The Spirit of Excellence is upon you. You are an inspiring keynote speaker in high demand for your empowerment speech. You are a bestselling author. You are a global highly sought-after Transformation Consultant. You are a highly recognized and rewarded International Business Strategist. You are a wealthy philanthropist. You are a channel of God's blessings to others; A financial pillar to nations. You will build many Empowerment centers worldwide to engage, encourage, equip, educate, empower, energize, enable, elevate and evolve others; transforming lives and communities; for His Grace and all for His Glory!"

Own your story, turn the page, start a new chapter, and manifest your new Vision to come alive!

Rehearse, Recite and Repeat your vision! Dream, Declare, Decide and Do it! Verbalize it, Visualize it and Venture into it!

I am not saying that there aren't times when an event in life hit me so hard that I scream, bawl (mourn bitterly), stress-eat, and unable to sleep. But these responses are short-lived. I will have a sad moment, but no longer will I have a bad day. Most times, I fast and focus on God because if I ever start eating, whenever I do, I am unstoppable! Whenever I can't understand, I pray and praise! God sees my tears, listens to my mourning and groaning and even hears my silence.

At times, I can be so broken, during those times, my prayers are short, sincere, and simple, *"O Lord, please help me!"* God always responds to my cry to strengthen me, lift my head, and send a word or a helper to encourage me, shift the atmosphere and give me peace.

At times, I hear the voices and chatter in my head, repeating my mistakes, what people said, negative thoughts flooding my mind; I start worshipping, praising, and thanking God. I post an inspirational message to encourage and refresh myself and others. I try to find something praiseworthy and admirable to think, imagine, and dream big.

I fondly recall one evening, amidst my storm and brokenness, while having dinner with the family, I said, 'I have a passion for building empowerment centers to equip, educate, and elevate people globally.' One of my sons, being a realist, looked at me with such loving care, yet seriousness, *'Mom, but you are so far away from that dream!'*

I could be unemployed with neither contracts nor clients, and I am declaring and decreeing that I am a highly sought after with multiple sources of income (smile); after all, dreaming is a form of planning, and your decisions will be carried out. I have a *Vision* statement, which establishes my core value, to guide my venture, equip my *Vow*; so, I consistently speak it into life.

When life surprises you, say this is only a bend in the road of life, I may not know what is around the corner, but I know who holds my tomorrow, and I am safe, secured, and sustained in His hands.

"For the rest, brethren, whatever is true, whatever is worthy of reverence and is honourable and seemly, whatever is just, whatever is pure, whatever is lovely and lovable, whatever is kind and winsome and gracious, if there are any virtue and excellence, if there is anything worthy of praise, think on and weigh and take account of these things fix your minds on them." (Philippians 4:8 (AMPC)

Eradicate Negative Attitudes; Enable Optimism!

Renew your mind by changing your attitude! Our attitude makes a big difference. Let your positive attitude be the thermostat that automatically regulates your temperature and response to events. Activate a positive attitude when there is a change in the 'heat' of life situations. Take an optimistic stance in your position, approach, belief, philosophy and the way you think, feel, perceive, speak and act about something or someone. Your attitude drives your mindset, demonstrates your behaviour and determines your altitude. However, attitude is a choice; it is in our power and control to change our perspectives and actions, and regulate our peace of mind. A negative attitude leads to a negative mindset, behaviour and result; likewise, positive attitude takes precedence over the facts, feelings, and focus; leading to a positive outlook, opinions, and outcomes.

Our attitude must reflect in our belief that all the Promises of God are YES and AMEN! When God says YES, it doesn't matter what the report of others is saying. One yes from God is all you need, and believe that it is complete – signed, sealed, and delivered. Whose report do you take? I receive only the revelation of God; I reject all other statements. The truth of God overrides, overrules, and over-shadows every fact.

For as many as are the promises of God, in Christ they are [all answered] "Yes," So, through Him we say our "Amen" to the glory of God.

~ 2 Corinthians 1:20 Amplified Bible (AMP)

Our attitude must reflect in your declaration that you can do all things through Christ who strengthens you. Declare, *"I can do all things, which He has called me to do through Him who strengthens and empowers me to fulfill His purpose—I am self-sufficient in Christ's sufficiency; I am ready for anything and equal to anything through Him who infuses me with inner strength and confident peace."* (Philippians 4:13 AMP)

Our attitude must reflect the view of God's Word. His thoughts, plans, and purpose towards us. Not man or circumstances; His plans for peace and well-being; not for disaster to give you a future and a hope. (Jeremiah 29:11)

How precious also are your thoughts to me, O God! How vast is the sum of them! If I could count them, they would outnumber the sand. When I awake, I am still with You.

~ Psalm 139:17-18 Amplified Bible (AMP)

Our attitude must reflect the fearlessness and faithfulness of Christ. The Almighty, All-Powerful, and the All-loving God, He is always with us to protect, provide, and redeem us. In all things, we are more than conquerors, and overwhelming victory is already ours. We are victorious! We shall possess our possession. The Great I AM dwells in you!

"Don't be afraid," the prophet answered. "Those who are with us are more than those who are with them."

When the servant of the man of God got up early the next morning and went outside, there were troops, horses, and chariots everywhere. "Oh, sir, what will we do now?" the young man cried to Elisha.

"Don't be afraid!" Elisha told him, "For there are more on our side than on theirs!" Then Elisha prayed, "O Lord, open his eyes and let him see!" The Lord opened the young man's eyes, and when he looked up, he saw that the hillside around Elisha was filled with horses and chariots of fire.

~ 2 Kings 6:15-17 New Living Translation (NLT)

Then Caleb quieted the people before Moses, and said, "Let us go up at once and take possession of it; for we will certainly conquer it."

~ Numbers 13:30 Amplified Bible (AMP)

Yet in all these things we are more than conquerors and gain an overwhelming victory through Him who loved us so much that He died for us.

~ Romans 8:37 Amplified Bible (AMP)

Our attitude must reflect our obedience to God's Word – His commandment, counsel, correction, and covenant promise. God blesses for our willingness and our reward includes, being at the head and never the tail, above only and never beneath. It is not over until you win! Do not serve or listen to any other gods other than the Lord, God Almighty, and The Sovereign God of the Universe.

So, whose voice is chattering in your head? Silence every other voice! *Cast down imaginations, and every high thing that exalted itself against the knowledge of God and bringing into captivity every thought to the obedience of Christ* (2 Corinthians 10:5).

> *The Lord will make you the head (leader) and not the tail (follower), and you will be above only, and you will not be beneath, if you listen and pay attention to the commandments of the Lord your God, which I am commanding you today, to observe them carefully. Do not turn aside from any of the words which I am commanding you today, to the right or to the left, to follow and serve other gods.*
>
> *~ Deuteronomy 28:13-14 Amplified Bible (AMP)*

Our attitude must reflect the greatness, divine nature, and goodness of God in our prayers, praising, and proclamation. We think, decide, act, and speak positive declarations over our lives and circumstances. All things are not only possible but are favourable with God; for the ones who trust and believe in Jesus.

> *Jesus said to him, "[You say to me,] 'If You can?' All things are possible for the one who believes and trusts [in me]!"*
>
> *~ Mark 9:23 Amplified Bible (AMP)*

Today, be empowered, equipped, and elevated by renewing your mind and making the choice of changing your attitude to reflect faith and expectation of God for a positive outcome as you trot along life's journey. God is creating everyday heroes and legends with our God stories as we overcome life events.

Your faith journey is your Story. It's for God's Glory. Never be ashamed of your story, own your moment! Look at the encouragement we receive from the Glory Stories of a few of the Faith Heroes in the Bible. Including Sarah, Abraham, Noah, Joseph, Moses, David, Daniel, Three Hebrew boys, Esther, Ruth, Gideon, Samson, Samuel, Rehab, Hannah, Mary - Mother of Jesus, The Woman at the Well, The Woman with the Issue of Blood, Jeremiah, Elijah, The Blind Man at the Pool of Bethesda, The Apostles, Mary Magdalene, Paul; the Most Prominent - **Jesus Christ, Our Risen King!**

God has quenched the flames of fire, and we have escaped death by the edge of the sword. Our weakness was turned to strength. We became strong in battle and put whole armies to flight.

~ Hebrews 11:34 New Living Translation (NLT)

Maintain Positive Thoughts

Negative emotions, thoughts, and bitterness ruin our relationships, rob us of peace and harm our bodies:

- Anger affects our liver
- Grief affects our lung
- Worry affects our stomach
- Stress affects our heart and brain
- Fear affects our kidney

"A merry heart does good, like medicine, but a broken spirit dries the bones."

~ Proverbs 17:22 New King James Version (NKJV)

"A cheerful heart is a good medicine, but a broken spirit saps a person's strength."

~ Proverbs 17:22 (NLT)

"A joyful heart makes a cheerful face, but when the heart is sad, the spirit is broken."

~ Proverbs 15:13

"The spirit of a man will sustain his infirmity, but a wounded spirit who can bear?"

~ Proverbs 18:14

"For I am afflicted and needy, and my heart is wounded within me."

~ Psalm 109:22

Jesus, The Undefeated Champion, Most Valuable Player, Chief Executive Officer, The King of the Universe; He has commanded us that in life's circumstances, we should be of good cheer, be courageous, be courteous to others, find comfort, confidence, and certainty in the truth that He has already conquered the world. The battle belongs to the LORD. Jesus has already fought each struggle and won the war. Therefore, we are Overcomers, Victorious Warriors, more than Conquerors; overwhelming victory is already ours through Christ, who loved us.

Our response strategy to eradicate any depression, worry, and anxiety during the waiting period is to practice - positivity, perseverance, praise, prophecy, and persistent in prayers.

Seek Forgiveness; Choose to Forgive!

Forgiveness can be hard work! However, choosing to forgive is imperative to your healing and restoration! There is incredible power in the act of forgiveness and repentance. We should want to forgive others because of the grace we receive from God, His love, mercy and forgiveness of our sins, mistakes and failure; guaranteeing us a new beginning, a clean slate and a fresh start. God does not punish us for all our sins; He does not deal harshly with us, as we deserve. For His unfailing love toward those who fear Him is as high as the height of the heavens above the earth. He has removed our sins as far from us as the east is from the west. (Psalm 103:10-12)

Forgiveness requires us turning away from our sins and seeking God's mercy; as well as us extending the grace and mercy of forgiveness to others. Let the wicked change their ways and banish the very thought of doing wrong. Let them turn to the Lord that He may have mercy on them. Yes, turn to our God, for he will forgive generously. Also, when you are praying, first forgive anyone you are holding a grudge against, so that Your Father in heaven will forgive your sins, too. (Isaiah 55:7, Mark 11:25)

Let's Pray

Heavenly Father, I confess of all my sins and repent of my misguided attitude and ungodly behaviour. I turn away from sinful actions and seek Jesus as my personal Lord and Saviour. I receive the sacrificial price He paid for my sins, past mistakes, and failures. Lord, I confess the scriptures of Psalm 51 (NLT) over my life – *"Have mercy on me, O God, because of your unfailing love. Because of your great compassion, blot out the stain of my sins. Wash me clean from my guilt. Purify me from my sin. For I recognize my rebellion; it haunts me day and night. Against you, and you alone, have I sinned; I have done what is evil in your sight... O Lord, purify me from my sins, and I will be clean; wash me, and I will be whiter than snow. Oh, give me back my joy again; you have broken me— now let me rejoice. Don't keep looking at my sins. Remove the stain of my guilt. Create in me a clean heart, O God. Renew a loyal spirit within me. Do not banish me from your presence, and don't take your Holy Spirit from me…"*

I want to become like you, to follow you, and be obedient to your commandments. Your Word in 1 John 1:9, says, *"If I confess my sins, You are faithful and just, to forgive me of my sins and to cleanse us from all unrighteousness."*

I believe, I receive and activate my forgiveness, freedom and faith in Jesus name.

Abba Father, this *violation* hurts like crazy, naturally, in my human capability, I am unable to forgive, but I no longer want to be a victim of bitterness and unforgiveness. I desire to forgive, move on, let go, and start over. Please, Holy Spirit, do this in me, through me and for me; as well as for my personal development, mental/emotional/spiritual healing, and relationships with others. If I fail today, please O Lord, strengthen me to try again, and again until I am free, in Jesus name.

Lord, Your Word says, *"If I forgive those who sin against me, my Heavenly Father will forgive me. However, if I refuse to forgive others, my Father will not forgive my sins."* (Matthew 6:14-15)

Also, Your Word in Luke 6:37 says, *"Judge not, and you shall not be judged. Condemn not, and you shall not be condemned. Forgive, and you will be forgiven."*

Lord, please forgive me for all my wrongs doings and judgemental views, and teach me to forgive others who have used, hurt, violated and offended neither me; even if no apology was given nor regret shown. *Lord, if you kept a record of our sins, who, O Lord could ever survive? However, you offer forgiveness that we might learn to fear you.* (Psalm 130:3-4)

O Lord, please teach me how you forgive and forget so lovingly, willingly and continually! Please help me love others as You have loved me. Though my sins are many, O Lord, You have forgotten them all and shown me, everlasting love. Now, I am brave, bold and determined to forgive others too, just as You have forgiven me, in Jesus name. Amen!

> *"I tell you, her sins—and they are many—have been forgiven, so she has shown me much love. But a person who is forgiven little shows only little love." Then Jesus said to the woman, "Your sins are forgiven."*
>
> *Luke 7:47-48 New Living Translation (NLT)*

"Come now, let's settle this," says the Lord. "Though your sins are like scarlet, I will make them as white as snow. Though they are red like crimson, I will make them as white as wool. I, even I, am He who blots out your transgressions for My own sake; and I will not remember your sins." (Isaiah 43:25, Isaiah 55:7)

Steps to Forgiveness

1. Do an inventory of all the people you associated with the *Violation.* What was the role they played and the pain they caused you?

2. Choose to forgive others. Choose to forgive everyone associated with the *Violation.* Declare I choose to forgive you, _____ for hurting me and causing me pain. I choose to let go of this bondage, set myself free and refuse to allow you to hold me captive any longer.

3. Recall and denounce all the negative thoughts and words spoken and actions due to the anger or fear during your *Venting*. I pray a crop failure over every negative word spoke, and I claim every divine promises, prophecy and great covenant of God over my life, my children, my household, my finances, my career, my ministry, our purposes, our future, and this day.

4. Seek God's forgiveness. I confess, repent of _____ and seek the mercy and grace of God's forgiveness through Jesus Christ.

5. Receive God's forgiveness. I receive my forgiveness, and I accept the gift of salvation. He whom the son set free, is free indeed! I am free!

6. Choose to forgive yourself. I now choose to forgive myself as liberated, and I am no longer a captive of my past or present situation or the fear of my unknown tomorrow. My time and seasons are in God's hands.

7. Today, *[insert date]*, mark my Day of Forgiveness. Now I turn my mind to focus on coming out of the *Valley*; moving on, letting go and starting over!

Efforts not excuses get the result, so, I choose to make progress and not make excuses!

I declare that I am ready for the climb to new dimensions on the Transformative Change process, and I victoriously take the next step to achieve my *Vision*. I make a *Vow* as my contract and commitment to Christ and myself to chayah, despite it all!

Where is another God like you, who pardons the guilt of the remnant, overlooking the sins of his special people? You will not stay angry with your people forever, because you delight in showing unfailing love.

Once again you will have compassion on us. You will trample our sins under your feet and throw them into the depths of the ocean!

Micah 7:18-19 New Living Translation (NLT)

Gain a Winning Mindset

Renewed Mindset allows you to reclaim your power, positivity, patience, and passion for propelling you to win and grow prosperously in your life, goals, and relationships. Motivate yourself to plan, implement, reflect, and dominate. Achieving your new vision and keeping the commitment to your Vow. Have an accurate and precise view of your future state, with a clearly defined mission and the unaltered desire to pursue it. Show grace, empathy, compassion, and kindness to yourself and others.

You must thrive on becoming the best version of you to make your best life and so that you can give of yourself willingly to others. Ignite the power of inner self to focus on continuous self-development: Positive self-image, self-care, self-talk, self-confidence, self-projection, self-improvement, self-awareness, self-reflection, self-discipline, self-esteem, self-love, self-discipline, and self-control.

It is not selfish, neither about what you are expecting of others because you are empty; instead, it's about what you can pour into others because you are full, complete, and whole.

You are a fountain to others, and never a drain!

Rebound Faith Declaration and Prayer

And my God will liberally supply (fill until full) your every need according to His riches in glory in Christ Jesus.

~ Philippians 4:19 Amplified Bible (AMP)

I know that my God causes all things to work together for good to those who love God, to those whom He calls according to His purpose... His thoughts are nothing like my thoughts, and His ways are far beyond anything I could imagine! For the Lord God, He is my sun and my shield. He gives me His grace, glory, favour, and honour. The Lord will withhold no good thing from those who do what is right... Moreover, I am sure of this, that He who began a good work in me will bring it to completion at the day of Jesus Christ.

I am richly blessed, redeemed, restored, and revived.

I am happy, joyful, grateful, peaceful, and wise.

I am healthy, wealthy, victorious, and prosperous.

I have a superabundant supply and heavily loaded with Heavenly Currency - Faith, Favour, Love, Honour, Grace, and Glory!

This same God, who takes care of me, will supply all your needs from His glorious riches, which He gives to us in Christ Jesus.

Heavenly Father, in Faith, we glorify you with our stories. Lord, please forgive us for focusing on the pain, the process, our pride, people, and pity rather than Your plan, promises, and purpose. Lord, You are preparing us and making our stories dazzling displays of the splendour of Your Glory, in Jesus name.

Lord, I look to you! Lord, I continue to seek You even when I don't understand, and everything makes no sense, and I am still required to stand! I look to you when after all I have done and still my breakthrough is yet to come, and my strength is gone. I listen to you; when all the music stops, in you O Lord, I hear my song of deliverance!

> *"The Lord your God in your midst, The Mighty One, will save; He will rejoice over you with gladness, He will quiet you with His love, He will rejoice over you with singing."*
>
> *(Zephaniah 3:17)*

Let's Pray:

> *For God so loved the world, that he gave his only begotten Son, that whosoever believeth in him should not perish, but have everlasting life.*
>
> *~ John 3:16 King James Version (KJV)*

Heavenly Father, Almighty God, King of the Universe, I bless Your name and thank you for everlasting life. I exalt you above all my fears, my troubles, my situations, my afflictions and exchange my heavy burdens for the light and easy yoke of Jesus. I stand on Your Word today for answered prayers, for supernatural deliverance, breakthroughs, miracles, and blessings. I declare that all things are working together for my good. I decree that I shall experience a divine intervention of God in my situation. I receive the anointing and grace for goodness, greatness, excellence, influence, magnificence, righteousness, promotion, prosperity, peace, joy, wisdom, worship, healing, and health. Today, I shall run and not be weary... Though youths grow weary and tired, and vigorous young men stumble badly, yet those who wait for the Lord will gain new strength; They will mount up with wings like eagles, they will run and not get tired, they will walk and not become weary. I declare and decree that everything I do today I shall prosper and renewed in strength. Today my life will thrive, my children will flourish, my household will prosper, my finances shall prosper, my career/business shall prosper, my calling/ministry shall establish, the work of our hands shall excel. We shall prosper as our souls prosper, in Jesus name.

Father; thank you for the promises in your Word to be with me through deep waters, to rejoice over me with gladness and singing, to be in my midst, to save me, to quiet me with your love, and to be my comfort in my affliction. Thank you for your only Son, Jesus, My Redeemer, My Saviour, My Healer, My Deliverer, My Strength, My Lord! Thank you for the gift of Salvation, the Cross, and the Empty Tomb. Please help me to work out my salvation with fear, trembling. I am a light for You in this dark world as you work in me. Today, I declare that I know that my Redeemer lives and I look to you in all I do. I confess that this is my comfort in my affliction, that Your word has revived me and given me life. (Psalm 119:50)

Glorify me, O Lord to bring glory to You, in Jesus name I pray, Amen.

> *Therefore, my beloved, as you have always obeyed, so now, not only as in my presence but much more in my absence, work out your own salvation with fear and trembling, for it is God who works in you, both to will and to work for his good pleasure. Do all things without grumbling or questioning, that you may be blameless and innocent, children of God without blemish amid a crooked and twisted generation, among whom you shine as lights in the world.*
>
> *Philippians 2:12-15*

4th Quarter

Live Zealously... Chayah!

Living Enthusiastically, Keenly and Passionately!

"She is clothed with strength and dignity, and she laughs without fear of the future. When she speaks, her words are wise, and she gives instructions with kindness. She carefully watches everything in her household and suffers nothing from laziness. Her children stand and bless her. Her husband praises her: 'There are many virtuous and capable women in the world, but you surpass them all!' Charm is deceptive, and beauty does not last, but a woman who fears the LORD will be greatly praised. Reward her for all she has done. Let her deeds publicly declare her praise."

~ Proverbs 31:25-31 New Living Translation (NLT)

It seems like only a few years ago, with two children, life brought me through a mighty storm. The winds and waves were raving; never in my wildest dream had I ever thought this would be my portion. After being married for ten years, I reached the point where separation was the best option due to the irreconcilable difference in my marriage; resulting in a four-year separation and family court battle for the divorce, final settlement, and custody of the children. During this season, I found myself in an ocean of hopelessness, discouragement, and depression.

After the divorce, I had to learn how to move forward, let go, and start over. Despite the self-doubt, insecurity, and uncertainty about making the right choice in relationships; I had to learn to trust and find love again. Accelerate the achievement of my goals personally and professionally, after such a significant setback.

Because of the extravagance of those revelations, and so I wouldn't get a big head, I was given the gift of a handicap to keep me in constant touch with my limitations. Satan's angel did his best to get me down; what he in fact did was push me to my knees. No danger then of walking around high and mighty! At first, I didn't think of it as a gift, and begged God to remove it. Three times I did that, and then he told me,

"My grace is enough; it's all you need. My strength comes into its own in your weakness." Once I heard that, I was glad to let it happen. I quit focusing on the handicap and began appreciating the gift. It was a case of Christ's strength moving in on my weakness. Now I take limitations in stride, and with good cheer, these limitations that cut me down to size—abuse, accidents, opposition, bad breaks. I just let Christ take over! And so, the weaker I get, the stronger I become.

2 Corinthians 12:8-10 The Message (MSG)

My story is a journey of faith to rebound from life challenges and overcome my defeat ad depression. Like, other adverse life events, going through a divorce can be traumatic; negatively impacting your peace, identity, financial stability, self-esteem, and especially your health – mentally, emotionally, and physically. I had to figure out how to reset, renew, re-establish; rebound and 'really' live not just for myself, but also for my children.

Today, I boldly tell my story both as a therapy and a testimony; as continuous self-improvement as well as paying forward to help others, who are hurting through adverse life changes. Owning, writing and telling my story is a form of expressive therapy for healing and personal growth. Sharing my story also helps and may have a positive impact on others. Telling my story also gave courage and confidence; making me bold and brave as I found my voice. Also, it challenged me to be able to articulate my story in a way that benefits and applies to you as a self-help tool. I had to analyze my situation and revisit the painful experiences and rejoice at the manifestation of the prayers and hope; giving Glory to God. I am therefore confident to express the strategies and solutions that worked for me as they should also work for you. Storytelling also helped me to pause and prioritize; look back and assess my setback; look forward and affirm my comeback! Sharing my story assisted me to overcome defeat and depression, with a new vision of Rebound Faith, and a vow to chayah to a definite place of peace, joy, hope, and victory. God word says that we overcome by the blood of the Lamb, and by the word of our testimony.

They say the only thing constant in life and experience is Change.

We are living a game-changing life. The challenges and life events are ever present. At times, we feel like just when we are about to get a shot at the net, we missed the chance, the opportunity pass, and defeat creeps in. However, how do we remain strong, stay or get back in the game; notwithstanding the opposition and attack? How do continue being resilient after the block, defeat, and setback? How do we get in the right position at the right time, blocking-out the enemies that are tormenting our mind, body, and soul? How do we gain the rebound and triumph victoriously? With every battle, you have faced in life, what is your rebound effectiveness?

Marring this road of life are many triumphs, trials, tests, troubles, temptations, tribulations, and transitions. It is said that we are either: going through one, overcoming one or heading for one.

"This river I step in is not the river I stand in."

- Heraclitus

The current of a river keeps the water always moving; the water is never the same. Therefore, the river (situation) you stepped in is never the same that you are standing it. It wasn't supposed to be this way – You were the most qualified one for the promotion and worked your butt off, yet you were overlooked and denied. You were not supposed to have these illnesses and diseases. The marriage was supposed to work out and not end in divorce, destroying the family and household. Not to mention the lies, the betrayal, the shame, and the people who wronged us. The love affair was not supposed to be abusive mentally and emotionally; it didn't start as a toxic relationship. The broken heart and brokenness were not supposed to happen. The pregnancy was not supposed to fail. Your loved ones were not supposed to die young, too soon, and so innocently without a cause. There was supposed to be enough money to cover the bills, to put food on the table, to take care of the children, and family expenses. The financial crisis and struggles were never part of the equation. The contracts were not supposed to end abruptly, but they walked you to the door. The business was supposed to be successful and not stop in bankruptcy. The closing of those deals was supposed to be a no-brainer and the clients on-boarded. Your children were not supposed to end up going through these troubles, the wrong association with the false friends, being at the wrong place at the wrong time; the captivity of drug, alcohol, addiction, not to mention the prison sentence. The depression and suicidal thoughts were never part of the equation. The demonic drama, destruction, and adverse life events happened. The enemy strategy is to kill, steal and destroy.

However, God! He has given you the victory; it shall be well! Jesus came to provide us with life, a more abundant and overflowing life! Rebound Faith is the Grit; the comeback power for you to endure, overcome, conquer, and chayah.

'U Power Up! Life Happens; Stay Strong!

Here is a replay of the very first time I was confident and courageous enough to publicly share my story zealously as a Speaker at a Women's Conference...

Her Story: The Zest for Life!

Jesus said to her, "Did I not say to you that if you believe [in Me], you will see the glory of God [the expression of His excellence]?"

~ John 11:40 Amplified Bible (AMP

His Story empowers Her Story!

On November 25, 2016, Black Friday, I was invited as a Keynote Speaker to give an inspirational speech at the Women Speak Out – Naked Not Ashamed - Christian Women Leaders, in Brampton, Ontario, Canada. It was all planned out on short notice, but I knew God has been preparing me for this, and I knew I had to act in obedience. I have so many testimonies to share about my survival and rebound through the many storms of life. This speaking engagement and event marked the very first time that I was courageous enough to share my Rebound Faith story publicly with a group of women, many of whom I have never met in my life; sharing my story had such a profound effect on these phenomenal women and empowered them. It propelled my desire and determination to never give up. I kept my faith to rebound from life events; it has not only transformed me, but continues to empower many others to chayah!

Hmmm, I thought, Black Friday reminds me of Good Friday, the crucifixion of Jesus and the great hope of His glorious resurrection on Easter Sunday. However, there are many spoilers for Easter. I hate spoilers! Spoilers should come with warnings, to protect people who didn't see the whole game yet, to prevent them from learning the information before they find out about it themselves. Today, we know the full story of Easter; not just the scene of Good Friday. We are confident that there is Easter Sunday because it's not only history but also '*His Story*'; such a glorious testimony in sharing and celebrating the truth of the Easter (before, during and after). However, imagine the feelings of fear of the disciples, Mary the mother of Jesus, Mary Magdalene, and all the other believers, who journeyed and witnessed the horrific death of Jesus, as He bore our sins, shame, and suffering on the cross; sacrificially dying in our place? Wouldn't the feeling of failure have overwhelmed them that all hope lost, thoughts of His covenant and promises broken, and Jesus being the Prince of Peace forfeited, as they had no evidence except by faith of Jesus' resurrection, which was coming only in the next three days of the future? Are we beyond thankful that Jesus endured and suffered for us and did not give up? When the pain became severe, Jesus the King of the Universe cried out to His Father.

> *He went away a second time and prayed, saying, "My Father, if this cannot pass away unless I drink it, Your will be done."*
>
> ~ *Matthew 26:42 Amplified Bible (AMP)*

Hallelujah! Christ did chayah! Today, He lives; resurrected and seated at the right hand of the Father interceding on our behalf. Because He lives, you can face tomorrow fearlessly and excitedly, and expect your chayah!

Even life's most adverse event is minor compared to the experience of Jesus Christ and His glorious victory over life and death. Nevertheless, there were many times I had cried out to God to let my cup pass, but not my will but His will be done! God will get the glory, and we get to partake in the rewards, benefits, and blessings for our obedience. By enduring and aligning our testimonies to Jesus' tremendous success, we bring praises for His name's sake.

I stand today as an Ambassador of Christ, a spokesperson, to declare that I am an Overcomer! By the Grace of God, I fought many battles and bounded my opponents. I overcame my many trials, troubles, and tribulations. By practicing and pioneering Rebound Faith to strengthen, survive, and succeed through an extremely challenging four-year separation, divorce, and family court battle that resulted in situational depression, leading to insomnia, panic attacks, and anxiety.

> *"Someone I loved once gave me a box full of darkness.*
> *It took me years to understand that this too, was a*
> *gift."*
>
> — *Mary Oliver*

My defeat, divorce, and depression were hard, painful, and lonely. Fear said there was no hope for the mess and madness; Faith whispers, there is hope and victory is abiding!

As painful as the present might be, or the past was, let us look ahead to the future as Jesus did! He knew the pain of the cross was great, but He had faith to outrebound the enemy. He was confident that as He looked to His Father, for the manifestation of the completed conquest, the already pre-determined win and predestined victory for our future which accomplished long before this battle began, and before even our creation and conception.

All Glory to God, today, I stand healed, delivered, and restored by His grace, goodness, and mercy. I know the unconditional powerful love of Jesus Christ as my Healer, Redeemer, Deliverer, Provider, and my Personal Lord and Savior. I can identify with many people who are suffering behind closed doors due to the stigma associated with depression and the judgement that comes with the marital status of divorce.

Today, I am more courageous to share about how my family court battle drove me into situational depression. I was on and off work on short-term disability and period of no-pay leave of absence. I had to pay spousal support from my disability income, with no award for child support for my children.

During the period when my short-term disability ran out, but I was not qualified for long-term disability, I went on no-pay leave as I was too unwell to return to work and needed self-care. Having neither food nor money, nor eligible for welfare (due to my past 6 figure income), I muscled up my little strength and courage to return to work. Upon return, news of my garnished salary greets me, as I ran into spousal support arrears. I was breaking and broken!

There were the brutal legal battles for the finances, the multiple motions dragging me in and out of the courthouse, the mental and emotional conflicts for my mind, and not to mention the custody battles for my children. After one eleven-hour mediation session of listening to all the lies, accusations, condemnations, and betrayal; I got a panic attack and stretched out on the floor, crying uncontrollably.

I am more than excited to share God's faithfulness during this very dark and long season of my life. How I lost everything and everyone; But God! I am now divorced, and I experienced first-hand my God as my Divine Defence Attorney in the courtroom. I ran out of money and could no longer retain a full-time lawyer; after going through four different lawyers. I know that I have an Advocate with the Father, Jesus Christ, the righteous. (1 John 1:6)

As I faced the *fact* of rejection from my husband, family, in-laws, and friends, I received the *truth* of the acceptance, and everlasting love of a Heavenly Husband, Father, Friend, Saviour and Redeemer.

"For your Maker is your husband, the LORD of hosts is his name; and the Holy One of Israel is your Redeemer, the God of the whole earth he is called."

~ Isaiah 54:5 English Standard Version (ESV)

I testify of the Lord, My God as my EVERYTHING: Peace, Protector, Source, Shepherd, Way-Maker, Defence, Creator, Best-Friend, Confidant, and The God of the Universe...

I have encountered and experienced the unwavering affection of my God, as my Heavenly Father and the Father for my children. As a single mother, I am confident that I am not raising my children alone, as God is with me to help me. I continue to pray for a Godly, faithful, and loving husband, an earthly-father for my children, a role model, a ministry-partner, and a Kingdom Enforcer. Now, I believe that God is preparing us to be ready for him, as he will soon locate us. Indeed, I am Prayed and Prepared for My Rib (maybe another book in the Rebound Faith series).

I share boldly about how I lost the family home in a very upscale neighbourhood (sold during the divorce and the money held in trust by the court until the time of the final award). I had nowhere to live with my children, my mother, and my dog. I had no stable income as I was on and off disability, and at times I was on unpaid leave of absence; I was indebted with legal fees, a terrible credit score, no room on credit cards, no credit line, and no savings remaining. I even applied for social welfare, and they declined my application because of my previous high income. However, God remembered me; He timely intervened. Listed on the market was a single-family home in a beautiful neighbourhood for lease. By faith, though unqualified by the facts and reports, having a poor credit score and no full-time job as I was on disability. I presented an offer for the leased property at an amount that was significantly lower than listed. God granted me the favour; the landlord accepted my proposal immediately, and we finally had a place to call home.

Within a few years, God miraculously transferred me from the tenant to the owner of the house. God has blessed me with a beautiful home, in a lovely affluent neighbourhood, where I now live with my children, along with our dog. You see, my dog, Ace, is integral to my Rebound Faith Story. God has used this dog which He told me to acquire for the boys during the divorce as a source of healing throughout the series of depression and panic attacks in the household. Only God! Jesus, He set me free. I can surely testify that He whom the Son has set free, is free indeed.

What a shout of triumphant and glorious Hallelujah, that day, when I witnessed the miracle with my own two eyes and heard with my very own ears, the manifestation of God's response to my years of prayers and waiting on the Lord. Mind you, there are no winners in a divorce, everyone loses, especially the children; but not having to pay spousal support from my income was a significant win for me.

Here is an extract of the FINAL AWARD:

> *"... the parties thereby releasing each other from any and all claims for support of themselves, whether under the family law and the divorce act, now and in the future, regardless of whether their respective financial circumstances may change in the future by reason of their health, the cost of living, their employment, or otherwise."*

My God, He delivered me, anointed me, and empowered me, and He is continuously blessing my children and me.

Neither my divorce nor my depression equated to failure; they are great life lessons and tools of my Rebound Faith strategy, story, and solution!

Never allow fear to paralyze you; for during the valley of depression; God is there – He promised never to leave you nor forsake you. Always remember that in the middle of the shadow of death, God is with you! He is walking beside you. God is carrying you in His everlasting strong arms. He is strengthening you. Jesus loves you with His eternal, unconditional love. He is singing songs of deliverance over you. The Lord is making a way of escape for you. He is breaking through your enemies like a flood. He is lining up the right people, placing you in the right position and organizing the right situations to bring you out of that tough, dark, and dry place; into a position of strength, hope, and victory; for you to chayah!

These are only a few of the storms that I have endured and experienced in my life, and there are many, many more. However, today, these are the highlighted historical events of God right-hand working in my life and authoring my story. I am unashamed of my testimonies and public declaration of my love for Jesus. I have matured in my faith to rebound through life's challenges and chayah. I look at the storms that I am facing today, the future and its surprises; and I testify of my Rebound Faith. I am fearless to share My Story of The Sovereign God of all Storms.

> *And suddenly a great tempest arose on the sea so that the boat was covered with the waves. But Jesus was asleep. Then His disciples came to Him and awoke Him and saying, "Lord, save us! We are perishing!" But He*

said to them, "Why are you fearful, O you of little faith?" Then He arose and rebuked the winds and the sea, and there was a great calm. So, the men marvelled, saying, "Who can this be, that even the winds and the sea obey Him?"

~ Matthew 8:24-27 New King James Version (NKJV)

I am thankful to God as I couldn't have successfully endured these battles without Him. I stand today as a trained soldier and a victorious warrior, an Overcomer and more than a Conqueror. I have my battle scars, badges of horror-to-honour, as evidence to show that I overcame that which was intended to kill, steal, and destroy me.

For He has rescued us and has drawn us to Himself from the dominion of darkness and has transferred us to the kingdom of His Beloved Son, in whom we have redemption [because of His sacrifice; resulting in] the forgiveness of our sins [and the cancellation of sins' penalty].

~ Colossians 1:13-14 Amplified Bible (AMP)

No matter what the devil, his demons, and agents of evil are planning against you and your children, it will not work. They will not succeed. Activate the spiritual covering and protection by the Blood of Jesus and the Fire of the Holy Spirit to surround you, your children, your household, your family, finances, career, calling, and future.

"For we wrestle; not against flesh and blood, but against principalities against powers; against the rulers of the darkness of this world, against spiritual wickedness in high places."

~ Ephesians 6:12 King James Version (KJV)

Being a Transformation Consultant, Prophetic Leader and Empowerment Speaker, I have reflected on my experience and sought God earnestly about the demonic attacks of my defeat and the divorce. My analysis concluded two powerful revelations; the battle was for my mind and my seed.

This profound wisdom gave me the insight, hindsight, and foresight to see who the real enemy is; confirm the truth that the enemy's attack us in the area God has anointed for exaltation. Equip me with grace to forgive, move on, let go, and start over. Ignite my power, resilience, endurance with the grit to survive, revive, and thrive. Confirm the truth of Rebound Faith that amid what seems like a complete defeat, there is the hope of restoration as Christ has already conquered the enemy, and therefore our future to chayah is secured. It is so good when you learn the game, that not by might nor by strength, but by His Spirit.

The Battle was for my Mind

Within only a few years, I experienced several adverse life events. I suffered the sudden death and burial of my biological father, there was trouble in my marriage and separation in the household, and my mother who came to support me during my trauma became gravely ill and had to return home immediately. During that season, not only my personal but my professional life as well was in turmoil. My career was also uncertain as the company I enjoyed and worked with as a full-time Director was losing its market leadership position in the industry. I had grown exponentially in my career; I was now on the senior executive management team, holding a prominent high-profile job in Corporate Canada. I was highly rated, recognized and rewarded as an excellent business strategist and transformational leader.

I am gifted, creative and talented with the anointing of the grace as a Prophetic Leader. I carry a legendary spirit of excellence; ability to understand vast information, knowledge and wisdom; insight, hindsight and foresight; the revelation of strategies, visions and dreams; potential to unravel mysterious, puzzling, challenging concepts and ideas, and bring to realization/ commercialization; capability to solve highly complex, complicated ambiguous problems in business, leadership and life. Therefore, my goal was to shift my career into management consulting. As such, I founded Nikimac Solutions Inc. as a boutique business consulting company while manoeuvring and managing life challenges.

The enemy's evil plan was therefore to destroy my mind. For therein lays my intellect, my intelligence, my emotional, mental, and spiritual capacity, competencies, capabilities and drive to think, dream, imagine, focus, conceptualize, and strategize. Prophecies over my life are wealth-creation, billion-dollar ideas, thought-leadership, innovative thinking, transformational leadership skills, talents, and creative global strategies for multi-sources of income, a financial pillar to nations, and a Kingdom builder. These gifts equip my God-ordained calling and His grace in me to transform life, leadership, and business.

Rebound Faith Prayer and Declaration

In the name of Jesus, God has not given me a Spirit of fear, but He has given me a Spirit of power, love, and sound mind. God's Spirit has given me the ability to succeed, the strength to make a living and the grace to achieve greatness. So, I remember the Lord God, for it is He who gives me the ability to produce wealth, riches, success, affluence, and influence for increased income and impact; O Lord, give me more of Your Holy Spirit and manifest Your great power within me. Let your grace be always upon me so others will share in your divine destiny and bring you Glory, in Jesus name, AMEN!

"For God did not give us a spirit of timidity or cowardice or fear; but [He has given us a spirit] of power and love and of sound judgment and personal discipline [abilities that result in a calm, well-balanced mind and self-control]."

~ 2 Timothy 1:7 Amplified Bible (AMP)

"But you shall remember [with profound respect] the LORD your God, for it is He who is giving you the power to make wealth, that He may confirm His covenant which He swore (solemnly promised) to your fathers, as it is this day."

~ Deuteronomy 8:18 Amplified Bible (AMP)

The Enemy Attacked my Seed

The seeds of my womb are breaking the bloodline of generational curses; fatherless households, single parenting, divorce, relationship, and family crisis; sickness, poverty, occult and ungodly associations and influences. Renouncing and cancelling the old covenants made with the gods of our forefathers and establishing a new generation of Glory-Carriers and Kingdom Builders for Jesus Christ. The devil is scared and mad; therefore, he is urgently doing everything and will use anyone to stop us and hinder our future generation.

- The Spirit of Pharaoh is holding us captive in bondage and slavery;

- The Spirit of Jezebel is seducing us and perverting our minds into sin, control, immoral behaviours, and apostasy;

- The Spirit of Athaliah is killing our seeds and devouring our future God-ordained destiny.

> *"And I will put enmity (open hostility) between you and the woman, and between your seed (offspring) and her Seed; He shall [fatally] bruise your head, and you shall [only] bruise His heel."*
>
> *~ Genesis 3:15 Amplified Bible (AMP)*

> *So, the dragon was enraged with the woman, and he went off to wage war on the rest of her children (seed), those who keep and obey the commandments of God and have the testimony of Jesus [holding firmly to it and bearing witness to Him].*
>
> *~ Revelation 12:17 Amplified Bible (AMP)*

However, what an awesome and fantastic promise of Victory!

> *The God of peace will soon crush Satan under your feet. The [wonderful] grace of our Lord Jesus be with you.*
>
> *~ Romans 16:20 Amplified Bible (AMP)*

Rebound Faith Prayer and Declaration

Lord, according to Romans 16:20, O God of Peace, rise and crush Satan under Your feet to utter disgrace. Let the grace of our Lord Jesus Christ be with my children and me. Blood of Jesus, cancel and terminate every demonic attack and diabolical schemes for our minds and seeds. The fire of the Holy Spirit, consume and permanently destroy every enemy, evil plan, the curse of the law, negative utterance, generational curse, old covenant, and diabolical plot over our minds and after my seed, in Jesus mighty and matchless name. Lord, we seek your forgiveness, Salvation, redemption, divine protection, security and ask that the covenant promises of Christ be made anew with us. We claim our identity as Children of God, Godly inheritance and heritage in our lives, destiny and future generation, in Jesus name; Amen.

Your Story is for His Glory!

Let us quickly reflect on Joseph's story in the Bible; He had a dream about his ordained dominion and authority. He journeyed and endured a 13-year preparation and re-positioning through many trials, troubles, temptations, tribulations, and triumphs. Sold as a slave, Joseph served in the palace, favoured, rewarded, wrongfully accused, and punished unfairly. Joseph remained faithful to God. He was never forsaken nor forgotten by God. At the appointed time, God acted. Joseph experienced a 24-hour turnaround from Prisoner to Prince. He woke up in the pit and then promoted to the palace, that same day. Years later, we still marvel at the fulfillment of the predestined prophecy God gave Joseph in his childhood dream. God organized, arranged and aligned the performance of His divine plan for Joseph to chayah!

So, no more shrinking and hiding and putting a limit on the Limitless God!

God is miraculously positioning you for a purpose.

As for you, you meant evil against me, but God meant it for good, to bring it about that many people should be kept alive, as they are today.

~ Genesis 50:20 English Standard Version (ESV)

God loves you unconditionally, and absolutely nothing can change that. His love is everlasting, steadfast, eternal and unfailing. He understands where you are at in the process of transformation. He has appointed a time for your miracle, deliverance, and breakthrough. Genesis 3:9-10, says, *"Then the Lord God called to the man, 'Where are you?' He replied, 'I heard you walking in the garden, so I hid. I was afraid because I was naked.'* God sees your nakedness, you are unable to hide from Him, for He knows everything about you; the good, bad, and the ugly; despite it all, He still loves you. He is calling you; answer Him! So, no more attempts at hiding from God, answer His call. Receive His love, power and favour! Be there when He shows up! Call unto Him, Abba Father! God says, *"Why was no one there when I came? Why didn't anyone answer when I called? Is it because I have no power to rescue? No, that is not the reason! For I can speak to the sea and make it dry up! I can turn rivers into deserts covered with dead fish."* (Isaiah 50:2)

But when the right time came, God sent his Son, born of a woman, subject to the law. God sent him to buy freedom for us who were slaves to the law so that he could adopt us as his very own children. And because we are his children, God has sent the Spirit of his Son into our hearts, prompting us to call out, "Abba, Father." Now you are no longer a slave but God's own child. And since you are his child, God has made you his heir.

~ Galatians 4:4-7 New Living Translation (NLT)

God is in your midst; you will not fall, fail, be forgotten, nor forsaken. He is with you to comfort you, to strengthen you, save you, to help you, to fight on your behalf, to rescue you, and to bless you. God hears every cry for mercy, strength, and help. He knows the pain, the shame, the suffering, the darkness, the isolation, the rejection, the intimidation, the insensitivity, the fear; the extreme difficulty in integrating back into society and the challenges faced to move forward.

Moreover, He is our loving God; He redeems, rewards, rescues, recovers, restores, revives and bounds us to live abundantly and zealously! They say the hotter the battle, the sweeter the victory! If you are in a hot war, get ready for your loving worship; for, the more terrible the struggle, the more glorious the triumph!

"Behold, you have admonished and instructed many, and you have strengthened weak hands. Your words have helped the one who was stumbling to stand, and you have strengthened feeble knees."

~Job 4:3-4 Amplified Bible (AMP)

It is an enormous psychological maturity and spiritual growth for me to share my story publicly because of the stigma associated with mental health within our culture, our corporate careers, the community, and even our church. However, today, I do not consider myself a victim of my circumstances, but a threat to the enemy; honoured for the privilege to be used by God as a disruption of this stigma. I am not telling my story for pity nor sympathy. My testimony is a Rebound Faith Story of

Transformation to engage, encourage, equip, educate, empower, energize, elevate, enable, and evolve you.

Deliberately, I focus my story away from detailed traumatic tales, the dramatic events of my divorce and blow by blow plays of the depression. Instead, I aim to allow you to get attracted to the faith to believe that the rebound in your life, in whatever circumstance that you are facing today is not only possible but very favourable for you. I endured, survived, revived, thrived, and chayah; God did it for me, and He will undoubtedly do it for you. I am excited to share with you the biblical principles and application of Rebound Faith as transformational and empowerment mechanism through life changes.

What the enemy intended for harm, God turned it around for good, to save many others! Do not be afraid, only believe, having faith for your chayah! You shall be restored and 'really' live! Living victoriously, righteously, prosperously and zealously! You are coming out! You are crossing over! It's restoration season! It's turnaround time! The day of your deliverance is hastily approaching. You're next in line for your miracle! You shall have great testimonies of mind-blowing miracles and receive many congratulations! The no-eyes-have-seen and no-ears-have-heard blessings are yours; good measure, pressed down, shaken together and running over, will be poured into your lap. (Luke 6:38)

> *"The Sovereign LORD has given me His words of wisdom so that I know how to comfort the weary. Morning by morning He wakens me and opens my understanding to His will."*
>
> *~ Isaiah 50:4 New Living Translation (NLT)*

For me, my high confidence and courage come from the truth that the battle is of the Lord. Jesus, by His divine nature, has given us all things for life and righteousness to enjoy abundant living. Jesus has fought the many battles and won the war. He has already defeated the enemy. We are merely partakers in His overwhelming victory. By His grace, our stories are for His glory! I release God's blessing upon you for your rebound! God is about to give you every wasted year back. Receive your chayah anointing and blessing today!

You are loved!

Let's Pray

Beloved; a rise and shine; for your light has come, and the glory of the LORD has risen upon you. You have risen with Christ, raised from spiritual death, sin, suffering, sorrow, sickness, shame to new life, and sharing in Jesus' Resurrection Power, Light, and Glory.

"Therefore, if you have been raised with Christ to a new life, sharing in His resurrection from the dead, keep seeking the things that are above, where Christ is, seated at the right hand of God. Set your mind and keep focused habitually on the things above the heavenly things, not on things that are on the earth, which have only temporal value. For you died to this world, and your new, real life is hidden with Christ in God. When Christ, who is our life, appears, then you also will appear with Him in glory." — Colossians 3:1-4 (AMP)

Hence, I put off my old self, who belongs to my former manner of life and is corrupt through deceitful desires, and I am renewed in the spirit of my mind, and I put on the new self, created after the likeness of God in true righteousness and holiness. I take hold of the power of the Holy Spirit which dwells in me and commands that Jesus Christ is Lordship over my life, my thoughts, my desires, and deeds. My experience reflects God's righteousness and aligns with God's Word, Will, and Way.

For God did not give me a spirit of timidity, cowardice or fear; but He has given me a sense of power, love, sound judgment and personal discipline, abilities that result in a calm, well-balanced mind and self-control. I rise in power, dominion, and authority which were given to me at creation and restored to me upon Jesus' resurrection.

I trample upon snakes and scorpions and declare that nothing shall harm me. I rise to take possession of the promised land. I overtake my enemies and command all evil spirits to come out. I claim national rights and reap the milk and honey of the earth. Oh, Lord, God of Israel, that you would bless me and enlarge my territory, extend my borders, and enlarge my coast! Let your hand be with me and keep me from harm so that I will be free from pain. Moreover, my God has granted my request!

In the name of Jesus, I bind the works of darkness and loosen the power of the Holy Spirit. I stand on the Rock of Salvation, being confident in control of the Holy Spirit, who lives in me and say, Satan, you can't prevail... Satan, you must fail! I command every Red Sea to give way. I command every wall of a hindrance to crumble. I declare the crooked path to make straight. I decree rocky trail to be smooth. I command every sickness and disease to dry up at the roots, wither and die, never to return to my body or my bloodline. I proclaim that the curse of poverty, joblessness, lack, failure, frustration, barrenness, and financial difficulty to flee and make room for God's abundant blessings, financial overflow, and supernatural breakthroughs.

In the name of Jesus, I command all spirits of infirmity, hurt, anger, wrath, bitterness, depression, mental illness, past, pain, pride, forgiveness, neglect, abandonment, doubt, unbelief, rejection, rebellion, guilt, shame, condemnation, deceitful desires, sexual sins, lust, ungodliness, loneliness, stubbornness, disobedience, defiance, denial, division, addiction, witchcraft, slothfulness, intimidation, as well as ancestral or generational curses to come out NOW, to be destroyed and consumed by the Fire of the Holy Ghost. I am God's servant, and He takes pleasure in my prosperity, peace, protection, and my promotion.

I command God's overflow blessings in my storehouse. The Blood of Jesus to devour all my devourers, to terminate all my terminators, to defeat all my defeaters, and to oppose all my opposes.

Your word says, if anyone is in Christ, he is a new creation; old things have passed away; behold, all things have become new. I declare that I am a new creation, and this is a new day, a new beginning, a new season... I receive fresh oil and a fresh anointing. I speak to this day to cooperate with the covenant promises, plan, and purpose of God concerning my life. I command this day to produce joy, success, prosperity, favour, promotion, honour, abundance and peace in my life and all my concerns. I declare the anointing of excellence, affluence, influence, and magnificence to come upon me. I command my insufficiency to line up with the All-Sufficiency God! I declare my power to line up with the All-Powerful God. I decree that my finances line up with God's overflow and abundant blessing. I command my seeds to produce, to be fruitful, multiply and provide a great harvest. I call upon the Lord, this day, for deliverance and the Lord hears for my cry for mercy and help; He has immediately delivered me, set me free, redeemed me, rescued me, saved me, healed me, and helped me. In the name of Jesus, I call forth the manifestation of the power, Shalom, and Salvation of the Almighty God! The Lord, my Way-Maker, He makes way for me, where there is seems to no way; sea parted, heavens open, floodgates open, windows open, channels open, and doors open for me! I reach out and touch the hem of the garment of Jesus, the Lord, my Healer. He heals everything that is hurting me, my children, my household, my family, finances, ministries/callings, careers/businesses, the work of our hands, and our destiny.

Today is the day the Lord has made. The day the Lord has acted. We will rejoice, be filled with joy and be glad in it!

Fear wanted to bring me down, but Faith says, *"I shall rebound, come alive and quicken to life. I shall chayah!"*

Thank you, Lord, in Jesus mighty name, I have prayed and now ready to receive, Amen!

Post-Game Review

The Manifestation of Rebound Faith to Chayah!

"This poor Woman called, and the LORD heard her;
He saved her out of all her troubles!" (Psalm 34:6)

At the appointed time, I emerged from that dark place. The storm had elevated me to a new position. I evolved into a new person with a Rebound Faith prophetic prayer strategy, a transformation process, a renewed mind, and an empowerment story for me to chayah!

There is no force fiercer, and no strength stronger
than that of a determined and disciplined Godly
woman with a plan, a promise, and the passion for
pursuing her Purpose!

273

Nicola's Spiritual Empowerment and Life Transformation Journey

The Violation	The Venting	The Valley	The Vision	The Vow
Separation and Divorce	The Legal Court Battles (Divorce, Finances, Custody)	Situational Depression	Rebound Faith: The Strategy and Solution	'U Power Up!
Family and Financial Crisis		Disability Income	Prophetic Prayer Strategy - 5R milestones	Life Happens; Stay Strong!
Death of my Father	Negative Self Talk (low self-esteem, self-worth)	Payment of Spousal Support from my disability income	Transformative Change Process - 5 V Stages	Rebound and 'Really' Live... Chayah!
Critical illness and major surgery of my Mother	Guilt, Fear of Future, Bitterness, Unforgiveness	Anxiety	Renewed Mind for Mental Wellness (Shalom)	
Loss of my Family Home		Panic Attacks		
		Insomnia	Rebound Faith Story – Testimony, Therapy, and Transformation	
Loss of my Corporate Executive job		Lack of Concentration		
Wrongful accusations and insults				
Neglect, rejection, abandonment				

The Fulfillment of God's Promises

God's continued manifestation of my Rebound Faith Prophetic Prayer Strategy.

Request to Revelation

As mentioned earlier, it was during the storms of 2011 when I founded Nikimac; all hell broke loose. My father also died in late 2010. I went back to Jamaica to bury him. The company I worked with and enjoyed the benefits of growing in my career had suffered a significant loss in market positioning, and there were uncertainties regarding my job. There was turmoil at home as the separation in the household began; the breakdown of my marriage became irreconcilable. It was an extremely stressful time, both personally and professionally.

God bless the love of a mother! My mother came to spend time with us to support me and help me take care of my children. Unfortunately, she had a fall, became too sick, and needed attention herself. She had to return home to be cared for with a full-time nurse as she underwent major surgery.

I couldn't make sense of all these adverse life events. I cried out desperately to God for help. I went to every altar call at many churches, conferences, prayer meetings, and Christian summits; I wept bitterly at the altar.

At first, I battled my storm in solitude in the wake of my divorce. It was during my lowest periods with no friends, no family, no work, and no money that I started encouraging myself through inspirational posts, writing prayer blogs and sharing them on my Nikimac Facebook page. Writing became therapeutic for me. The mechanism and therapy I also used to overcome my depression, discouragement, and disappointment. I would share posts, like them, share them, and like them again. I was my audience. I preached to myself. I prophesied to myself; I was the Preacher and the congregation. I said AMEN and AMEN, again and again. I tagged people and frequently posted throughout the day, especially at nights when I was unable to sleep (due to insomnia). Many of my contacts became extremely annoyed. They would message me about flooding their newsfeed with Bible verses, prayers, and inspirational posts; others unfollowed, blocked or unfriended me; However, kicking off the beginning of my Rebound Faith journey. I began to earnestly and fervently seek God in prayers and fasting. My Facebook posts brought encouragement and refreshment to others; it was refreshing, and I was growing deeper. I held God accountable to His Words. Father, You said, *"If I seek you, I will find you, if I seek you with all my heart…"*

Revelation to Response

God began to reveal Himself to me and would give me profound revelations of His Word. His Words brought me comfort, encouragement, light for my dark unknown paths, covenant promises of blessings, the hope of a better and prosperous future. I started to power up the faith to outrebound my enemies!

I stood on God's word for my mom's healing. I researched scriptures in the Bible that had to do with healing; I personalized and prayed back the scriptures.

By the grace of God, He has granted her extended life, and she also testifies of His glory. I applied the Rebound Faith principles during her storm as she became extremely weakened, suffered from two strokes, a mild heart attack, diabetes, and high blood pressure, as was being prepped for surgery to remove her larger intestines… I taught her scriptures and personalized it with her name: "Audrey Young-Lynch, you shall not die but live to declare the glory of God!" *I shall not die, but live, and declare the works of the LORD.* (Psalm 118:17 KJV)

On her hospital bed, the doctors asked to gather the family to prepare for the worst news. I asked Mom, what is the scripture, in the weakest, faintest voice, with all the strength she had, she recited the scripture – *"I shall not die but live to declare the glory of God!"*

I have also demonstrated this with my son, Nick. Often, as he faced his academics and football games; he would call or message me to ask for prayers, and I would ask him, declare it, and he would repeat – *"I, Nick Stanley, can do all things through Christ who gives me strength!"* It changes the atmosphere, changes his perspective and changes his frantic tone to peace.

With my son, Matthew, I always remind him that he is a Gift of God. Whenever I pray for him, I would ask him, what does your name mean? Even if he is asleep, he would whisper – *"Gift of God!"*

These were seeds of my Rebound Faith; knowing, trusting, and learning to take God at His Word as my only Source of Truth. I was broken, burdened, broke, battered, and blue! I said to myself, *"If I only touch His garment, I will be made well!"* (Matthew 9:21)

I heard God's voice as He said, *"My precious child, I love you! I will never leave you. I am actively watching over my Word ready to perform them... My Word shall not return to me void and unfulfilled. For the plans and thoughts that I have for you; plans to prosper you, and not to harm your plans to give you hope and successful future."* (Jeremiah 29:11)

Response to Receive

I meditated on His Words and promises... His Words gave me life, hope, purpose, faith, joy, peace, and strength. He promised me an expected end to my troubles and a victorious rebound. If I trusted Him, He would deliver me so that He would get the glory. *At the appointed time, it happened!*

One morning, on June 16, 2014, I was looking for my Bible in my bed. Didn't I say He was my Comforter and my Husband (smile)? I found my Bible, opened under the sheet and He revealed the WORD that completely transformed my Rebound Faith experience to the chayah manifestation.

> *"Is this true?" the king asked her. And she told him the story. So, he directed one of his officials to see that everything she had lost was restored to her, including the value of any crops that had been harvested during her absence.*
>
> *~ 2 Kings 8:6 New Living Translation (NLT)*

I responded to God's revelation by writing down the verse in my prayer journal and by faith claimed the manifestation, *"I thank you Lord for Your All-Powerful word. Lord, I believe it! I receive it! I activate it! In Jesus name; Amen."*

Many of the actions God asked me to take were untraditional and condemned by the experts, but I obeyed. Many times, the process and the outcomes looked like total defeat and not a victory in sight; I cried but remained faithful. My lost and the captivity were brutal. I was fighting for my future, my finances, my children, and my health.

God divinely intervened. He manifested His divine power in the physical realm to carry me through. He blessed me with a competent, knowledgeable and supportive team of caregivers. I had a loving doctor, a God-fearing therapist, and several faithful pastors. He led me to an Arbitrator and Mediator. In addition to when the battle got hot, in the nickel of time, He provided me with a lawyer, who was a Man of God, and without an upfront retainer.

"This poor Woman called, and the LORD heard her; He saved her out of all her troubles!" (Psalm 34:6)

Receive to Rejoice

As I shared before, but to summarize the matter, my separation began in January 2011, family court and divorce battle came to an end in January 2015, the award came in, and I got custody of my boys, and I was able to return to work on a graduated schedule. However, the money from the sale of the million-dollar house went to legal fees, debts, and towards my final pay-out…. I got a tiny portion. It was bittersweet as I no longer had to pay spousal support and the settlement was final. I cried out to God, what about the house; I was leasing, and in faith, I had put an offer for purchase on the leased property, but now it seems as if I wouldn't have the money to move forward. I cried out to God, "Lord, how am I going to close it, insufficient deposit, no source for additional money, poor credit score, maxed out credit cards, massive financial debt, low disposable family income as my salary was the disability income for the last 3-years, no savings…."

Fear said, 'stacked against me were all the odds,' while Faith said, 'The stage is set for a miracle, a mighty move of God, that He may get the glory and transform many lives.'

So, one afternoon, while putting my shoes on in my mudroom to go pick up my boys from school, with mixed emotions, confused yet contented, I enquired of the Lord, *'How will I let go, move forward and start over?'* I heard the tender, loving voice, of the LORD distinctly, as I questioned Him of the outcome of the family case. I had a training to recognize His voice; as Father (God), my Redeemer (Son), and my Counselor (Holy Spirit). My Abba said, **"If I did it any other way, they would have said, they did it!"** I looked around and again; He repeated these same words to me. It was clear as daylight, God has spoken with authority and promised me divine restoration.

- *Call unto me, and I will answer thee, and show thee great and mighty things, which thou knowest not.* ~ **Jeremiah 33:3 (KJV)**

- *My sheep hear my voice, and I know them, and they follow me: And I give unto them eternal life, and they shall never perish, neither shall any man pluck them out of my hand.* ~ **John 10:27-28K (KJV)**

Remember the WORD in 2 Kings 8:6 that God gave me during the storm in June 2014, well My God, Amazing and Awesome LORD; He continues to manifest His WORD for the Rebound and our chayah!

I am winning the battles, conquering the enemy, taking the spoils and plunder of the war and God is bestowing me with His grace, honour, and favour to chayah!

- My Faithful Heavenly Father opened doors supernaturally, I was miraculously qualified for my mortgage, and I closed my home in the spring of 2015. I transitioned from a tenant to an owner of a beautiful family home in an affluent executive neighbourhood.

- I am enjoying the renovation and landscaping projects at home, and God is using these restructuring processes to give me revelations of His transformation power in His children's lives.

- My boys are maturing into God-fearing responsible happy, handsome and healthy young men.

- My ex-husband and I have forgiven each other (only the Holy Spirit could have done this... trust me!) We now have a respectful and civil relationship to co-parent our children. We often, share a coffee and even a laugh.

- God stirred my comfort-zone, and I left my full-time job in the Fall of 2015 as an employee, shifted me to an employer to lead Nikimac Solutions Inc., the company I founded during the 'storms' on November 20, 2011.

- I received my first client and first contract, then another, and another. I am having an amazing experience, mutual opportunities for growth, learning, and development. God helped me to deliver exceptional work in the engagements successfully. I continue to provide consulting and coaching to individuals, entrepreneurs, government, and corporations; mentorship and motivation globally and generationally!

- I am nurturing and helping thousands of people globally through various life transitions, speaking engagements, inspirational media, motivational talks, mentorship, and events.

- I expanded Nikimac focusing as a Transformational and Empowerment Community providing three strategic services: Transforming Business. Leaders. Life!

- I am continuously working on the business development of Nikimac Solutions Inc. to acquire new contracts and clients, as well as expanding our services globally. Not without challenges, but I got Rebound Faith to power me up and box-out oppositions for the victory, by His Grace and for His Glory... Nikimac shall chayah!

• I am a highly sought-after Management Consultant, by Corporate, Government, and Entrepreneurial organizations for strategy definition and deployment, business and digital transformation, product development, project management, change implementation, and transformational leadership development.

• I have launched *upowerup.com*, with the compelling tagline, *Life Happens; Stay Strong!* It is the Life Transformation, Spiritual Empowerment and Social Responsibility arm of Nikimac Solutions Inc. Being the Visionary behind several innovated and transformational programs to engage, encourage, equip, evolve, enable and elevate individuals, families, and communities. 'U Power Up Programs include:

    o Hosting *21 Days of Daniel Fasting* (launched in January 2017) based on God-inspired revelation, *"God is Closing the GAP!"* All glory to God for the many testimonies experienced globally.

    o Leading a Family, Life, and Relationship series, *"Prayed and Prepared for My Rib,"* exploring the Biblical principles of marriage, character, conduct, attributes, and actions of Kingdom men and women in relationships; sharing real-life stories of real people quest to experience and express love.

o   Helping individuals, ministries and affinity groups to facilitate vision board workshops/parties and create their own vision board. The *Empowerment Vision Board* is powerful and effective, application of Godly principles; providing the clarification, creative visualization, and manifestation of your envisioned future goals.

Unbelievably to you but I am a bit shy, so was a bit timid at first to host these 'U Power Up Programs. However, they were well received, and the participants were engaged, encouraged and empowered. Righteousness gives you boldness and confidence to be unashamed of the gospel and Jesus. *I'm a corporate girl who loves Christ Jesus!*

●   In 2018, I partnered with another believer to pioneer a community and movement known as "Legends and Legacy" to connect, change and challenge Christians to align their Professions with Purpose for excellence in Ministry and Marketplace. With the compelling slogan: *"Live like a Legend; Leave a Legacy!"*

●   I am planning on authoring several books in the Rebound Faith - Spiritual Empowerment and Life Transformation Series; Chayah is the first one.

●   Moreover, the list goes on! As Psalm 40:5 (NLT) says, *"O Lord, My God, You have performed many wonders for us. Your plans for us are too numerous to list. You have no equal. If I tried to recite all your wonderful deeds, I would never come to an end of them"*

I still encounter challenges, surprise changes, and unexpected setbacks, because this is life on earth. When I fail or fall, and I have been unable to achieve my goals, I change the plan but not the vision. I have dropped on my face numerous times, but I cry out to the Lord and continue to keep going. Each time, I get up, straighten my crown which got shifted during my fall, and move forward. The fall nor my failure do not define me; what describes me is how well I come back after the setback... I shall arise; I am falling forward and standing tall above every trial. The storms have deposited in me the grit to survive, revive and thrive! The questions, anxiety, fear, panic, weaknesses, and intimidation will come to my mind and thoughts with the lies of the enemy, but I quickly replace them with the Truth of God.... *Thus, says the WORD of the LORD! You should destroy sophisticated arguments, every noble and proud thing that sets itself up against the real knowledge of God and you take every thought and purpose captive to the obedience of Christ.* (2 Corinthians 10:5)

I am forever grateful; the process was painful, but powerfully revealing the glory of God. God is indeed faithful; He continues to complete His work in me. Mature my Rebound Faith to box-out my oppositions for me to rebound and 'really' live and chayah!

If God did it for me; He will unquestionably do it even more significant for you.

In those times when it feels like your world is shattering, the sky is falling, and everything you do, even with good intentions held negatively against you, remember to practice mindfulness; nothing is permanent! Pause and breathe, inhale and exhale! Let it all out, empty yourself by breathing out the negativity, anger, confusion, chaos, self-pity, self-destructive thoughts. Breathe in positive thoughts, peace, power, patience, endurance, resilience, beauty, and joy. Smile and remain silent! Kneel and let God stand-up! God got this under control and what's in His power is never out of control. Let God handle it. It's fixed! It's complete! It's finished! It's healed! It's provided and protected! Things are already better!

You are what you believe, think, speak, decide, and act! You are growing, glowing, and glorifying God.

You must consistently pray and accept God's Word: *"Lord God, I thank you for the new opportunities (open doors) and the missed opportunities (closed doors). My God, He is the Alpha and the Omega, the First and the Last; He knows the Beginning and the End. My time is in His hands. Moreover, my God will meet all my needs according to the riches of His glory in Christ Jesus. For the Lord God is a sun and shield: The Lord will give grace and glory: no good thing will He withhold from them that walk uprightly. Also, we know that God causes all things to work together for good to those who love God, to those who He called, prepared and equipped according to His purpose. 'No' means the next opportunity! God is doing something new to bring Greater Glory to His Kingdom and guess what; I get to be a partaker in that, in Jesus name I pray, praise and proclaim. Amen!" (Philippians 4:19, Psalm 84:11, Romans 8:28).*

Rebound Faith Prayer and Declaration

I decree and declare that the remaining weeks of this month, as well as the rest of this year, are going be great. You shall have an excellent testimony, supernatural miracles, and breakthroughs after breakthroughs to the Glory of God. You shall finish this year strong and start next year empowered. You shall testify that this last year maximum is this year's minimum, because, year-over-year, you are growing, multiplying, increasing, and expanding exponentially. God shall open new doors for you that no man can shut though you had little strength, you have not denied Him. God shall increase your income, your impact, and your influence. You and your children are blessed and flourishing. You are the head and not the tail, top and not the bottom, above and never below. The spirit of excellence surrounds you, favour chases you down, the peace of God encamps about you, and with long life and abundance, God has satisfied you and showed you His salvation. God delights to prosper you as your soul prospers. His goodness, grace, mercy shall follow you all the days of your lives. No matter the storm, God is Greater! He quiets the winds and the wave. God rejoices over you with songs and singing. He will make a way where there seems to be no way. God can do everything but fail, and you can do all things through Christ who strengthens you. You know that God didn't bring you this far to leave you, forget you, fail you, and forsake you.

Jesus gently whispers, *"Yes, there's still a chance for Rebound! For the Lord, He is your Shepherd!"*

> *The LORD is my Shepherd [to feed, guide, and shield me], I shall not lack. He makes me lie down in [fresh, tender] green pastures; He leads me beside the still and restful waters. He refreshes and restores my life (myself); He leads me in the paths of righteousness [uprightness and right standing with Him--not for my earning it, but] for His name's sake. Yes, though I walk through the [deep, sunless] valley of the shadow of death, I will fear or dread no evil, for You are with me; Your rod [to protect] and Your staff [to guide], they comfort me. LORD; You prepare a table before me in the presence of my enemies. You anoint my head with oil; my [brimming] cup runs over. Surely or only goodness, mercy, and unfailing love shall follow me all the days of my life, and through the length of my days, the house of the Lord [and His presence] shall be my dwelling place.*

> *~ Psalm 23 Amplified Bible (AMP)*

In the mighty, and matchless Jesus name, I pray, praise, and proclaim His provision, protection, peace, promotion, promises, purposes, plans, prosperity, and Providence in my life, the lives of my children, household, family, finances, business/career, ministry/calling, works of our hands, and destiny, AMEN!

I enjoy praying and talking with my LORD; I have an intensely intimate relationship with Jesus. I love to cover myself and everything concerning me with the Blood of Jesus (smile). Ask my boys! We are like driving in the car, and I am whispering a prayer, *"O LORD, please cover us with the Blood of Jesus. AMEN!"* They are looking at me, like, Mom, am I not driving carefully? I smile and say *"Of course, you are, but we always need God's protection."*

So here I am today, responding to my Calling and being committed to the same Unchangeable, All-Powerful, Almighty, Sovereign, Faithful, Loving God, to walk with you through your storms…. However, you know what? Our God, He is faithful, and before you get there, He has already provided.

God said to tell you, *"My steadfast love is unfailing, unconditional, everlasting…Come to me, all you who are weary and burdened, and I will give you rest. Take my yoke upon you and learn from me, for I am gentle and humble in heart, and you will find rest for your souls, for my yoke is easy, and my burden is light. Cast your cares on the LORD, and He will sustain you; He will never let the righteous be shaken or moved.* (Matthew 11:28-30, Psalm 55:22).

Beloved, therefore to wake up this morning knowing that God is on our side is enough. We arise and shine ready to possess our possession. We take territorial rights for that which God has already ordained and predestined for His Glory and our goodness. We get prayed up, put on the full armour, kick the devil in his teeth; we exercise our power, authority, and dominion in the fullness of His grace. No matter how we feel, we get up, get dressed, get going, take up our mats and move forward, declaring, *"This is the day the Lord has made, and I shall rejoice and be glad in it!"*

Chayah from Devastation and Depression to Deliverance!

So, you have relived my Rebound Faith Story as some of the prayers and declarations are real from my prayer journal, Nikimac Solutions Inc. Inspirational Devotions, as I walked through my journey from devastation and depression to deliverance.

I know that there are many testimonies of everyday legends (like you) as well as Bible Heroes with the divine encounter of Jesus to change us from ashes to beauty. Each day, we are living our own mind-blowing miraculous stories of you exercising Rebound Faith; let us continue to survive, revive, and thrive; Rebound and 'really' live...Chayah!

The Life Transformational Touch

Let's look at the Woman with the issue of Blood, Her Rebound Faith Story: Outcast, Ostracized, and Overwhelmed from Prolong Sickness.

Here is a Rebound Faith story of another woman, with given no name, yet she painfully suffered a prolonged sickness for 12 years, known famously as "The Woman with the Issue of Blood." She had numerous doctor appointments, spent all she had but found no permanent cure and but did not receive complete healing.

However, on one appointed day, this beautiful woman muscled up her Rebound Faith to chayah! When she decided to seek Jesus as a solution and source to stop her suffering, shame, and she reached out for the life-transformational touch; His power to heal and deliver.

There is no force higher than a determined woman with a prayer and a plan. That day, she decided to present her pain to His divine power which propelled her chayah; restored to health and life!

> *And a woman who had [suffered from] a hemorrhage for twelve years [and had spent all her money on physicians], and could not be healed by anyone, came up behind Him and touched the fringe of His outer robe, and immediately her bleeding stopped. Jesus said, "Who touched me?" While they all were denying it, Peter [and those who were with him] said, "Master, the people are crowding and pushing against you!" But Jesus said, "Someone did touch me because I was aware that power [to heal] had gone out of me." When the woman saw that she had not escaped notice, she came up trembling and fell down before Him. She declared in the presence of all the people the reason why she had touched Him, and how she had been immediately healed. He said to her, "Daughter, your faith [your personal trust and confidence in me] has made you well. Go in peace (untroubled, undisturbed well-being)."*
>
> *~ Luke 8:43-48 Amplified Bible (AMP)*

She decided to live victoriously and move through the stages of her **Rebound Faith Transformative Change Process** (5 Vs).

Violation: The prolonged issue of the blood! Sickness!

Venting: Long periods of suffering; many doctors, and no permanent cure; an outsider and the outcast; absence/limitation in everyday life.

Valley of Depression: She experienced similar symptoms and stigma of mental illness; ostracised, discouraged, isolated, disliked, and rejected. She was desperate for deliverance and a change in her physical and psychological health.

Vision: Her desire is to be permanently healed and to be made whole and to seek Jesus as her Healer.

Vow: Determined and disciplined for her deliverance, no matter what it takes; pressing through the crowd amid her shame, suffering, and stigma to get to Jesus; breaking religious customs, laws, and the stigma with each step and every step to get to Jesus for that one stolen touch.

She decided to live righteously by presenting her pain to Jesus' power and applying the **Rebound Faith Prophetic Prayer Strategy (5 Rs).**

Request: Her ask was with the activation of her attitude and her actions of physical touch. With only a mere touch of her infirmed body to the hems of her Savior's garment.

Revelation: A powerful experience and divine encounter of Jesus, the Great Physician, the Healer, the Redeemer... Jesus said, *"Who touched me?* Also, Jesus said, *"Someone did touch me because I was aware that power to heal had gone out of me."* (Luke 8:45-46)

Response: When the woman saw that she had not escaped notice, she came up trembling and fell before Him. She declared in the presence of all the people the reason she had touched Him and immediately healed. She received holistic wellness and freedom. (Luke 8:47)

Receive: Jesus said to her, *"Daughter, your faith, your personal trust, and confidence in me has made you well. Go in peace, untroubled, undisturbed well-being."* (Luke 8:48)

Rejoice: Giving thanks and sharing the testimony of her suffering and her immediate healing to a new life.

The woman decided to live prosperously with a Renewed Mind to claim God's Shalom: His peace, Salvation, healing, well-being for her miracle to revive, to recover, and restore her health and life.

The woman's faith healed her at that moment; she made up her mind to seek Jesus's help for rebound. She owned her moment! She renewed her mind, shifted her focus to the positivity; her every action, thought, feeling, attitude and emotion concentrated on what is possible with Jesus. *"If these rumours I heard of His miracles are correct, I want my breakthrough."* She persevered for 12 long years; her perseverance through the crowd, drowned the noise, negativity, and her fears. She powered up through her past to grasp the future. She stole the touch that equipped her transformational story; so compelling that we are still talking about it even to this day. She courageously faced the circumstances, the community, and the crowd. She met the very fears that had her bound due to her condition.

The woman tells of her troubles which marked her faith journey and declared her healing which represented her new beginning. Jesus confirmed that her faith, her confidence, and assurance in Him had made her well. He released the blessings, goodness, and glory over her; His SHALOM – His peace, wellness, health, prosperity, and all that is good in her life... His anointing for her to chayah! She decided to live zealously by

291

owning and sharing her Rebound Faith Transformation Story to chayah!

> *A woman who suffers from "issue of the blood" as per Leviticus 15:19-20 would suffer in silence as their role, rules, and rituals dictate a stigma that she should be ashamed of publicising her story. Her state of unstoppable bleeding is one medically impossible. Therefore, God had sustained her during these years. But it would leave her ostracised as an outsider or an outcast; physically, mentally, financially, and emotionally devastating to anyone.*

> *"When a woman has a discharge, and the discharge in her body is blood, she shall be in her menstrual impurity for seven days, and whoever touches her shall be unclean until the evening. Moreover, everything on which she lies during her menstrual impurity shall be unclean. Everything also on which she sits shall be unclean."*
> *~ Leviticus 15:19-20 English Standard Version (ESV)*

She was facing her circumstance in the city and amidst the crowd, yet no one noticed her presence, or her pain or her posture reaching out for Jesus' power. The woman with her "unclean" illness was in close contact with believers and non-believers but all too busy to notice her; as she touched them, therefore, they too are also tainted.

However, when you touch Jesus, He sees and speaks life, healing, and restoration! Jesus said, *"Who touched me? ...Someone did touch Me; for I perceived that healing power had gone forth from Me."* (Luke 8:45-46)

I am somewhat delighted with the vagueness of the story; no name, title, status, creed associated with 'the woman' and her adverse condition was also vague. Let's conduct an analysis and analogy with other violations; we often encounter in life. Bring the similarities to be drawn from this testimony of her sickness of the "issue of the blood" with different emotional and mental illnesses like depression, addiction, and abuse (sexual, domestic, bullying). These people with these issues often go unnoticed, and the shame prevents them from seeking the necessary treatment – physically, mentally, emotionally, and spiritually.

Her "unclean" status caused by her sickness is very similar to mental illness today. Mental illness is stigmatized culturally and socially in the community; yet ironically in the crowd at the "crown of grace" was where she sought and took a stance for her healing – disrupting Jesus' schedule, the stigma, and society; yielding the breakthrough solution.

What motivated her to change this day? One day, she woke up with a renewed mind; fierce and on fire, she decided that her burning desire for success be more significant than her deepest fear of failure and with that new perspective; she shifted from an Outcast to an Overcomer!

Each day, including today, gives a new chance to choose a change. We have a choice to remain in our situation or to move forward to seek better, to gain hope, and to become greater. Our attitude drives our actions; our actions produce reactions. We calculate our chances and consequences and make clear decisions to take steps that create a brighter and more prosperous future.

The woman moves through the crowd with an inconsolable hopefulness that pushes her out of her "valley of despair" as led by the Holy Spirit to explore divine healing for her situation.

Her desire and motivation to be healed could be internally driven or triggered by an external factor; the imperative of her story though is that she pushed through the "noise" of her circumstances amid her pain, shame, and suffering. She powered up her Rebound Faith to chayah; the strength, stamina, and courage to protest her illness; despite the weakness of her physical body. She made her prayer request through the feebleness of her body, a physical touch of Jesus, and the honest declaration of her belief; immediately she was healed. Her rebound faith displayed in her deliberate actions, her determined attitude, and His divine attributes.

The psychological impact of such a prolonged sickness, suffering, and separation will no doubt impact one's physical, mental, emotional, spiritual, and social well-being. The good news of the story is that no matter how long you have suffered and lived isolated due to your situation; you may have tried numerous treatments/solutions to pacify or survive the pain. There is absolute deliverance in seeking God for immediate Salvation and the ultimate gift of eternal life; and who knows, His grace may also leave you with a fantastic, remarkable and miraculous healing. Jesus didn't reprimand, condemn, nor reject her. He responded with love for redemption, recovery, and restoration.

This woman took a stance to disrupt the stigma and sought her healing; leaving evidence, witnesses and onlookers astonished that she broke traditions - religious, cultural, and societal barriers. Opening the door that despite the disaster or devastation that triggered the depression/mental illness, there is no need to quietly suffer while there are treatments available physically and spiritually for your deliverance.

Let's Pray:

Almighty Father, thank you for your Word that brings life and hope. May my pain drive my motivation today, to pursue my purpose despite the setback, the delays or the denials; Lord, I surrender to you. Lord, take away this prolonged "issue" as well as the pain, shame, and suffering that are the by-products of it. I request my deliverance, financial breakthrough, healing, and restoration. I muscle up my rebound faith and power up my strength to reach out today to touch you, despite how condemned I am, how guilty I feel, or how messed up my situation is. Your Word revealed that you are the Healer and Redeemer, and I claim by faith for my rebound to victory.

In the name of Jesus, I declare that I will no longer be ashamed or stigmatized by my enemies. My life has purpose, significance, influence, and impact. The Lord shall open the windows of heaven and doors of opportunity, gates of goodness and greatness for me. In the name of Jesus, I reverse every evil pronunciation, curse, plot, plan, demise, and the diabolical scheme to the sender. By God's grace and for His glory, I shall revive; chayah! I shall not leave in flight as God shall be my rear guard. I shall be at the right place at the right time; my arrival shall break boundaries, shatter barriers, and extend borders. My mind-blowing miracles will establish new protocols. My testimony shall be a generational and global blessing. I am blessed and highly favoured, admired, preferred, and respected everywhere I go. God makes me the salt and light. I am the head and never the tail. I am at the top and never the bottom. I am growing from strength to strength, rebounding from shame to fame, from sickness to wellness, from insult to result, and from overlooked to overbook. God shall prepare a table and feast for me in the presence of my enemies, and my cup shall overflow with His glory, in Jesus name.

Today, I believe that with one touch, the power to heal has released and I receive it. I stand joyfully, rejoicing and thanking You for Shalom. I hear you loving and gently voice – saying to me, *"My Child, your faith, your confidence and trust in Me has made you well! Go, enter into peace, untroubled, undisturbed well-being."* (Luke 8:48)

I believe, I receive, and I activate the manifestation. I am blessed because I know that there will be a fulfillment of what spoken of the Lord to me.

Almighty God, Father, I repent and confess of being too busy to notice the pain of others. I admit my judgement of others, my impatience, and unkindness when I have no idea of their suffering and the prolonged condition that they are carrying. Frequently, we judge saying that they haven't tried hard enough to get out of their situation or toxic relationships or addictions. Lord, please forgive me. Today, I pray that amidst their suffering, they will find You as the source of their strength to survive, to be empowered, and the hope to seek the help, and the faith to rebound. I ask all this in Jesus name. AMEN!

Claiming God's Promises for Your Rebound to Chayah!

On July 26, 2017, I was sitting on the Go Train heading to downtown Toronto, Ontario, Canada, I was excited and in awe of God's faithfulness. It was my very first day of a Government Contract I landed after months of seeking, praying and waiting. This day, the Holy Spirit led me to Isaiah 45:19-21.

Interestingly and coincidentally, through many trials, troubles, tribulations, and temptations, precisely one year later, July 26, 2018, the Holy Spirit led me to the very same scriptures to confirm His Word. Again, God's word encouraged, empowered, and equipped me with the strength to carry on, the wisdom and revelation to respond with Rebound Faith to every season of wilderness, barrenness, and unfruitfulness; igniting my Vision and Vow to chayah!

God's word is alive, active, powerful, and influential! God's word provides insight, hindsight, and foresight for you to see your *Vision* through His Sight. His Light guides you on the venture and His Might anchor you as you make the *Vow* to pursue your God-ordained Vision.

> *"I have not spoken in secret, in the corner of a land of darkness; I did not say to the descendants of Jacob, 'Seek Me in vain [with no benefit for yourselves].' I, the Lord, speak righteousness [the truth—trustworthy, a straightforward correlation between deeds and words], declaring things that are upright.*

Assemble yourselves and come; Come together, you survivors of the nations! They are ignorant, who carry around their wooden idols [in religious processions or into battle] and keep on praying to a god that cannot save them.

Declare and present your defence of idols; Indeed, let them consult together. Who announced this [the rise of Cyrus and his conquests] long before it happened? Who declared it long ago? Was it not I, the Lord? And there is no other God besides Me, A [consistently and uncompromisingly] just and righteous God and a Savior; there is none except Me."

~ Isaiah 45:19-21 Amplified Bible (AMP)

Let us examine what God is saying to you this day:

"My Beloved Child, I have not spoken in secret about your rebound, to revive, restore, redeem, rescue, recover, reset, and renew you to 'really' live... Chayah! I did not call you to a fruitless service. I have called you to live an abundant life; to live victoriously, righteously, prosperously, and zealously! I have not told you to seek me in vain, for nothing, with no benefit to you. I have promised a just reward for you! I speak righteousness and truth! I am trustworthy, faithful, and straightforward having alignment and correspondence to My character, conduct, actions, and attributes to manifest My Word. I declare things that are upright. I am actively watching over My Word, ready and hasty to perform and fulfill it. (Jeremiah 1:12)

So, my Precious Child, gather yourself and come alive! You are a survivor! You are more than a conqueror! You are a victorious warrior! Indeed, you are a winner! Pray to Me, the God, who can and will save you! Believe in Me, the Only Wise God; The Creator! The Sovereign God, who knows the Beginning and the End. The Almighty God, who knows and prophesied the past, present, and future, long before it happens! Your loving Abba, Heavenly Father! Your Redeemer, Deliverer, Provider, Protector, Healer, Shepherd, Promise-Keeper, Way-Maker! The Great I Am! Know that there is no other god besides Me! I am consistently and uncompromisingly; the Righteous God and Saviour. None can compare to Me, for there is none except Me!

My Beloved Child; do not be afraid nor doubt, only believe, declare, and decide to chayah!"

Achieve your Game-Changing Success

So, how do you continuously power up from the current state of being stuck in mediocrity, affliction, infirmities, troubles, and temptations? How do you box-out every opposition and rebound to the desired future state? How do you continuously survive, revive, and thrive in the next dimension?

The zeal of the LORD of Hosts will accomplish this! (Isaiah 9:7)

So, continue to trust and take God by His Word. The Lord says, *"Have you seen all this great army? Behold, I will hand them over to you, and you shall know without any doubt that I am the Lord. Moreover, I will guide you along the best pathway for your life. I will advise you and watch over you."* (1 Kings 20:13, Psalm 32:8)

The Lord frustrates the devices and schemes of the crafty, So that their hands cannot attain success or achieve anything of lasting worth. The Lord will disappoint and expose every demonic game plan, plot and operation set up in disguise to defeat and destroy you and all concerning you. (Job 5:12)

So, learn and implement the Principles of Rebound Faith for Spiritual Empowerment, and Life Transformation provided in this book to guide you to chayah. Rebound and 'really' live with the application of a *Prophetic Prayer Strategy* to pull you through the *Transformative Change Process*, with a *Renewed Mind for Mental Wellness* and sharing your *Rebound Faith story* for His glory. Being confident, resilient and resolute of God's plan for your future, call upon God and seek Him to direct you *"Call to Me and I will answer you and tell you and even show you great and mighty things, things which have been confined and hidden, which you do not know and understand and cannot distinguish."* (Jeremiah 33:3)

Pray, praise, and prophesy your future state; possess your position of victory! Applying the Rebound Faith Prophetic Prayer Strategy (5Rs) - Request, Reveal, Release, Receive, and Rejoice; surrender your will to His. Declare, *"O Lord, Your will be done on earth as in Heaven, in my life and my situation, guide my steps, O Lord. For this, I give you thanks for I know you hear me when I pray to You and will navigate me along the paths of life; for the steps of a good and righteous man are directed and established by the Lord, and He delights in his way and blesses his path."* (Psalm 37:23)

Forgive, let go and move forward to a higher dimension! Venture victoriously through the stages of the Transformation Process (5 Vs) from the Violation, the Venting, and Valley of depression; *'U Power Up* making the impressive comeback! Your *Vision* and *Vow* have produced a new level of faith, focus, and fortitude. Declare: *"Lord, with all my heart I have sought you, inquiring of you and longing for you; do not let me wander from your commandments, neither through ignorance nor by willful disobedience."* (Psalm 119:10)

Be at peace throughout the journey and the Wait! Have a *Rebound Faith* Renewed Mindset for Mental Wellness (Shalom) with Positivity, Perseverance, Praise, Prophecy, and Prayers. Declare: *"O Lord create in a clean heart, O God, and renew a right and steadfast spirit within me. Do not cast me away from your presence and do not take Your Holy Spirit from me. Restore to me the joy of your salvation and sustain me with a willing spirit. Then I will teach transgressors your ways, and sinners shall be converted and return to you."* (Psalm 51:10-13)

Speak life! Inspire positivity with positive declarations, decrees, decisions and deeds over your life, thoughts, emotions, and relationships. Shift the atmosphere and energy in your favour! Dream big, if you can imagine it, it can exist! Ignite God's power and give purpose to your vision.

Stay Positive or Stay Silent! Positive thoughts and self-talks produce positive emotions; positive emotions produce joy, success, and peace!

Be intensive and intentional with the zeal to live. Pursue the passion for achieving your purpose-driven life! Own your moment and tell your Rebound Faith Story of transformation to empower others.

SELF-TALK: I declare - "I know who God is and the magnificence of His power to lavish me with His love. I know that my identity is in God, as my Father and my King. I know that the only wise and living God holds my future. The Way-Maker God is doing a new thing. Today, I am authoring a new Chapter, and my story will end in victory. I have a fresh new beginning; God's power to guide me through every rough path, valley, and hindrances in the maze of life. As I cry out to God, God hears the cry of His children, and He promises to deliver them out of all their troubles. I testify, right now in advance of my breakthrough, that I have cried, and the Lord heard me and saved me from all my troubles. (Psalm 34:17, Psalm 34:6)

Therefore, the Bible is the Blueprint for experiencing a successful Game-Changing Life Transformation; having unwavering faith in God for your rebound. The grit that despite it all, you shall chayah; come alive, survive, revive, and thrive to live abundantly; victoriously, righteously, prosperously, and zealously!

The biblical principles for Rebound Faith are also grounded and aligned with the scriptures written in Ephesians 6:10-18. So, when getting dressed, each morning, program in your routine to put on the whole Armor of God and be ready for the battle! Throughout the day; not if, but when the enemy comes in like a flood and reminds you of your past sins, failures, human limitations, weaknesses and mistakes; rebuke him and tell him of his defeated future. Recite your Rebound Faith declaration: *"Jesus has already won the war, and this battle is His. Therefore, I am confident that I am a Winner, an Overcomer, More than a Conqueror and a Victorious Warrior with Christ Jesus!"*

Moreover, at the end of each day, despite it all, thank God for everything and declare your victory and reclaim your rebound to chayah through Christ.

Live Victoriously – Progressing through the Rebound Faith Transformative Change Process (5 Vs). Being ready and focused with the Spiritual Weapons to fight from a position of victory in each stage of the transformation; from the Violation, silencing the Venting, coming out of the Valley of depression alive with a new Vision and a Vow to chayah!

Live Righteously – Activating the Rebound Faith Prophetic Prayer Strategy (5 R's); being fervent in prayers and praises; maturing through the Request, Revelation, Response, Receive, to Rejoice; revealing your unshakeable faith, a Godly-character of Righteousness (in the right standing with God through Christ being repentant and obedient). Applying the Truth of God's Word, the Matchless Name of Jesus, the Blood of Jesus and the Consuming Fire of the Holy Spirit.

Live Prosperously - Seeking Rebound Faith for Mental Wellness (Shalom). Having a Renewed Mindset for positivity in speech, thoughts, and emotions to attract, affirm and activate prosperity, peace, and promotion into your life and soul. Know that the real enemy is the devil, his demons, and evil forces. Stay alert as the battle is for your mind! Mental wellness is your new wealth; you are becoming abundantly wealthy! Claim God's promises for your *Shalom*: every goodness, greatness, fullness, welfare, happiness, and completeness of life; salvation, health, well-being, peace, joy, and prosperity.

Live Zealously – Glorifying God enthusiastically with your Rebound Faith Empowerment and Transformation Story. Experiencing the game-changing power of your story to change lives, heal minds, and win souls. Praying, praising and proclaiming God's grace, glory and goodness. His divine manifestation in your life - Freedom, Miracles of Healing, Strength, Provision, Promotion, Affluence, Wealth, Influence, Excellence, Restoration, Redemption, Deliverance, Breakthroughs, Protection, and Security.

Rebound Faith Declaration and Prayer

O Lord, You promise my deliverance from devastation and depression, and from every defeat, demise, and diabolical scheme of the enemy. Lord, I call upon you today for the performance of your Word of the release and freedom from the violation, venting, and valley; every worry, sadness, brokenness, captivity, poverty, persecution, wrongful accusation, negativity, injustice, sin, sickness, disease, lack, crime, violence, disaster, trouble, trial, temptation, and tribulation... I declare that the God is my refuge, shelter, and strength, a help always near in times of great difficulty. The Lord helps me and delivers me; He delivers me from the wicked and saves me because I take refuge in Him.

> I, [insert your name], decree and declare the entire scriptures of Psalm 91 over my life. The Lord is my light and my salvation— Whom shall I fear? The Lord is the refuge and fortress of my life— Whom shall I dread. When the wicked came against me to eat up my flesh, my adversaries, and my enemies, they stumbled and fell. Though an army encamps against me, my heart will not fear. Though war arises against me, even in this I am confident... My God's promise and plan of my deliverance are BIGGER than every problem and pain that I am facing... God is with me, and He is more than able... He will never fail, forget nor forsake me. I dwell in the shelter of the Most High and I will remain secure and rest in the shadow of the Almighty, whose power no enemy can withstand. I will say of the Lord, "He is my refuge and my fortress, My God, in whom I trust with great confidence, and on whom I rely!" He will save me from the trap of the fowler, and from the deadly pestilence. He will cover me and completely protect me with His pinions, and under His wings, I will find refuge; His faithfulness is a shield and a wall, a hedge of protection, surrounding all around me and all concerning me. Because I have made the Lord, who is my refuge, even the Most High, my dwelling place, no evil will befall me, nor will any plague come near my home, my children, household, family, our finances,

career/business, calling/ministry, destiny/purpose, nor the works of our hands.

Lord, You are actively watching over your WORD ready to perform it... For God, You said in Isaiah 55:11, *"So shall My Word be that goes forth out of my mouth: it shall not return to me void, but it shall accomplish that which I please, and it shall prosper in the thing I sent it to do."* Therefore, upon on the truth, authority, dominion, power and the unfailing promise of Your Word, I stand!

I confess Jeremiah 15:20-21 for Your divine protection, power, redemption, mercy, defense, deliverance, salvation, and a hedge of security covering my life, the lives of my children, my household, family, friends, our finances, career/business, calling/ministry, the works of our hands, and destiny, in Jesus name... *Also, God will make me to this people a fortified wall of bronze; They will fight against me, but they will not prevail over me, For the Great I Am, He is with me always to save and protect me. So, God will rescue me out of the hand of the wicked, and God will redeem me from the grasping palm of the terrible and ruthless tyrant.*

I confess Isaiah 60:16-18 for Your grace, glory, favour, goodness, transformation, miracles, virtue, prosperity, peace, promotion, influence, affluence, magnificence, wealth and riches in my life, the lives of my children, my household, family, friends, our finances, career/business, calling/ministry, the works of our hands, and destiny... *I will suck the milk of the [Gentile] nations and suck the breast (abundance) of kings; Then I will recognize and know that the Lord, is my Savior and my Redeemer, the Mighty One of Jacob. Instead of bronze, He will bring gold, and instead of iron, He will bring silver, and instead of wood, bronze, and instead of stones, iron and [instead of the tyranny of the present] He will appoint peace as my officers, and righteousness my rulers. Violence will not be heard again in my land, nor devastation or destruction within my borders, But I will call my walls Salvation, and my gates Praise to God.*

Almighty, Sovereign God, please manifest your Word in my life, O Lord, in Jesus name, as I pray, praise and make these prophetic utterances, AMEN!

In conclusion, my Beloved, be strong in the Lord [draw your strength from Him and be empowered through your union with Him] and in the power of His [boundless] might. Put on the full armour of God [for His precepts are like the splendid armour of a heavily-armed soldier], so that you may be able to [successfully] stand up against all the schemes and the strategies and the deceits of the devil; for our struggle is not against flesh and blood [contending only with physical opponents], but against the rulers, against the powers, against the world forces of this [present] darkness, against the spiritual forces of wickedness in the heavenly (supernatural) places.

Therefore, put on the complete armour of God, so that you will be able to [successfully] resist and stand your ground in the evil day [of danger], and having done everything [that the crisis demands], to stand firm [in your place, fully prepared, immovable, victorious].

So, stand firm and hold your ground, having tightened the wide band of truth (personal integrity, moral courage) around your waist and having put on the breastplate of righteousness (an upright heart), and having strapped on your feet the gospel of peace in preparation [to face the enemy with firm-footed stability and the readiness produced by the good news].

Above all, lift up the [protective] shield of faith with which you can extinguish all the flaming arrows of the evil one. Moreover, take the helmet of salvation, and the sword of the Spirit, which is the Word of God.

With all prayer and petition pray with specific requests at all times on every occasion and in every season in the Spirit, and with this in view, stay alert with all perseverance and petition interceding in prayer for all God's people.

~ Ephesians 6:10-18 Amplified Bible (AMP)

Beloved, I faithfully believe that God is ready to bless you and you are now prepared to Rebound and 'Really' Live... Chayah!

God did it for me; now it is your turn!

God began a good work in us; He will see it to completion, and nothing can stop what He has ordained and predestined to prosper. By His grace, we author our stories for His glory!

To be continued...

63010158R00172

Made in the USA
Columbia, SC
07 July 2019